rescue
from MORMON CHAINS

redemption
in CHRIST JESUS

Grit 'n Grace

Lance Earl

GraceNotes by
Grace Earl

The Authors are not so much Lance and Grace. Instead, *Jesus Christ* is the Author and Finisher of their saving faith. He patiently led them on a long trek from the dead works of religion to the riches of divine grace and the gift of eternal life.

This book is the story of their journey to faith in the biblical Christ. They wrote it to lift the eyes of the reader from the common yoke of human effort to the Son of God; crucified for our sins, buried and raised from the dead! It has no other purpose. May God bless the reader to that redeeming end!

Pastor Ronald Tabor

COPYRIGHT

Grit 'n Grace

Copyright ©2021 by Lance Earl

All rights reserved. No part of this publication may be reproduced, stored in a retrieval system, or transmitted in any form or by any means - electronic, mechanical, photocopy, recording or any other - except for brief quotations in printed reviews, without the prior permission of this publisher.

Publisher: The Word Ministries, Inc.

Cover Design: Lance Earl
Cover Image: Lance Earl
Interior Design: Lance Earl
Grace Notes: Grace Earl

BIBLE TRANSLATIONS

This work includes scripture quotations from the following bible translations because they are available without copyright entanglements. Quotations have been primarily selected for purposes of readability.

King James Version (KJV) is an English translation of the Christian Bible for the Church of England, begun in 1604 and published in 1611 under the sponsorship of King James I of England.

American Standard Version (ASV) is rooted in work that was done with the Revised Version, a late 19th-century British revision of the King James Version of 1611.

World English Bible (WEB) is based on the American Standard Version of the Holy Bible which was first published in 1901.

Young's Literal Translation (YLT), 1898, by Robert Young who also compiled Young's Analytical Concordance. This is an extremely literal translation that attempts to preserve the tense and word usage as found in the original Greek and Hebrew writings.

Darby Bible (Darby) was first published in 1890 by John Nelson Darby, an Anglo-Irish Bible teacher associated with the early years of the Plymouth Brethren. Darby's purpose was to make a modern translation for the unlearned who have neither access to manuscript texts nor training and knowledge of ancient languages of the scriptures.

DEDICATION

In the depths of soul-crushing sorrow, she held my hand. We danced in the light of new hope.
 Without complaint, she poured over endless drafts and rewrites until her eyes crossed. Her love and dedication made this book possible.
 I love you, Gracie!

Contents

COPYRIGHT	iii
BIBLE TRANSLATIONS	v
DEDICATION	vii
PREFACE	ix
INTRODUCTION	xi
FOREWARD	xv

I	A HOUSE ON THE SAND	1
1.	DOES TRUTH MATTER?	3
2.	SHADOW OF THE TEMPLE	9
3.	IS MY TESTIMONY REAL?	13
4.	THE LEAST OF THESE	17
5.	FORGIVENESS GRANTED AND REFUSED	23
6.	DID I DO ENOUGH	29
7.	OF BLUE, BEARDS, AND BLASPHEMY	39
8.	CALLED OF GOD OR MEN	47
9.	THE CHANGING TEMPLE	55

II	A FALLEN HOUSE	63
10.	A TESTIMONY OF JOSEPH SMITH	65

11.	THE REAL JOSEPH SMITH	71
12.	TESTING JOSEPH SMITH	79
13.	THE GAG ORDER	87
14.	TAKING THE TEMPLE	93
15.	THE DARK YEARS	97

III	SIFTING THROUGH THE RUBBLE		105
	16.	IS THE GOSPEL EVERLASTING?	107
	17.	WHITE AND DELIGHTSOME	111
	18.	NOT QUITE WHITE	117
	19.	A CURSED CHURCH	123
	20.	HOW DO I REPENT?	133
	21.	FIG LEAF APRON	143
	22.	HIGH PRIEST	151
	23.	MAKING OTHER GODS	157

IV	LEANING ON THE ROCK		163
	24.	THE WORDS	165
	25.	RED LETTERS	169
	26.	EXCOMMUNICATION	177
	27.	PERSONA NON GRATA	187
	28.	GIVEN OVER TO THE COURTS	193
	29.	PEACE IN PERSECUTION	201

V	A HOUSE ON THE ROCK		209
	30.	GRACE	211

31. ETERNAL MARRIAGE 217
32. PEACE WITH GOD 221
33. A PARTING PRAYER 227

PREFACE

Together, Grace and I wandered in the wilderness of Mormonism for exactly forty years. In that dreary and burdensome wasteland, God found and saved us. He led us over the river and into the land of promise. God reached down and lifted us high.

Shortly after our escape, I began writing this book. As it approached completion, I read through the chapters and realized, *This will not please God!* Primarily, that work focused on Mormonism as the consummate evil that persecuted me. I trashed the whole thing and started again.

As I neared completion of the second draft, I read through the chapters and realized, *This will not please God!* In this attempt, I cast Jesus in a leading role, but I remained the star. Consequently, I trashed the whole thing and started again.

In this, my third attempt, I am doing things with a new focus. The gospel is the plot, and Jesus has the leading role. I share the story of our rescue to glorify God singularly. I pray He will approve.

This book is about a big, big God who honors every promise and rewards a wretch like me with infinite grace. I also write of other gods. "God" and "Lord" will represent our biblical God, while "god" and "lord" will be used to indicate false gods. Other pronouns representing deity will likewise use an upper case or lower case first letter to identify God or other gods.

INTRODUCTION

Grit

I am fascinated by the simple faith of a seemingly insignificant man, a man who was blind from birth. Those who encountered him wondered why his eyes were dark and who was responsible. Most saw him as definitive evidence that someone had sinned. They argued that his blindness was God's just response to someone's evil works.

Jesus understood this man as only God can. The blindness was not a curse; it had never been so. The man was born blind that *the works of God may be manifest*.[1] What appeared to be a natural consequence for grievous sin was instead a gift from God. This gift is not for the blind man alone. It was for countless millions who have and will come to know Jesus through this man's story.[2]

Can you imagine the endless sorrow that marked each day of this man's miserable existence? He had been born blind and consequently struggled with every associated challenge and limitation. He was of age.[3] As a result, he endured blindness for twenty years or more.[4] He lived in a nation that saw his blindness and attributed it to sinful indiscretions by this man or his parents. It is difficult to comprehend the ridicule, shame, abuse, and even physical persecution he surely knew at the hands of neighbors who should have loved him.[5]

I was born blind and remained sightless for the first sixty years of my life; I was blind ... born that way! There are two kinds of blindness, physical and spiritual. The man in our story suffered from the first type and possibly the second. My blindness was spiritual. Having never experienced the light, I had no comprehension of the darkness that enveloped me. In that darkness, I walked

---

[1] John 9:3
[2] Romans 10:17
[3] John 9:21 & 23
[4] Numbers 1:45
[5] John 9:2

the wide path leading to certain destruction.[6] Having never seen illumination, I denied my blindness and insisted, before the world, that my vision was clear.[7]

Having known only abuse, the blind man may have interpreted Jesus' action as more of the same. Jesus made mud of spit and dust and applied it to the man's eyes. Will spit and grit in a man's eyes fail to produce pain? Onlookers may have seen this as more *rightly deserved* abuse. The blind man probably assumed the same and initially saw his encounter with Jesus as more persecution. Perhaps the first moments of his encounter with Jesus brought only the anticipation of pain. For he had known and could comprehend of nothing different.

I came to know Jesus, and, at first, there was pain. The cost of knowing Him seemed too high. Hence, I almost could not bear to pay! I tore away everything I loved and knew and thought I knew, casting it all at the foot of the cross. This tearing produced pain I had not previously imagined. Loved family and lifelong friends turned to walk away forever. Because of this, my heart broke. These things caused deep cuts and lasting scars that are not fully healed.

Heeding the counsel of Jesus, the blind man stumbled and fumbled toward the *pool of Siloam*.[8] Tears must have streamed from sore, muddied, and gritty eyes as he groped in darkness. With every miserable step, he pressed forward, ever reaching, and ever searching for living water.

Kneeling together, Grace and I blindly felt our way toward Jesus. Our physical eyes could see, but we had never seen Him, known Him, or experienced His light. If we could see at all, we saw only darkness. Yes, we could see with physical eyes, but sightless were our spirits. "*Take everything if that is the cost to open our eyes!*" we cried, "*take it all and show yourself to us!*"

Grace

After many tears and seemingly endless searching in the darkness, after groping along the way, after each stumble and fall, after much pain, the blind man and we found the light we craved. The blind man and we lifted newly seeing eyes and gazed into ... light. Comprehension rushed in as we perceived what we previously could not imagine. Hearts leaped, and praise fell from our lips. Upon having our eyes opened, we, and the blind man, forgot our pain. Because a child had been born.[9] So it was for this once blind man[10] and for us. At that moment, Grace and I became children, a son, and daughter, of our holy God.[11]

There is much we do not yet fully understand, even though we see the light of God. We continue pursuing truth, but not in darkness. In illumination, which is the *Glory of God*, we search and seek, we find, and we see! And when

---

[6] John 12:35 & Matthew 7:13
[7] Mat 13:13 & Mar 4:12
[8] John 9:7
[9] Genesis 3:16 & John 16:21
[10] John 9:38
[11] John 1:12

INTRODUCTION

we cannot see it all, we, and the once blind man, cry out, *I know not: one thing I know, that, whereas I was blind, now I see!*[12]

On his way to the pool, the blind man must have experienced painful grit. Pain is often the motivator that moves a man or woman toward Jesus. We felt the same. At the pool of living water, he and we experienced infinite grace. His story, and ours, are the basis for this book.

Our prayer, dear Father, is that You will use this book for Your glory. May it be a tool in your hand to reach ears for the justification of souls that now languish in the bondage of Mormon chains. May it help others pass from the grit of muddy blindness into the clear light of Your amazing grace.

Amen.

---

[12] John 9:25 (KJV)

FOREWARD

When I think of Lance Earl, I recognize a man full of passion and commitment. Lance puts it this way in this insightful and surprisingly honest book, *Grit 'n Grace*; "I was a columnist, I was a blogger, I was a public speaker, I was a political activist, I was a constitutional instructor, and, I was a Mormon."

Lance, along with his seven younger brothers, were active Mormons. He admits to a few bumps in the road. Still, he took Seminary, had a temple marriage, served as an Elder's Quorum President, Gospel Doctrine Teacher, substitute Seminary teacher, became a High Priest, and a veil worker in the Temple.

Grit N' Grace is an appropriate title for this book and the journey on which Lance has been. "Grit" for "muddy blindness" and "Grace," well, I think Lance is using a double meaning here. First, "Grace" is Lance's lovely, supportive wife of forty-four years. Second, "Grace" is the unearned gift of favor, mercy, and eternal life we receive from a loving God when we give our lives to Jesus. The book explains how Lance moved from muddy blindness into the marvelous light of Jesus. Lance discusses his discoveries and the impact they had on his spiritual life.

The reader will learn of a "Gag Order" and other troubling occurrences with church leadership where Lance had to choose between obeying the LDS Church or following his conscience. It isn't surprising Lance chose the latter. This book, in my opinion, is Lance's way to "voice" his side of the story to friends, family, and ward members. It will also help many people understand more about the Church of Jesus Christ of Latter-day Saints from an investigated and well-studied perspective.

I interviewed Lance eight months after he left the church in 2017 and then again two years later. I was impressed with Lance's desire to know the truth. His story and mine parallel in some ways. I was raised in the Mormon church and discovered doctrinal, theological, and historical problems with the LDS narrative. I, like Lance, was afraid to tell my wife what I learned. We are both grateful for sweet companions who joined us in our journey.

Grit 'n Grace is full of personal stories and anecdotes. For example, Lance and Grace were teaching an LDS Sunday School class when they realized the teacher's manual did not teach of Jesus.

One of Lance's insightful comments is: "Mormon history is a repeating pattern of compromise." He explains how this compromise relates to doctrinal changes relative to polygamy, blacks, the priesthood, the temple ceremony, and, sarcastically, all from an unchanging God.

There is a funny story about Pentecost. Also, a tender story of Lance's faithful, LDS grandmother who said in her last days: "I didn't know if I did enough." But the best part of Lance and Grace's story is about finding and accepting the biblical Jesus.

Finally, there is a general misconception by the LDS community about those who leave the church. They assume apostates are looking for an easy way to "eat, drink and be merry" without any responsibilities. Nothing could be further from the truth. I think Lance and Grace represent the best examples for refuting this false notion. They are active in the Christian community, including a prison ministry where they teach a twice-weekly Bible study for maximum-security inmates. They are great examples of a Christian commitment to share the good news of Jesus and how He saved us when we could not save ourselves.

I am sure you will find this book informative, honest and reflective of a truth seeker who found the Good Shepherd and joined his flock.

E. Earl Erskine

Host

The Ex Mormon Files

Part I

A HOUSE ON THE SAND

Living and Loving a Lie

Part 1

A HOUSE ON THE SAND

CHAPTER ONE

DOES TRUTH MATTER?

> Truth rises when people follow God and reject men's teachings. For these few, they have anchored their houses on the Rock of Jesus Christ, and mercifully, their shelf is bare.
>
> *Lance*

Pilate asked Jesus, "What is Truth?"[1] If a more critical question exists, I can't imagine what it might be. I was born into an imagined truth that sought my destruction for sixty years and more. Evil, disguised as truth, entangled me in the tentacles of hell. Incredibly, the victimized cling, with passion and dedication, to the very tentacles that choke life.

I had been born into what I believed was the greatest gift of god, the only true and living church on the face of the earth. I was confident in my Mormon god, my church, and the men who lead it. After all, we were god's chosen people, and only we had the whole truth.

> And also those to whom these commandments were given, might have power to lay the foundation of this church, and to bring it forth out of obscurity and out of darkness, **the only true and living church upon the face of the whole earth**...
> – *Doctrine & Covenants*, 1:30, emphasis added

I had the only truth, the whole truth ... or, so I believed. Consequently, my truth meant everything to me. As a young man, I didn't know that Mormon truth is infinitely fluid and malleable. I never knew what I never knew. Mormon

---
[1] John 18:38

truth is a moving target. Consequently, I came to know what I could not know and believed what I could never establish in the Bible or Mormon scripture.

Mormon knowledge is a collection of claims unproven. By the power of emotion, false beliefs become accepted truth. Study, research, and reason are not the building blocks of Mormon doctrine. The basis of LDS truth is imagination, illusion, and a heart's transient flutter.

It is strange now to look back with understanding and wonder, how do otherwise intelligent and accomplished people allow this to happen?

1.1 Truth According to Mormon Leaders

Three Mormon leaders have adopted strangely untrue approaches to the truth. Russell M. Nelson is the recognized prophet of *The Church of Jesus Christ of Latter-day Saints*. Dallin H. Oaks is second in seniority, and he will take control at the death of Nelson. Boyd K. Packer died a few years ago. Before his death, he was senior to Nelson and Oaks. Consequently, if Packer still lived today, he would be the Mormon prophet, with Nelson and Oaks holding the successive two positions in the Mormon hierarchy. These men, who are the top Mormon officers, have a unique and troubling perspective on truth. In order of seniority, they said,

> There is a temptation for the writer or the teacher of Church history to want to tell everything, whether it is worthy or faith promoting or not. Some things that are true are not very useful...
> – Boyd K. Packer. "The Mantle Is Far, Far Greater Than the Intellect" Talk, August 22, 1981

> Some truths are best left unsaid.
> – Russell M. Nelson. "Truth—and More" Talk, Brigham Young University, August 27, 1985 & Russell M. Nelson, "Truth—and More", Ensign, January 1986

> Not everything that's true is useful.
> – Dallin H. Oaks, "An interview with Dallin H. Oaks" (Interview by PBS) July 20, 2007

These teachings, at best, leave the Mormon people on incredibly shaky ground. These damaged people are they who build their homes on the sand.[2]

The Mormon devout store their truths in carefully separated piles. One is for useful truths, and another for those that are useless. They struggle to divide useful and useless truths because the standards for discerning such things shift

---
[2] Matthew 7:26-27

DOES TRUTH MATTER?

frequently. Each Mormon man and woman anchor their lives on the instability of shifting sands. Consequently, lines between useful truth, useless truth, and untruth are in constant motion. The constant movement of LDS foundations leaves the people with no certainty of their standing before God.

Mormon prophets move the lines and redefine the usefulness of many gospel standards. When this occurs, the people must adapt to new realities. Believing their prophet to be the mouthpiece of God, the people have no choice but to accept every new doctrine without verification. Mormon prophets speak, and lies take root in the people's minds and hearts.

> Another way to seek a testimony seems astonishing when compared with the methods of obtaining other knowledge. We gain or strengthen a testimony by bearing it. Someone even suggested that some testimonies are better gained on the feet bearing them than on the knees praying for them.
> – Dallin H. Oaks. "Testimony" Talk, General Conference, April 2008

Telling and retelling a lie is the pattern that establishes Mormon truth. By continuous, repetitious regurgitation, the people accept untruths that enslave both heart and mind. When serious concerns arise, a prophet's word, true or not, will belay all doubt.

> I suggest that research is not the answer.
> – Dallin H. Oaks. Devotional, Young married couples in Chicago, February 2, 2019

Faithful members reserve a pile for all truths considered *useful* and *faith promoting*. If a doctrine or teaching feels good and aligns with the current prophet, it will go in this pile. These truths empower the Mormon people with a delusion of faithfulness. These are the truths that feel good but cannot be verified!

Juries and judges often base their verdicts and sentences on sworn testimony. Statements given under oath are presumed to be truthful. To knowingly mislead the court is a serious crime we call perjury. One sworn statement has the power to tip the scales of justice and dramatically alter someone for a term up to and including life. In extreme cases, such a lie may cause loss of life. False testimony, relative to God, will rob men of eternal life. Upon perjury, all Mormon truth rests.

Lance

The second pile is for truths that do not support Mormonism's current position. These truths challenge, convict, and even condemn current Mormon dogma. These will trouble devout church members, yet they are often set aside and ignored. When a Mormon dares to investigate the items in this pile, he will find the truth. It is often the most essential and challenging truth that leads a person to hard-won maturity in Christ. By these hidden treasures, men and women find salvation and peace with God!

One last quote from the Mormon prophet is deeply troubling in its scope and destructive power.

> To anyone who, because of "truth," may be tempted to become a dissenter against the Lord and his anointed, weigh carefully your action...
> – Russell M. Nelson, "Truth—and More", Ensign, January 1986

This final quote from Russell M. Nelson deserves particular and individual attention. God is truth.[3] Satan is the lie.[4] Since God is truth, it follows that all truth will lead to God. It will never lead a person to be a dissenter against the Lord. However, the truth will lead the honest in heart into dissension against false gods, false gospels, and false prophets!

Those, like myself, who were once members of *The Church of Jesus Christ of Latter-day Saints*, often refer to the pile of uncomfortable truths as the "shelf." This shelf is where we piled all the truths that troubled us. This is the place where we heaped things we didn't want to acknowledge.

1.2 A Brightness of Truth

Every Mormon man and woman has a shelf littered with troubling issues; I am sure of it. Items stored there include ugly chapters of Mormon history and surprising reversals of doctrine. These make up the dark underbelly of Mormonism. People desperately ignore absolute truths, which are, from the Mormon perspective, neither *useful* nor *uplifting*. Unanswered questions heap higher and higher. Every shelf has a load limit. To be sure, shelves sag, groan and ultimately fall. Like the house built on the sand, great will be the fall thereof.[5] On that fateful day, fallen truths and troubling unknowns must be examined.

Thankfully, Jesus, who is truth, will be waiting. With Him to guide, the honest will begin a journey toward light. In that illumination, shackles fall, and the weight of bondage lifts. Finally, finally, these precious people are made free.

> [31] Then said Jesus to those Jews which believed on him, If ye continue in my word, then are ye my disciples indeed; [32] And ye shall know the truth, **and the truth shall make you free**
> – John 8:31-32 (KJV), emphasis added

Truth rises when people follow God and reject the teachings of men. These faithful few readily accept the light and truth[6] they have craved for so long. In

---

[3] John 14:6 & John 17:17
[4] John 8:44
[5] Matthew 7:26-27
[6] 2 Timothy 2:15

that light, they anchor their houses and lives on the Rock of Jesus Christ[7], and mercifully, their shelves are bare.

[7] Matthew 7:24-25

CHAPTER
TWO

SHADOW OF THE TEMPLE

> And so I knew, and I knew that I knew. I never knew why I knew, how I knew, what I knew, or how I came to know that which I knew and never knew.
>
> *Lance*

Growing up Mormon in a Mormon society is a heady thing. Family, church, school, and community combine to fill a young man's mind with pomp, pride, and grandeur.

As a Mormon youngster, I had a church that set me above all other people. I believed that god would raise me up to equal his stature and status. Trusted adults, honored leaders, and loved family members often rehearsed a familiar Mormon couplet, *As man now is, God once was; as God now is, man may be.*[1] I grew up with the certainty that *I will someday be a god with power and authority.* This belief filled my imagination with delusions of eventual deity.

The prospect of becoming a god should have made me a better person. Instead, hatred and judgment filled my heart. I lived in a world, as I supposed, of inferior beings. My Mormon god did not love the Christian people enough to welcome them as new gods among the gods. Because explicitly, he numbered them among the church of the devil.[2]

---

[1] The Church of Jesus Christ of Latter-day Saints, *Teachings of the Presidents of the Church Lorenzo Snow*(Salt Lake City: n.p., n.d.) 83
[2] *Book of Mormon*, 1 Nephi 14:10

2.1 A Mormon Boy

I was born as a multi-generational Mormon boy. Both sides of my family tree reach back to the early days of the church. Stories from my family history speak of valiant men and women who suffered intense hardships as they crossed the plains, fleeing from tobacco-stained, rum-soaked, anti-Mormon persecutors. Our story speaks of forebearers in association with the prophet Joseph Smith. One gave money to the prophet for the promise of a long life. Another spoke of the day she gazed into the lifeless face of Joseph Smith, her murdered prophet.

I grew up on a constant diet of Mormon hymns such as *"Come, Come Ye Saints"*,[3] *"We Thank Thee, O God, for a Prophet"*[4] and *"Praise to the Man"*.[5] Of course, there were hymns that spoke of Jesus. These, however, were rare compared to those that praised and exalted men over God. Nevertheless, Mormonism's secular music reached my heart by lifting up and glorifying men instead of God.

I remember family reunions in company with cousins I loved more than life. These were wonderful and carefree days. At these reunions, my grandmother worked to organize *family genealogy meetings*.[6] Desperately, she struggled to ingrain, in the hearts of the children, a profound love for our Mormon heritage. She tried to secure an emotional attachment to our Mormon forebearers and an unquenchable commitment to Joseph Smith. We, her grandchildren, poked each other, wiggled, and giggled during the presentations. Consequently, she often became discouraged by our inattentive play. Nevertheless, her efforts affected me profoundly, even if she never knew it. I was all in, lock, stock, and barrel.

My great-grandpa Gunnell was my hero, though I knew him only as a kind and frail old man. He was the son of a Mormon polygamist, a dry-land farmer who helped settle southeastern Idaho. He toiled to scratch a living from the dust, suffering many hardships along the way. Above all, he was a devout Mormon leader. I grew up on stories of his unshakable faith in the prophets and gods of Mormonism; in that order, I suppose. Grandpa Gunnell was, to me, bigger than life.

As a boy, I remember trips to Salt Lake City. The temple spires rose above the city as a monument to the greatness of *my people*. As we sped along the interstate, I never tired of gazing at it with a kind of awe and self-exalted pride. It was, in my view, the temple of our most high god. At nighttime, the temple energized me! Its spires, bathed in brilliant white light, glowed like heaven itself.

In my young life, my chest swelled with pride for all things Mormon.

---

[3] Mormon hymn 30 *Come, Come, Ye Saints*
[4] Mormon hymn 19 *We Thank Thee, O God, for a Prophet*
[5] Mormon hymn 27 *Praise to the Man*
[6] 1 Timothy 1:4

2.2 A Valiant Son

I was sitting in a priesthood meeting when I learned who I was, according to Mormon doctrine. I was fourteen years of age and held the office of teacher in the Aaronic priesthood. My instructor explained that we all lived in a pre-mortal world as spirit sons and daughters of our Heavenly Father and one of his goddess wives.

Jesus and Lucifer, our elder brothers, got in a bit of a scrap over who should rule the yet uncreated Earth. The conflict between these two would-be rulers spread to us, the other spirit children of Heavenly Father. One by one, every brother and sister chose a side, aligning with Lucifer or Jesus. Lucifer lost the battle. As a result, god cast him and his followers from heaven to become the Devil and his demon angels. We who were loyal to Jesus knew we performed well in the pre-existent heaven based on skin color and our birthplace.

Those with black skin were the shirkers and ne'er-do-wells of the pre-mortal world. Because they were not valiant, God sent them here with a permanent curse of blackness.[7]

The Mormon god saw others as somewhat better than the black people. These include native Americans, Hispanics, Asians, and all people with skin darker than my own. The underlying principle is that god curses the weak and wicked with dark skin. Sometimes, god cursed people for a weak performance in the pre-existent world. Others, he cursed for different reasons. Unlike black people, who presumably sinned before they were born, native Americans received a *skin of blackness* for evil deeds after their births.[8] In the Book of Mormon, these people are the Lamanites. Today, we know them as native Americans.

Next in line are white people born to non-Mormon families. They are those who fought on Jesus' side. However, god considers them less because of a somewhat lackluster performance.

My instructor explained, god sends the most valiant spirits to righteous, white Mormon homes. We were the best of the best, saved for these latter days because we were more valiant and more loved by god. That self-righteous delusion held me captive for most of my life.

2.3 An Empty Assurance

For years, I believed every Mormon teaching to be true. I would have died in their defense.

Why did I know? How did I know? The church systematically groomed me from birth, and I never questioned a thing. I trusted those things because I had been taught that the prophet could never lead me astray.[9] I knew these things

---
[7] See chapter: White and Delightsome
[8] *Book of Mormon*, 2 Nephi 5:21
[9] *Doctrine and Covenants*, , Excerpts from Three Addresses by President Wilford Woodruff Regarding the Manifesto

to be true because of the burning I felt in my bosom[10] when I looked on the temple, heard stories of great-grandpa, learned of my pioneer heritage, sang a Mormon hymn, and each time I gazed at my white skin in arrogant pride.

Amid these assurances, there was no particle of proof. No scripture backed my position. If there had been supporting scripture, it would not have mattered because I relied on Mormon fables. I believed the Bible to be corrupt and did not trust it.[11] For this reason, God help me, I never knew of the biblical requirement to test the tales of our religion against the word God had previously revealed.[12]

I knew, and I knew that I knew! I never knew why I knew, how I knew, what I knew, or how I came to know that which I thought I knew. Defend the unknown I did without knowing why. All my knowing was in defense of what I could not defend. Oh, the tension!

2.4 Test Every Spirit

Words cannot describe the freedom that lifts and enlightens a man when God removes the burden of legalism. There is a magnificent assurance that comes with a proper understanding. Oh, the solace that attends a man who can biblically refute or affirm every teaching.

I know God's truth. When I hear a new or different teaching, I turn to the Bible and separate truth from error. The everlasting gospel[13] has been established by Jesus, who fulfilled the law. It was given once for all God's people.[14] Like John, I live with an unshakable assurance that even now, in this very moment, I have eternal life.

> And this is the witness, that God has given to us eternal life; and this life is in his Son.
> – 1 John 5:11 (Darby)

---

[10] *Doctrine and Covenants,* 9:8-9
[11] See Chapters: Does Truth Matter?& Is My Testimony Real?
[12] See Chapter: Testing Joseph Smith
[13] See chapter: Is the Gospel Everlasting?
[14] Jude 1:3

CHAPTER
THREE

IS MY TESTIMONY REAL?

> Repetition breeds familiarity.
> Familiarity breeds acceptance.
> Accepted things feel like truth
> even when they are not.
>
> *Lance*

We all have beliefs that shape our lives, behavior, and relationship with God and men. One trouble arises when men embrace beliefs that manifest violently.

Religion fueled two of the largest mass murders in North America. The culprit was a sinfully twisted belief in a false god. Men, driven by a firm conviction that they were acting in God's will, accomplished the Devil's work and people died.

On September 11, 1857, at Mountain Meadows, Utah, Mormon faithful shot, stabbed, and hacked 120 men, women, and children to death. Each murderous man was driven by faith in Brigham Young, a temple covenant of vengeance, and allegiance to Mormon priesthood keys. These keys rendered their leaders "*infallible*", or so they thought.

On another September 11th in New York City, in a Pennsylvania field and at the United States Pentagon, 2,996 died. Muslim radicals, acting under their own religious imperatives, justified what God condemns.

What do these atrocities share in common?

Testimony!

3.1 A Biblical Basis for Testimony

From the first biblical writer to the last, the Word of God teaches that we must find and establish truth using the Bible as an authoritative standard.

Deuteronomy 13:1-5 provides an understanding of methods by which we can test for false gods. This passage declares that we prove our love for God when we employ this standard of truth. Logically then, we do not love God when we reject this standard. Deuteronomy 18:20-22 establishes a means by which we might find protection from false prophets and false prophecies. Acts 17:11 declares, by testing all things against the truths God previously revealed, men become noble. It directs us to test even the most trusted teachers, apostles, and prophets. Galatians 1:6-9 teaches that we may recognize those who pervert the gospel by comparing their words to the gospel previously delivered to the saints.[1]

In summation, 1 John 1:4 demands that we test every spirit. God commands us to test every teaching and every claim according to the patterns He provides. God will not change His mind or His will because He is not a God of confusion,[2] nor is He a changing God.[3] Therefore, those things God has established in His word will not be changed, modified, deleted, uprooted, or reversed. On His word, we find, comprehend, and trust all things because He is the Rock of our salvation.

> [1]I will love thee, O Lord, my strength. [2]The Lord is my rock, and my fortress, and my deliverer; my God, my strength, in whom I will trust; my buckler, and the horn of my salvation, and my high tower.
> – Psalms 18:1-2 (KJV)

3.2 Gaining a Mormon Testimony

Mormon leaders encourage the people to profess a false belief in Joseph Smith and *The Church of Jesus Christ of Latter-day Saints*. The people continue these false professions until a false belief is solidified in their hearts and minds. The Mormon testimony is a statement of faith in which a person claims a perfect knowledge of things not known.

> It is not unusual to have a missionary say, "How can I bear testimony until I get one? How can I testify that God lives, that Jesus is the Christ, and that the gospel is true? If I do not have such a testimony, would that not be dishonest?" *Oh, if I could teach you this one principle: a testimony is to be found in the bearing of it!*
> – Boyd K. Packer. "The Quest for Spiritual Knowledge" Talk, Seminar for new mission presidents, June 25, 1982

---

[1] 1 Corinthians 15:1-4
[2] 1 Corinthians 14:33
[3] Hebrews 13:8

Is there a time when bearing witness to an unknown is the right thing? Perjury in a court of law carries with it fines and imprisonment. Perjury is a high crime in the courts of man. How much more condemned is it then, in the court of God? Astonishingly, some men claim to be prophets and apostles of Jesus Christ while encouraging such deceitfully dishonest behavior.

Mormon parents lead their small children to the pulpit and coax them through standard Mormon testimonies. As soon as the child can speak, the indoctrination begins. This is wrong on many levels. First, the children testify of things they cannot comprehend. Second, for the child's lie, parents give hugs, Bishops reward with a somber and robust handshake, and the congregation pats their little heads. Oh, how quickly the child learns that a bit of untruth brings substantial rewards.

Repetition breeds familiarity. Familiarity breeds acceptance. Accepted things feel like truth even when they are not. In the end, the Mormon masses bear a powerful witness of what they believe but do not know. Their faith statements have no basis in God's established pattern for discerning truth and error.[4]

The Mormon people are my people, as the Jews were Paul's. Along with him, I echo the desire of my heart;

> Brethren, my heart's desire and prayer to God for ~~Israel~~ (**the Mormons**) is, that they might be saved. For I bear them record that they have a zeal of God, but not according to knowledge. For they being ignorant of God's righteousness, and **going about to establish their own righteousness**, have not submitted themselves unto the righteousness of God.
> – Romans 10:1-3 (KJV), word substitution, emphasis added

3.3 A Testimony Built on the Rock

self-delusion noun
the act of deluding oneself or the state of being deluded by oneself especially concerning one's true nature, abilities, feelings, etc.
– George Merriam & Charles Merriam, *Merriam-Webster*(Springfield: Encyclopaedia Britannica, 1831) Number one definition

I once based my testimony on self-affirming-delusion as taught by Boyd K. Packer. The Bible describes my Mormon testimony perfectly;

> [10] And with all deceivableness of unrighteousness in them that perish; because they received not the love of the truth, that they might be

---
[4] 1 John 4:1

saved. ¹¹And for this cause **God shall send them strong delusion, that they should believe a lie**: ¹²That they all might be damned who believed not the truth, but had pleasure in unrighteousness.
– 2 Thessalonians 2:10-12 (KJV), emphasis added

And every one that heareth these sayings of mine, and doeth them not, shall be likened unto a foolish man, which built his house upon the sand:
– Matthew 7:26 (KJV)

When the winds and rain of doubt came, my Mormon testimony did not stand, and great was the fall of it.⁵ That testimony rested on the unstable foundation of lies told to me and lies I told myself.

I have a new testimony. The Bible perfectly describes this new one as well.

Therefore whosoever heareth these sayings of mine, and doeth them,
I will liken him unto a wise man, which built his house upon a rock:
– Matthew 7:24 (WEB)

When the winds of hatred, anger, and persecution came, my testimony stood. Furthermore, it stood firmly on the rock that is my Lord and King!

---

⁵Matthew 7:27

CHAPTER
FOUR

THE LEAST OF THESE

> None offered assistance on that cold winter night. They saw his filthiness, his wretchedness, but they never saw him.
>
> *Lance*

"When ye are in the service of your fellow beings", the Book of Mormon hero King Benjamin said, "ye are only in the service of your God".[1] There was a time when this principle meant everything to me. These words I believed were actual and of God. On that belief, I bet everything. I still remember the bitter day when I learned the Mormon church didn't share my feelings.

The Ogden Temple was the first Mormon temple dedicated in the state of Utah. The Salt Lake, Manti, and St George temples were dedicated in the Utah Territory over 78 years earlier. Therefore, this new temple was a big deal for the Mormon people, as you might imagine.

So, on a frigid December evening in 1971, I stood in a long, slow-moving line. We were on location to tour the Ogden temple. My grandparents, mother, and brothers accompanied me on this outing. The adults hoped to instill in my brothers and me a love for the temple. They brought us there in anticipation of a life-changing event. My life changed, but not as they had expected. Instead of leaving that place with a burning desire to return, I went home deeply troubled.

Besides the expected Mormon contingent, others from outside the faith were there. They came to see the temple interior which was generally closed to outsiders. Their curiosity to see firsthand drew them near.

Those who attend temple open houses have no worthiness standard. All are welcome. Open houses represent a public relations opportunity for the church.

---

[1] *Book of Mormon*, Mosiah 2:17

Non-Mormons, shepherded by the Mormon faithful, get a firsthand look at the extravagance that will be theirs if they join up. Once dedicated, the temple will be closed to all but the most worthy church members.

Being a fifteen-year-old boy, I didn't know much. Suffering from a delusion shared by many teenagers, I presumed to know everything. In reality, I was a dumb kid trying very hard to grow up. Being schooled in Mormonism, I received the Mormon priesthood and served first as a Deacon. Later, I advanced to the office of Teacher. These ordinations were automatic, occurring because I had a birthday and never because I had a calling, desire, or appropriate gifting. In short, I only knew what the Mormon leaders wanted me to know. That wasn't much. Nonetheless, gallons of Mormonism flowed in my veins. My beliefs filled me without the benefit of truth.[2]

So, there I was one wintry night standing in a line of freezing people. It's been many years; I still remember the bitter cold. It cut through layers of warm winter clothing. It was a cold that sunk to the core of a person, especially a skinny fifteen-year-old kid like me. I slapped my sides and stomped my feet to keep warm. Still, I was freezing. That's when I saw something that brought me up short.

A man standing in line caught my eye. He was about thirty, with long hair and a beard. Everything about his appearance marked him as an oddity, even in a large and diverse group. His clothing was simple and tattered. He wore a loose, lightweight, and oversized shirt or tunic for a coat. It was off-white and made of a coarsely woven fabric. He was clearly different from others in the crowd, most of whom were presumably Mormon. It wasn't his dress that caused me to stop and gaze. It wasn't his unkempt hair and beard that drew my eyes back to him again and again. His feet! I couldn't believe his feet! Try as I might, I couldn't stop looking ... at his feet!

I looked again and saw what I struggled to comprehend. *His feet were bare!* I had difficulty believing what I could not deny. Uncovered feet waited quietly on ice-encrusted concrete.

4.1 Cast Out

It seemed to take forever, but finally, we approached the temple doors. I was so cold that I no longer had much interest in seeing the temple. However, I was very, very ready to be inside and warm. I noticed movement in the line ahead. The crowd parted as the man with no shoes slowly retraced his steps down the frozen sidewalk. There was no sign that he was angry. He didn't seem offended. Instead, he was calm, at peace, and unsurprised. His stride seemed to have purpose as he moved, head up and eyes forward. What kind of man was this? Why would any man receive this abuse and be ... unoffended?

I stepped aside and gazed up at him as he passed. This man, perhaps the least of these, had quietly waited as long as any. He had been peaceful, respect-

---

[2]See chapter: Is My Testimony Real?

ful, non-assuming, and he suffered more than us all. Yet, when he reached the temple doors, men in suits, men in sturdy shoes, men in warm coats turned him away. They sent him out into the night with no warm covering for his body and without shoes for his feet. A judgment quickly rendered, I suppose! A man, whom they did not know, was too unworthy, too unclean, and too disgusting to be treated with respect. Their actions proclaimed his repugnance so vial, so offensive that Jesus Himself would not and could not love him.

> He doesn't respect the persons of princes, nor respect the rich more than the poor; for they all are the work of his hands.
> – Job 34:19 (WEB)

In the darkness that night, I was deeply troubled. I still think of that man with his bare, frozen feet. And still, I am afflicted. By this man's rejection, I experienced for the first time, ugly self-righteousness in the Mormon people. I desperately wanted to love the church, but I despised, loathed ... **hated!** what I witnessed that night.

> They shall **put you out of the synagogues**; but the hour is coming that every one who kills you will think to render service to God;
> – John 16:2 (Darby, emphasis added)

I have since wondered about others who saw this sad situation. Can you imagine what it would have been like if a man had said "wait, brother" while unbuttoning his heavy winter coat? Can you imagine the scene if a man sat down on a bench to remove his shoes and stockings?

Can you imagine the lasting impression such a scene would have made in my fifteen-year-old mind? How might it have changed my life if such generosity had come from a man I loved and respected? Oh, the awe and wonder that would have washed over and even warmed me. Only God's love can exceed compassion such as that. But that unprecedented act of love never happened, and I remain broken-hearted!

None offered assistance on that cold winter night. They saw his filthiness, his wretchedness, but they never saw him. They never saw or loved *the least of these*.

> And the King shall answer and say unto them, Verily I say unto you, Inasmuch as ye have done it unto one of the least of these my brethren, ye have done it unto me.
> – Matthew 25:40 (KJV)

4.2 Heaven Sent

The Word of God is most beautiful in my sight. It penetrates my heart and illuminates my mind. Two thousand years before my story, Jesus told it in a parable. It is most awe-inspiring to see the seamless tapestry of God's infinite work appear before my very eyes.

> ¹⁰Two men went up into the temple to pray; one was a Pharisee, and the other was a tax collector. ¹¹The Pharisee stood and prayed to himself like this: "God, I thank you that I am not like the rest of men, extortionists, unrighteous, adulterers, or even like this tax collector. ¹²I fast twice a week. I give tithes of all that I get." ¹³But the tax collector, standing far away, wouldn't even lift up his eyes to heaven, but beat his breast, saying, "God, be merciful to me, a sinner!" ¹⁴**I tell you, this man went down to his house justified** rather than the other; for everyone who exalts himself will be humbled, but he who humbles himself will be exalted.
> – Luke 18:10-14 (WEB), emphasis added

I have many questions about the happenings of that night. One, however, stands above all others. This singular question rings in my ears and moves around my mind without resolution.

I can't explain it, but I have no recollection of saying anything to the surrounding people. I don't think I pointed this man out to my family. Equally strange is this, I don't remember anyone around me noticing or saying a word about the strange man who came on that bitter winter night. There is an odd sense that this experience was mine alone. It is as if he came for me. I didn't fully comprehend, and I can't explain, but there was something significant in the happenings of that frigid evening.

I have never spoken of this experience with anyone, including those who attended me that night. They have been equally silent to me. I am curious to know if they saw it or if their eyes were made blind. Somehow, it seems inappropriate to ask. It's almost as if this was a sacred, closely-held experience. And so, I am left to wonder ... and wonder. I now tell what has never been told before except in Grace's ear.

I keep this experience in my heart and my head as a personal treasure. I play and replay it in my mind while I quietly wonder at the significance. There is a strange sense that this simple, humble, quiet, and uniquely dignified man was from above. Was he sent for me? Did he come to plant a seed? Did he come to drive a wedge and divide me from the curse of Mormonism?

Was he a man or an angel? I can't even say that he was not Jesus. One thing I do know, the memory of this obscure man causes me to reflect on the majesty of my Lord. I reflect on Jesus in the house of Caiaphas[3] and the palace of Pilate.[4] Bound, mocked, struck, scourged, bloodied and wearing that horrible crown. Even then, Jesus was magnificent!

That this man was God-sent seems plausible. When I remember the barefoot man on a frozen sidewalk in a city with a temple, I remember another night in another city with a temple. Jesus stood patiently, quietly, and with dignity as he suffered. He, like the other, was without offense. Men in fine clothes sent

---

[3] Matthew 26:57
[4] John 18:38

Jesus and the other man away. The first to die on a cross and the other to die in the cold. I cherish the memory of both!

CHAPTER
FIVE

FORGIVENESS GRANTED AND REFUSED

> In the blackness of my despair, there was ... light. A crazy, warm illumination filled my heart. I began to breathe again.
>
> *Lance*

I was around fifteen years old when I took a hard left turn from Mormonism and plunged headlong into sin. In the first quarter of my junior year, I walked out of high school, never to return. I moved out of my parent's home and adopted a lifestyle of my choosing. It was the tail end of the Hippie generation, and I wanted to get mine before it was too late. Regrettably, that culture is the sum of two foolish mantras, *"Peace, Love & Dope"* along with *"Sex, Drugs and Rock & Roll"*

These generational idioms seemed noble enough because I was a selfish, foolish, and shortsighted boy. Living in the hippie utopia is not as easy as one might think. Even hippies need money. By nature, hippies are irresponsible and impudent lovers of self. Breaking and entering proved to be an efficient way to meet financial needs without actually getting a job. Of course, taking what belonged to another did not quite align with *"peace & love"*. But who's perfect?

5.1 Turning from Sin

In time, I desired to return to the god I formerly knew. There had been much sin in a brief span of years. I felt driven to make things right, but I didn't know how to begin. My multi-year love affair with crime proved incredibly difficult to reconcile. Being a frequent drug user, my memory of illegal events is a blurry and hazy fog. I have no clear recollection of what, when, or where. Consequently, making things right was and is impossible.

There were the girls. There were so many nameless, faceless conquests.

No longer was I willing to live in the darkness I had created. I had to get out and get free, or sin would certainly own me. To be better than my former self proved problematic. Failure hindered every effort. Old friends drew me back into darkness with no noticeable resistance on my part. I sank easily back into the sludge I never entirely abandoned. I was still the person I no longer wanted to be. Each failure brought fresh pain and a renewed sense of hopelessness. Drugs and debauchery were my release, though temporary at best. Sin was the addiction I embraced, again and again. I despised and loved my sin. The old me resisted change and was victorious over the person I hoped to become.

5.2 Turning to God

One morning, I was sitting on the edge of my bed. Self-derision is a dark place on a long rocky road. In this place, a person's vision becomes unclear, and life becomes hardly worth the effort. I felt so low, so devastated. Great sobs racked my soul. My chest heaved as every breath came with difficulty. Revulsion and disdain overwhelmed and held me down. Broken, chained, and hopeless, I cried out.

I had not prayed for a very, very long time. I was running out of options because so far, nothing had worked. The dark me remained strong and active. The new me was conquered and devastated. Day after day and week after week, nothing changed. Rise one step, fall back three. I had nowhere to turn. Between the shudder of each sob, I gasped, "I'm sorry, I'm sorry, I'm so sorry!"

Help Me Jesus!

I struggled to understand what happened next. There was no comprehension. No words can describe what God did for me and in me. In the blackness of my despair, there was ... light. A crazy warmth filled my heart. I began to breathe again. Jesus was there, and he was accepting me. He lifted me from the blackest pit into the light of new hope. Peace replaced anguish. Joy replaced misery. Hope overcame hopelessness. The healing blood of Jesus washed over me. For the first time in a very long time, there was life. I was new. Thank you, God! Thank you, Lord Jesus!

5.3 Learning from Bartimaeus

In Mark 10, we read the story of the blind man, Bartimaeus. He, a picture of hopelessness, sat daily near the Jericho gate. Indeed, despair filled his endless, empty days. Petitioning passersby for crumbs and coins was all this man had, and it was not enough.

One day, Jesus passed through Jericho on his final journey to Jerusalem.

> And when he heard that it was Jesus of Nazareth, he began to cry out, and say, Jesus, thou son of David, have mercy on me.
> – Mark 10:47 (KJV)

Even when the crowd turned on him and hatefully demanded silence, he cried all the more. Threatening and angry hisses from the people did nothing to quiet him. Through their rebuke, he called all the louder, "*Jesus, son of David ...*"! Jesus, hearing the commotion, stopped and called to Bartimaeus.

When called, this blind beggar, who possessed nothing, showed us the true meaning of faith. Through Bartimaeus, we begin to comprehend the power of simple but unshaken faith. Rising to his feet, he cast his cloak away and rushed to Jesus.

The cloak was disgusting, filthy, and a tattered rag. For Bartimaeus, it was the entirety of his worldly goods. It provided some protection from long, cold nights. Spreading it on the ground, he could avoid sitting in the dirt. He may have laid it before him as a receptacle of cloth to collect alms cast in his direction. For Bartimaeus, that filthy rag was all he possessed.

Why did he cast his cloak away? Faith drove him to do what some might call reckless. Faith was his motivation. His cloak was of value to a blind man, but it held no value to the seeing. Bartimaeus believed Jesus could open his dark eyes! Doubting nothing, he left his rag behind and stepped out in faith!

The rest of this blind man's story guides us all. Praise God!

5.4 Turning from God to Men

What I did next was unbelievably foolish and predictably Mormon. I'm embarrassed to admit the truth. But I must, if only to expose how controlled and subservient I had become to Mormonism. Before describing my religious foolishness, let us again consider the blind man.

With no eyes, Bartimaeus saw truth more clearly than my Mormon eyes. Utterly sightless, he saw more than I did with two good eyes!

Belief in Jesus leads to a healing of physical infirmities and spiritual sickness as well. Jesus came especially to heal and give me sight. He came to bring eternal life. Jesus healed Bartimaeus in both ways. By contrast, I rejected Jesus and received neither healing nor life.

On the edge of my bed, I, like Bartimaeus, noted the presence of Jesus. With my whole heart, I wanted a healing. Like the blind man, I cried out, "*have mercy on me*"! When the ever-present demons of my own making rebuked me, I cried all the louder, "*Jesus, Jesus have mercy on me*"!

Unlike Bartimaeus, I did not have a fullness of faith. The darkness of my Mormon ways blinded my eyes. I could not see. Because of my inability to see, I believed a multitude of lies. Religious traditions rendered me sightless. In my mind, Jesus was too weak and too limited to heal or redeem without the assistance of mortal men.

I saw and understood only the demands of Mormonism. Turning to my Bishop, I gave myself into his hands. I relied on him to do what the Mormon Jesus could not. When I should have trusted, I clung to a filthy cloak of Mormonism. Pulling it tightly around me, I accepted Jesus subject to religious requirements. I lacked the faith to cast it away, and I could not trust in Jesus alone. He is the light of the world. Regrettably, precious little of that light reaches those lost in caverns of legalism.

Mormon leaders convened a disciplinary council. Dutifully, I appeared and confessed every sin before my Bishop and three other men. They demanded every dirty detail of every self-centered act. I gave up every shameful secret. Looking back, all I see is the demand for justice and the absence of mercy.

After hearing my confession, they counseled together. God, they said, revealed that I was to be disfellowshipped. There were stipulations. They required me to attend weekly church meetings. However, I could not speak or pray, nor could I take the sacrament. These restrictions made sense to me then. But now I wonder, *who needs communion with God more than a humble, penitent, hurting sinner?* Essentially, this corrective action amounted to a scarlet letter, a shunning that other Mormons recognized and instantly understood. Essentially, I was a leper.

Several well-meaning people, including my Bishop, gave me a copy of *The Miracle of Forgiveness* by Spencer W. Kimball. This book is a pinnacle of evil with power to drive a struggling sinner into a hopeless depression.

> That transgressor is not fully repentant who neglects his tithing, misses his meetings, breaks the Sabbath, fails in his family prayers, does not sustain the authorities of the Church, breaks the Word of Wisdom, does not love the Lord nor his fellowmen. A reforming adulterer who drinks or curses is not repentant. The repenting burglar who has sex play is not ready

Reflections

We were new Christians who had the privilege of ministering in a maximum-security women's prison. We brought communion to Sunday services. Thirty-three women asked for and received baptism.

The Mormons were also there with a long list of restrictions. Inmates did not receive the sacrament [Mormon communion]. Nor were they able to be baptized. My heart broke to see Christianity's necessities denied where there was so much need.

When I reflect on the miracle of seeing God change so many good sisters, I also think about the hopelessness of those inmates under Mormon control.

Lance

for forgiveness. God cannot forgive unless the transgressor shows a true repentance which spreads to all areas of his life.
— Spencer W. Kimball, *The Miracle of Forgiveness*(Salt Lake City: Bookcraft, 1969) 203

... Eternal life hangs in the balance awaiting the works of men. This progress toward eternal life is a matter of achieving perfection. Living all the commandments guarantees total forgiveness of sins and assures one of exaltation through that perfection which comes by complying with the formula the Lord gave us. In his Sermon on the Mount he made the command to all men: *Be ye therefore perfect, even as your Father which is in heaven is perfect.* (Matt. 5:48.) being perfect means to triumph over sin. This is a mandate from the Lord. He is just and wise and kind. He would never require anything from his children which was not for their benefit and which was not attainable. Perfection therefore is an achievable goal.
— Spencer W. Kimball, *The Miracle of Forgiveness*(Salt Lake City: Bookcraft, 1969) 208-209

It is normal for children to try. They fall and get up numerous times before they can be certain of their footing. But adults, who have gone through these learning periods, must determine what they will do, then proceed to do it. To "try" is weak. To "do the best I can" is not strong. **We must always do better than we can.** This is true in every walk of life.
— Spencer W. Kimball, *The Miracle of Forgiveness*(Salt Lake City: Bookcraft, 1969) 264-265, emphasis added

What are we to understand from this? Not only is the sinner required to turn from his sin, but he must also lead a perfect life. For the Mormon people, no quarter is given. No flexibility is allowed. Kimball does not recognize that people are broken, scarred, and prone to sin. Overcome every weakness or to hell with you is the book's overriding message.

The requirement is not to walk with the Lord, leaning on and trusting as we go. To do "*Better than we can*" is the demand. Perfection is the only acceptable objective. Anything less is sin.

So what is the sinner to conclude? When a person becomes perfect and has no need for grace, god will grant it. Does God give grace to only those who have no use for it? What of those who do not achieve perfection and consequently do not qualify for grace? Are they condemned to hell?

Nephi, the most beloved prophet from the Book of Mormon, wrote:

> [17]Nevertheless, not withstanding the great goodness of the Lord, in showing me his great and marvelous works, my heart exclaimeth: O wretched man that I am! Yea, my heart sorroweth because of my flesh; my soul grieveth because of mine iniquities. [18]I am encompassed about, because of the temptations and the sins which do so easily beset me.
> – *Book of Mormon*, 2 Nephi 4:17, 18

I once considered Nephi to be a wholly righteous man. If sin haunts even him, what shall the rest of us do?

It is such a strange thing. I humbled myself before Jesus and confessed my sin in a desperate plea for forgiveness. When He came to me, acknowledged and forgave me, I was appreciative but not believing. I remained convinced that Jesus Christ was incapable of the finished work unto salvation and eternal life.

Because I doubted, his gift did not come to me. It was not because he failed, but because I could not believe and receive. In the end, I thrust Jesus aside and turned myself over to men. I subjected my life to the demands of deluded men who thought themselves capable of doing the work of my Lord and King.

So, I did the best I could, which was "not strong", but "weak". When I later reported my progress to the men who stood in judgment over me, I was not fully honest, because I had never quite achieved perfection. I never got close. I guess my failures amount to one more thing I must repent of, but never can. Crazy as it may seem, the act of Mormon repentance led to new lies and additional sin.

For nearly two years, as a disfellowshipped Mormon, I dutifully followed the instructions of men. Meanwhile, rejecting the simple promises of Jesus. But then, I was a Mormon, and Mormons seldom read and never comprehend the Bible. Every Sunday, I carried the Bible in my hands. The assurances of Jesus were so close, but I never opened the book to see what they might be. Because of a lie, my eyes were blind to the promises of God. Jesus was so close, but men and dogma stood between Him and me.

On the edge of my bed, I could have had it all. In that shabby little room, Jesus Christ found me. He offered everything. He came for my healing and happiness, and I never saw it. Instead, I drew a cloak of Mormonism tightly around my broken soul and waited for men to make me right! They never did!

CHAPTER
SIX

DID I DO ENOUGH

> I came to realize that I was indeed my Grandma's grandson. Together, we attempted to be saved according to the gospel of Joseph Smith.
>
> *Lance*

My grandmother was an incredible woman. In her, I found love without guile or limits. In my most trying times of failure and shame, harsh judgment was not in her nature. We often sat at her kitchen table, where her gentle love blessed the life of this troubled teen. Grandma was an exceptional woman!

Two giant apple trees stood in Grandma's yard. As a young boy, I loved to snitch the salt shaker, climb to the top branches, and feast on green apples. Grandma did all in her power to dissuade me from this activity. Her endless warnings of an upset stomach went unheeded. Consequently, I ate sour apples until her prediction became my reality. Sour stomach or not, green apples and my sweet Grandma bring to mind treasured boyhood memories.

As a grown man, I still climbed those trees every springtime. With tools in hand, I clipped and pruned each one in anticipation of the coming summer harvest of sweet red apples.

This chore was not complete until I was hot, sweaty, scratched, and scraped. When my feet hit the ground for the last time, Grandma joined me with an ice-cold pitcher of her signature drink. The combination of lemonade and homemade apricot nectar is surprisingly good. Together, we sat in the shade, sipped cold drinks, and cherished our time together. Predictably, her eyes inspected my work while she insisted on paying me. Grandmas are funny that way. And this is where the fun began, at least for me. I refused the money which was always a point of frustration for her. That's when the bartering started. These negotiations are among my favorite memories. The last time we haggled, I agreed to accept a hot cherry pie as payment in full.

Before Grandma was able to deliver, she suffered a massive stroke that left her bedridden for the rest of her days. She often mentioned her deep regret at not making good on her debt. Her sorrow broke my heart. Even so, by her last act of love, I came to appreciate her all the more.

6.1 Fear of the Lord

It wasn't long before the severity of that stroke took my Grandma. A few days before her death, we had an extended visit. As we talked, I perceived her deep agitation. Finally, I asked, *"Grandma, what is it?"* In all my life, I have never heard words that so deeply shattered my heart. The pain in her voice distressed me then and distresses me still. From the depths of stark terror, she shared her misery, *"I can't go to Jesus"*. Gaping at her, I could only ask, " *Why?*"

Even before she replied, my heart joined hers in a deep and fearful self-examination. Something essential was missing. Being steeped in Mormonism, I had no idea what that missing component might be, but its absence was evident. Something of eternal importance was beyond her grasp ... and my understanding. A disquieting panic gripped grandmother and grandson alike!

When her answer came, it shook me more deeply than before. The wrenching of my soul was complete. I had nothing to soothe her fearful heart or my own. She said, *"I don't know if I did enough!"*

Today, I understand what that missing quality was. A glorious peace attends those who are in Christ. I can see what I couldn't see then, and in it, I find indescribable rest. Ever will my heart ache because I had nothing of comfort, hope, or assurance to ease the anxiety of my beloved and dying Grandma.

> *Grace Notes*
>
> Being Mormon meant always doing. Do this; do that. I felt the endless burden of every calling, my visiting teaching, my duties as a Mormon wife and mother. Was I doing enough? My heart knew I was not. The weight of it all doubled and redoubled.
>
> When Lance and I laid everything we knew at the foot of the cross, the burden lifted! I fell in love with the Bible! It taught me all that "doing" was unnecessary. God gave us grace! A gift, freely given through infinite love! I am so free. Yes! I did enough when I gave my heart to Jesus. He wanted nothing more!
>
> *Grace*

DID I DO ENOUGH

> ⁴Rejoice in the Lord always! Again I will say, "Rejoice!" ⁵Let your gentleness be known to all men. The Lord is at hand. ⁶**In nothing be anxious**, but in everything, by prayer and petition with thanksgiving, let your requests be made known to God. ⁷**And the peace of God, which surpasses all understanding, will guard your hearts and your thoughts in Christ Jesus**.
> – Phillipians 4:4-7 (WEB)

Should Grandma be admitted into Heaven? If I get to decide, I will let her in for her fried chicken alone! It was that good! Plus, she still owes me a pie!

The Word of God is undeniable, and the news is not all good. In reality, Grandma did not do enough, nor have we. Her shortfall can be difficult to accept because she dedicated her life to Mormon good works. Being a good wife, a good mother, a good grandmother, a good worker of Mormon genealogy, a zealous temple worker, and the ultimate fryer of chicken will never reconcile anyone with God.[1] The reality is clear and final. All she did to earn the approval of God was never and will never satisfy justice.[2] Likewise, all the things she failed to do, the very failures that haunted her final hours, were not enough to turn our loving and holy God away.[3]

In the months and years that followed, the words of my dear grandmother have haunted me. If Jesus is a God of love, she should have been running to Him in joyful abandon. Instead, she approached him with desperate fear and trembling. There was nothing of the hope the Bible suggests. There was only a spirit of mortal terror. Where God's love should have filled her with optimistic joy, she knew only hopelessness.

Because of her words, I examined myself for the first time. What I found left me shaken. I discovered that her words, her fear, and her doubt were mine as well. Passage after Mormon passage tumbled through my mind and burdened my heart. These millstones pulled me ever deeper into the same dark abyss that held my grandmother's heart.

> ... for we know that it is by grace that we are saved, **after all we can do**.
> – *Book of Momon*, 2 Nephi 25:23, emphasis added

> Yea, come unto Christ, and be perfected in him, and deny yourselves of all ungodliness; **and if ye shall deny yourselves of all ungodliness**, and love God with all your might, mind and strength, **then is his grace sufficient for you**, that by his grace ye may be perfect in Christ; and if by the grace of God ye are perfect in Christ, ye can in nowise deny the power of God.
> – *Book of Mormon*, Moroni 10:32, emphasis added

---

[1] Romans 3:10-12
[2] Matthew 7:21-23
[3] Isaiah 54:10

Keep my commandments continually, and a crown of righteousness thou shalt receive. **And except thou do this, where I am you cannot come.**
– *Doctrine & Covenants*, 25:15, emphasis added

Now, add the seven steps of Mormon repentance[4] to comprehend Grandma's hopelessness. Step 3 of the Mormon repentance process demands that *she must forsake her sins*. Who can do that? Certainly, the apostle Paul was unable.

For I don't know what I am doing. For I don't practice what I desire to do; **but what I hate, that I do** ...
– Romans 7:15 (WEB), emphasis added

I reflected on Grandma's words repeatedly and contrasted them against my fears. I came to realize that I was indeed my Grandma's grandson. Together, we attempted to save ourselves according to the gospel of Joseph Smith.

We believe that through the Atonement of Christ, all mankind may be saved, by obedience to the laws and ordinances of the Gospel.
– *Articles of Faith*, 3

Because we followed Joseph Smith, we fell prey to the curse of the law. The law we tried to follow was the very thing that condemned us both.

For whosoever shall keep the whole law, and yet offend in one point, **he is guilty of all**.
– James 2:10 (KJV), emphasis added

By following Joseph Smith, we surrendered our hope in the cleansing power of Jesus. We turned from God and placed our trust, hope, and eternities in the hands of corrupt men, and false prophets.

It is better to trust in the Lord than to put confidence in man.
– Psalms 118:8 (KJV), emphasis added

We were enemies of God, my grandmother and me. Nevertheless, that didn't stop love.

[8]But God commendeth his love toward us, in that, while we were yet sinners, Christ died for us. [9]Much more then, being now justified by his blood, we shall be saved from wrath through him. [10]For if, when we were enemies, we were reconciled to God by the death of his Son, much more, being reconciled, we shall be saved by his life. [11]And not only so, but we also joy in God through our Lord Jesus Christ, by whom we have now received the atonement.
– Romans 5:8-11 (KJV)

---

[4]See chapter: How do I Repent? & The Church of Jesus Christ of Latter-day Saints, *Gospel Principles* N.p: n.p, n.d Ch 19

6.2 The Counterfeit

Generations before Grandma was born, professing Christians fell prey to the devil masquerading as an *angel of light*[5]. They heard and believed the words of Joseph Smith and others who pretended to be *ministers of righteousness*[6] so that the people might turn from God. Why did they leave the true faith? John provides the answer.

> They went out from us, but they were not of us; for if they had been of us, they would no doubt have continued with us: but they went out, that they might be made manifest that they were not all of us.
> – 1 John 2:19 (KJV)

In my family tree, these first Mormons were never genuine followers of Jesus. Oh, they may have professed to be Christian, but they had not been born again.[7] They were not made new.[8] They had never been *saved through the washing of regeneration and renewing by the Holy Spirit*.[9] These people led my family into darkness because they never knew that Jesus is "*He*",[10] the way, the only truth and the only life.[11] They were never a part of the body of Christ. Because they were not of us, it was a simple thing for Satan, the thief, to complete his dark work.

> The thief cometh not, but for to steal, and to kill, and to destroy: I am come that they might have life, and that they might have it more abundantly.
> – John 10:10 (KJV)

There can be no counterfeit unless there is also an original. We cannot recognize counterfeits by studying the qualities of a counterfeit. We can only recognize counterfeits when we are intimately familiar with the original. When the original is known, no false copy will deceive.[12] This is precisely the failure of the first Mormons of my family and every generational Mormon to follow. They never intimately knew Jesus, and He, therefore, never knew them.

> [22]Many will say to me in that day, **Lord, Lord,** have we not prophesied in thy name? and in thy name have cast out devils? and in thy name done many wonderful works? [23]And then will I profess unto them, **I never knew you**: depart from me, ye that work iniquity.
> – Matthew 7:22-23 (KJV), emphasis added

---

[5] 2 Corinthians 11:14
[6] 2 Corinthians 11:15
[7] Bible, *John 3:3*
[8] 2 Corinthians 5:17
[9] Titus 3:5
[10] John 8:24
[11] John 14:6
[12] See chapter: Is the Gospel Everlasting?

Generational lies became the foundation upon which my family stood. My dear Grandma knew nothing different. From her birth, she knew only deception. Consequently, Mormon lies seemed good and faithful in her eyes. Having never known the truth, she believed the Bible was corrupt. She lived before this current information age, never owning a computer or an Internet connection. She lived the entirety of her life in Utah, where institutional Mormonism was the predominant standard of truth. Despite her placement in a nest of lies, she believed and followed God according to her best understanding.

6.3 Finding Hope

In Luke 16, we read the parable of the Rich Man and Lazarus. This parable has particular application to my grandmother's story.

This rich man was a practicing Jew with a knowledge of God. How do we know this? From Hades, he cried out, *"Father Abraham"*. He understood his relationship with Abraham and was, therefore, familiar with the Torah. It follows that he was a synagogue attending, covenant-keeping Jewish man. We can assume he was a follower of a corrupted law that bore God's name, but no longer bore his image.

From one perspective, the news relative to my grandmother is quite frightening. My grandmother believed herself to be a follower of Jesus Christ. She prayed in the name of Jesus Christ but did not pray to Him. Faithfully, she strived to do all the works of Mormonism. Throughout her life, she made and kept Mormon covenants. She attended a church that bore the name of Jesus Christ but not His image. Finally, she carried the Bible in her hand all the days of her life. Tragically, she was taught and came to believe it was corrupt and not trustworthy. She had been told and believed that plain and precious parts of the gospel had gone missing. Consequently, she always had the Bible in her hand, but she was afraid to trust it! These are the lies that stole her peace.

Grandma is a modern copy of the rich man. The Word of God is undeniable. It presents a real possibility that Grandma is with the rich man in Hades. If she is, then I know she is pleading for her family as the rich man cried out for his.

> [27] I ask you therefore, father, that you would send someone to my children's homes; [28] for I have four children and many grandchildren, that he may testify to them, so they won't also come into this place of torment. [29] Her answer will be, they have Jesus, Peter, Matthew, John, Paul, the apostles and the prophets. Let them listen to them.
> – Luke 16:27-29, modified for Grandma

Every day of her life, Grandma knew only prison walls. Bars and chains held her mind and heart. Captivity bound her fast and would not set her free. Jesus, who knows all things, is aware of Satan's entanglements that held her bound. And, Jesus is love.

There is hope. When people have not heard the good news of the gospel, God will judge by a different standard. A light, placed in every heart, clearly testifies of God's goodness. Creation boldly and loudly testifies to every man that God reigns and rules the heavens. If these two things are all a person has, they are sufficient for any who acknowledge and fear God.

> That was the true Light, which lighteth every man that cometh into the world.
> – John 1:9 (KJV)

> For the invisible things of him since the creation of the world are clearly seen, being perceived through the things that are made, even his everlasting power and divinity; that they may be without excuse.
> – Romans 1:20 (WEB)

After healing the servant of a Roman centurion in Capernaum, Jesus taught a remarkable truth about the salvation of those who were not of Israel.

> [10] Verily I say unto you, I have not found **so great faith**, no, not in Israel. [11] And I say unto you, **That many shall come from the east and west, and shall sit down with Abraham, and Isaac, and Jacob, in the kingdom of Heaven.** [12] But the children of the kingdom shall be cast out into outer darkness: there shall be weeping and gnashing of teeth. [13] And Jesus said unto the centurion, Go thy way; and **as thou hast believed, so be it done unto thee**.
> – Matthew 8:10b-13a (KJV), emphasis added

Peter took the gospel to Cornelius, a Roman centurion at Caesarea. After Cornelius received the Holy Spirit, the Bible records this statement about people of every nation who may never hear the word of God. It reads:

> but in every nation he who is fearing Him, and is working righteousness, is acceptable to Him;
> – Acts 10:35 (YLT)

Jesus offers hope. There is good news for every man, woman, and child who live their lives without hearing the gospel. God will find any acceptable who live up to the light in them, and the testimony of creation placed before them.

> If I had not come and spoken unto them, they had not had sin: but now they have no cloak for their sin.
> – John 15:22 (KJV)

6.4 Comes the Schoolmaster

One hope rises above all. As this dear lady weighed her obedience against the laws and ordinances of the Mormon gospel, her failures became painfully clear.

Some believe the Bible is incorrectly translated. Because of this doubt, they will know the terror, sadness, and misery experienced by my Grandma. These people think salvation comes by compliance with laws and ordinances of a false gospel.[13] Their only hope relies on personal works and Mormon standards they can never meet.

We who know God see Grandma's fear as a glorious cause for rejoicing. The law reveals our wretched inability to meet its demands. In it, we see the reflection of who and what we are. In that reflection, we comprehend the impossibility of saving ourselves, so we seek a Savior. The law leads us all to Jesus.

> Wherefore the law was our schoolmaster to bring us unto Christ, that we might be justified by faith.
> – Galatians 3:24 (KJV)

As Grandma approached the day of her death, Jesus was calling her, drawing her. She measured her good works and found no peace, no assurance, and only fear. God uses the law to help us see ourselves for the wretches we genuinely are. I like to believe Grandma saw her reflection and cried out to God in total surrender. She is redeemed if she did this simple thing. I know she wanted Jesus, and I know He wanted her.

> who desires all people to be saved and come to full knowledge of the truth.
> – 1 Timothy 2:4 (WEB)

With incalculable gratitude, I picture her reaching, crying, yearning for Jesus and I see Him drawing, receiving, and redeeming her as Boaz redeemed Ruth. By the way, my dear sweet grandmother's name is Ruth.

---

[13] *Articles of Faith*, 3

Reflections

More than all others, this story has caused my family to react in anger. They claim Grandma never said these things to me because she never uttered the same to them. This anger has caused me to ask, why me? The answer is this, *God was in it!*

Because Grandma's panic produced a similar fear in me, I could not say that she had done enough. If I had, it might have ended her walk toward salvation. I believe God led Grandma to share her fear with me because I was the only one who could not give the standard and blatantly false Mormon assurances. I offered no relief from the fear that gripped her heart because I could not ease the anxiety her words planted in mine. Grandma spoke to me because God was working to save us both. Of this, I am sure!

Lance

> He shall be to you a restorer of life, and sustain you in your old age...
> – Ruth 4:15a (WEB)

I have many questions pertaining to the salvation of Grandma. Because I don't have the answers, I must leave her in the hands of God whose love never fails.[14] This I know, if I find her in Heaven, I will embrace her, kiss her, and my joy will be complete.

If my sweet grandmother is in Heaven, and I pray she is, her prayer will be for her family. She will desire that they come to the truth and join her in the place of eternal rejoicing.

6.5 The Gift

Through my dear Grandmother, God gave a gift of immeasurable worth. Indeed it is a *precious pearl of great price*. I add my prayer to hers that God might save us all.

God is light. That light has illuminated me. I will never say, as did my sweet grandmother, *"I don't know if I did enough"*. It will never be about what I do, how much I do, or how well I do it. It will always be about *what Jesus did*. And so, I live with unquestioned confidence and joyous hope in the Lord of Lords and King of Kings!

> Out of Zion, the perfection of beauty, God hath shined forth.
> – Psalms 50:2 (Darby)

With trusting anticipation in my most holy and awesome God, I look to the future. I glory in the possibility that Grandma and I will one day sit together at a table, in God's house, in the Holy City over a steaming hot slice of cherry pie.

---

[14] Psalms 136:1-5

CHAPTER
SEVEN

OF BLUE, BEARDS, AND BLASPHEMY

> God painted the sky the same shade of blue as my shirt. He put hair on a man's head and hair on his chin. And, if my memory is correct, he said, *"It is good".*
>
> *Lance*

Grace and I were in attendance at a Stake Conference of *The Church of Jesus Christ of Latter-day Saints*. These are semi-annual, regional meetings for the combined membership of a Mormon Stake. A Stake consists of three to five thousand people who are members of five to ten wards.

The Stake President's first counselor stood to address the assembled congregation. I quickly realized he was in a bit of a snit. He was running under a full head of steam and tearing into many at will, including me.

Before I get into the meat of this man's message, I must describe my appearance on that particular Sunday morning. My hair was closely cropped and neatly combed. On my chin, I sported a short and carefully trimmed goatee. I was wearing a pale blue dress shirt and tie, dark slacks, and black leather shoes. I capped it all with a dark sports jacket. Now that you have a reasonably clear picture of how I was turned out that day; we can continue.

The speaker began making wild statements about the wrong color of shirts worn by some men. He emphatically demanded that a clean white dress shirt was the only acceptable Sunday attire for men. He stated that God would deny blessings to the man and his family if he violates this dress code. Things were getting very serious in a big hurry. As you may guess, I looked at my shirt and became decidedly uncomfortable. I had a sensation of eyes drilling through my offensive blue shirt and into my back. I envisioned people nudging spouses and whispering, "Look at Brother Earl's shirt!" The speaker's intent, I think, was to make me and others feel dirty. The attempt was initially successful!

The speaker turned his attention to long hair. I ran my hand over my head and thankfully, I dodged that bullet. According to this man, God has the same low opinion of men who wear their hair longer than ... what? At any rate, long hair on a man will result in the cessation of God's blessings. Barbershop avoidance is apparently a sin.

The instant he finished his rant on hair, he launched the third wave. God hates whiskers! I reached up and touched my chin ... *ohhhh crap!* The goatee was still there! The same claim of God's withheld blessings applied to men with excessive facial hair. And facial hair of any sort was considered excessive!

As seconds drug on endlessly, I moved beyond discomfort and found myself knee-deep in righteous, indignant anger. These standards are not in the Bible nor any Mormon scripture! Under the direction of the Stake President, this man of imagined authority was creating false doctrine as he went. He was firing random shots into the crowd and striking many without justification or doctrinal support. Even worse, he had forcefully shoved God aside and presumed to speak for Him!

God painted the sky the same shade of blue as my shirt. He put hair on a man's head and hair on his chin. And, if my memory is correct, he said, *"It is good"*.[1]

7.1 When Men Speak Over God

I couldn't imagine that things could get worse. Sometimes a man looks back at himself and wonders, *How could I have been so unbelievably wrong?* Things got far worse in a hurry! Things got blasphemously worse. Having grown tired of attacking men, he turned his wrath on almighty God.

The speaker boldly stated, *"You may say that Jesus had long hair and a beard, but I tell you now"*, he turned and pointed at the Stake President, *"Jesus never knew President (Name of Stake President inserted)"*.

My head snapped up. My eyes focused on the face of the Stake President. It split into a toothy grin! I looked at my sweet wife. Her face was ashen, drained of color. *"Did you hear that?"* She nodded, she heard it too and muttered in reply, *"That was Blasphemy!"*

A heretic taught thousands that Jesus would have been a better God with the right sort of mentoring. He named the Stake President as the mentor who would deliver a better dressed, neatly trimmed, and cleanly shaven Jesus. The suggestion that this Stake President can improve on Jesus is heresy!

A Fire Started to Burn.

As the meeting continued, blasphemy echoed in my ears and smoldered in my heart. As a Mormon, I didn't know God, yet something in me began to

---

[1] Genesis 1:31

burn. Something was wickedly wrong. *"You may say that Jesus had long hair and a beard, but I tell you now, Jesus never knew ..."*

The Fire Became an Inferno!

Looking at the surrounding faces, I saw no evidence that anyone noticed. With the dazed dullness of caged animals, they fixed dead eyes on the speaker. Mind-controlled slaves drank the Kool-Aid and accepted every lie as it fell from the lips of the Devil.

> Thou hast loved evil rather than good, lying rather than to speak righteousness. Selah.
> – Psalms 52:3 (Darby)

Seething, we moved through the crowd after the closing prayer. The people, utterly satisfied and totally fulfilled, shook hands and slapped backs. Everyone mechanically did his or her part in the Mormon machine. Like cogs in a wheel, they went around and around, ever-moving, ever-circling, and never arriving. Each confidently wore the mask of righteousness. Those with white shirts, short hair, and shaved chins had a triple justification for self-righteous piety. The scene was exasperating above all we had witnessed that day.

Grace and I appeared to be the only two troubled by men who made Jesus small and exalted themselves. Were we the only ones whose hearts cried *blasphemy* as these men invented other gods?

> he who opposes and exalts himself against all that is called God or that is worshiped, so that he sits as God in the temple of God, **setting himself up as God.**
> – 2 Thessalonians 2:4 (WEB), emphasis added

Grace Notes

Blasphemy!

Talk about chastisement! The men were told they robbed their families of blessings because of shirt color and hair, of all things. The more I listened, the more livid I became. What does that have to do with Jesus?

When the speaker suggested that Jesus would have benefited if our Stake President had mentored him, I was stunned! I turned to Lance and blurted, "That was blasphemy!"

At that moment, my faith in Mormonism died. My life as a Mormon ended. Lance wasn't ready to come out yet, so I supported him. But no church that blasphemes the name of God can be true!

My heart I give to God. He may mold it according to His pleasure. I praise Him every second of every day!

Grace

In the parking lot, a woman approached with a bright smile. She gushed, "wasn't that a wonderful conference!" Grunting a barely civil reply, we increased our pace.

Stupid Woman!

7.2 Same Game, Different Perspective

The Church of Jesus Christ of Latter-day Saints has a long history of diverse but substantially identical events. Allow me to share two which I personally witnessed. I experienced the first from the perspective of a zealous and dedicated member of the church. The second I witnessed after Jesus freed me from the chains that bind and blind. Viewing each from a unique perspective gave me pause for reflection and introspection.

At a General Conference, the then President of the Church, Gordon B. Hinckley, dropped a bombshell that put the church in a spin. His announcement wildly shook many girls and women who suddenly found themselves at odds with the prophet and his teachings.

> Likewise the piercing of the body for multiple rings in the ears, in the nose, even in the tongue. Can they possibly think that is beautiful? It is a passing fancy, but its effects can be permanent. Some have gone to such extremes that the ring had to be removed by surgery. The First Presidency and the Quorum of the Twelve have declared that we discourage tattoos and also "the piercing of the body for other than medical purposes." We do not, however, take any position "on the minimal piercing of the ears by women for one pair of earrings"—**one pair**.
> – Gordon B. Hinckley. "Great Shall Be the Peace of Thy Children" Talk, General Conference, October, 2000, emphasis added

After Grace and I had been born again, President Russell M. Nelson lit a fuse that convicted nearly every church member. His words identified almost everyone as Satan pleasing and Jesus rejecting sinners. Even more far-reaching was the condemnation of every Mormon prophet who came before. These sixteen former prophets and presidents of *The Church of Jesus Christ of Latter-day Saints*, Nelson identified as enemies of Jesus and the soldiers of Satan. According to a few uttered words, the church stopped, turned 180 degrees, and reversed its direction of movement.

> What's in a name or, in this case, a nickname? When it comes to nicknames of the Church, such as the "LDS Church," the "Mormon Church," or the "Church of the Latter-day Saints," the most important thing in those names is the absence of the Savior's name. **To remove the Lord's name from the Lord's Church is a major**

victory for Satan. When we discard the Savior's name, we are subtly disregarding all that Jesus Christ did for us—even His Atonement.
– Russell M. Nelson. "The Correct Name of the Church" Talk, General Conference, October, 2018, emphasis added

With a single spoken word, millions who had been worthy Mormons when Nelson began to speak were sinners by the time he said amen. With no modification of behavior and no faith degradation, once faithful Latter-Day Saints became dregs and outcasts in the church. In an instant, men, women, and children became active participants in victory after victory for Satan. And if they are in partnership with Satan, what is to become of their relationship with Jesus?

> Woe unto them that call evil good, and good evil; that put darkness for light, and light for darkness; that put bitter for sweet, and sweet for bitter!
> – Isaiah 5:20 (KJV)

Mormons are an amazingly mechanical people. They handle the fluidity of Mormon standards with ease, never seeming to comprehend that changing doctrine conflicts with the steadiness of an unchanging God. Being universally indoctrinated, they rush to catch up, accept, and comply. Blindness robs them of reason, leaving them unable to test and unwilling to study the Word of God. Hence, they endlessly and blindly follow with no motivation to obtain God's truth. They spin, grind and march blindly on the wide way toward the broad gate and certain destruction.[2]

> [21] Test all things, and hold firmly that which is good. [22] Abstain from every form of evil.
> – 1 Thessalonians 5:21-22 (WEB)

7.3 Men Condemned of Men

Here we see and comprehend the danger of man-made religion. Mormonism is an impossible gospel[3] that adds confusion and contradiction to the *simplicity that is in Christ*.[4] False religion passes ultimate power to weak men. Weak men with power become tyrants, ever seeking more power. The Bible has prophesied, warned, and prepared us with solutions to identify false teachers. God excuses none for not seeing and dealing with wolves in sheep's clothing.[5] And yet, sixteen million Mormons never seem to notice the danger.

---
[2] Matthew 7:13-14
[3] See chapter: Is the Gospel Everlasting?
[4] 2 Corinthians 11:3
[5] Matthew 7:15

> ¹⁰Two men went up into the temple to pray; one was a Pharisee, and the other was a tax collector. ¹¹The Pharisee stood and prayed to himself like this: 'God, I thank you, that I am not like the rest of men, extortionists, unrighteous, adulterers, or even like this tax collector. ¹²I fast twice a week. I give tithes of all that I get.'
> – Luke 18:10-12 (WEB)

Two men stood before the congregation one Sunday morn; one was a Stake President, and the other his puppet. The puppet stood, glorifying himself and his master like this: God, I thank you, that we are not like other men, wearers of blue, hair like a woman, or even those with chins of stubble. We fast every month, pay our tithes, attend the temple and beat our chests while judging other men according to our law, never yours!

The destructive pattern of Mormonism repeats again and again. Foolish men empowered by stupid men soon become the judge, jury, and executioner of all.

One sabbath day, the disciples of Jesus plucked heads of grain and began munching kernels of wheat. Not unlike my stake President and his counselor, pompous men rushed in to attach sin to this simple and unassuming act. Pharisees of old and their modern-day counterparts are all about the law and absolute compliance with every minute point.

In Jesus' day, the law was about to be fulfilled but had not yet been. Because the law remained in full effect, the Pharisees may have had an excuse. Even so, Jesus pointed out, "one

Reflections

I wish the heresy of this stake conference had been an isolated incident. Tragically, the disease goes merrily on.

> Only your unbelief will keep god from blessing you with miracles to move the mountains in your life.
> – Russell M. Nelson. Talk, General Conference, April 4, 2021

Oh the pain this will cause. I see a solitary soul kneeling at the bed of a perishing spouse, a couple clasping hands and praying for a dying child, and a mother weeping for a son or daughter lost to sin. I see millions more praying at the base of immense mountains. I see them racked with guilt when mountains remain unmoved. What kind of monster teaches that miracles depend on broken people instead of the power of Almighty God?

God promised to sweep away the mountain of death and sin. That certain knowledge reduces all other mountains to insignificant bumps on the path to life.

Lance

greater than the temple is here".⁶ Jesus continued by pointing to a passage they should have known well.

> But if you had known what this means, **I desire mercy**, and not sacrifice, **you would not have condemned the guiltless**.
> – Matthew 12:7 (WEB), emphasis added

Jesus was referring to a passage from the Torah. By their failure to understand the scripture they used as a weapon, Jesus put them firmly in their place.

> For I desire mercy, and not sacrifice; and the **knowledge of God more than burnt offerings**.
> – Hosea 6:6 (WEB), emphasis added

I found a modern pharisaical equivalent in this Stake President and his counselor. The Pharisees had a written law to support their position.⁷ Their interpretation was twisted, but the Pharisees at least had the law as a fallback position.

Jesus fulfilled the law, and we must put that fulfillment in proper perspective. These Mormon leaders' sin exceeds that of the Pharisees. These men live in the church age, in the time of grace. Yet, at that stake conference, they extended no grace. Where they should have extended mercy, they condemned. Their condemnation lacked support from any passage of scripture, Mormon or otherwise. These men abuse the people more severely than the notoriously twisted Pharisees of Jesus' day.

Being convinced in his mind and by the will of a Stake President, this Mormon leader took it upon himself to define new sins never contemplated by the whole of Mormon and Biblical scripture. Fueled by the illusion of other men's sins, he presumed to stand in place of Jesus and pronounce judgment on the people. He falsely prophesied that God would deny blessings until Mormon men turn from the sin of blue, hair, and whiskers'.

7.4 Salvation Lost

According to Mormon doctrine, heaven consists of three kingdoms. The highest is the Celestial Kingdom, where men go to become a god. In that kingdom, he will create and populate a world, aided by many plural wives. The middle part of heaven is the Terrestrial Kingdom, where weak Mormons and good non-Mormons go. The lowest kingdom, the Telestial realm, is reserved for evil men such as Adolf Hitler and the Book of Mormon villain Korihor.

Each kingdom is a place of the Mormon god's glory. Church leaders taught me, *The Telestial kingdom is so wonderful that I would kill myself to get there.*

---

⁶Matthew 12:6
⁷Exodus 20:8-11

Tradition told me that Joseph Smith first uttered these words. I cannot confirm that he said this, but I know leaders taught it to me.

Here's the rub. If the Mormon god's blessings cease when a man commits certain sins related to hair and shirt color, how can he bless a man with any degree of glory? If you believe this Stake President and his counselor, you must accept that god will cast a man out of the darkest corner of the lowest heaven. Why? Because the Mormon god withholds all blessings from men who commit such *grievous sins*.

7.5 Salvation Found

The ever-present burden of sin and Mormon repentance is daunting.[8] From thin air, church leaders imagine and pile on new sins. Words like venom fall from their lips and overwhelm the people.

> A sepulchre opened is their throat; with their tongues they used deceit; poison of asps is under their lips.
> – Romans 3:13 (YLT)

Let us consider a more straightforward theology. Jesus asked, "why take ye thought for raiment?"[9] He continued, "Wherewithal shall we be clothed?"[10] What if we turn our focus from the outer man and look to the inner man instead? What if we stop judging him for showing up improperly dressed and praise God that he showed up at all? What if we stop judging through our eyes and try to see through the eyes of God?

There is an incredible peace that attends all who repent, not according to the pattern of Mormonism, but as faithful followers of Jesus.[11] When I turned to God in love, fear, and surrender, He poured on mercy and grace without limit. Through the apostle John, I have God's promise.

> He that hath the Son hath the life; he that hath not the Son of God hath not the life.
> – I John 5:12 (ASV), emphasis added

I am set free from silly men in sheep's clothing with this grand assurance. For this, I endlessly lift the name of God with shouts of endless praise. God who loves me has made me free; free to wear blue, free to grow my hair, free to shave or not, and free in all things through Christ my Lord.

---

[8] See chapter: How do I Repent?
[9] Matthew 6:28
[10] Matthew 6:31
[11] See chapter: How do I Repent?

CHAPTER
EIGHT

CALLED OF GOD OR MEN

> Which one of your gods screwed up? Which one got it wrong ... your Monday god or your Friday god?
>
> *Lance*

On one particular Sunday, the Bishop's first counselor asked to meet with me. Meetings such as these were always a bit tense because they typically indicated a new calling was in the works. When a man serves according to the purpose God puts on his heart, the service is joyful, rewarding, and often productive. In Mormonism, this is seldom the case because callings come from men who desperately try to fill an endless list of positions. Consequently, the Mormon leader routinely stuffs a round person into a square hole.

There was always a suspicion that Mormon callings did not originate in Heaven. The church teaches that Mormon leaders make all callings under direct inspiration from their god. That is the ideal, but the Mormon people often repeat a familiar couplet, "Callings come by perspiration, not inspiration." To fill every calling in the ward and stake is an endless and frustrating task. Having served in many leadership positions, I have experienced this for myself.

The counselor pointed me to a chair where I settled in and waited for the other shoe to drop. He explained that the ward leaders submitted my name to the lord for a specific calling. In great solemnity, he explained, *god himself*, called me to teach Sunday School for the sixteen-year-old youth.

What a relief! This time, the dreaded call to the nursery, to nag the men about home teaching, or to be a quorum secretary didn't materialize. I enjoyed working with the youth and readily accepted. Even if it had been the calling I dreaded most, I would have quickly accepted. The individual has no real say about where the Mormon god will call him or her to serve. The requirement to accept every calling is hardline Mormon dogma. Anything less is considered rebellion against the Mormon god, and I dared not deny him.

Most LDS people spend many years in callings for which God, the real God, never called them. Undeniably, most callings become an act of serving the Mormon machine rather than service to God.[1] At least this time, the call was to do something for which I had passion, gifting, and desire.

That next Sunday, I taught for the first time. The Sunday School President sat in to audit my performance. After I released the class, the critique began. He felt things had gone very well and confirmed that I was the right man for the job. I ended that day feeling rather proud of my outstanding work.[2]

That was the way with me. I did the work; therefore, the credit was mine. I patted myself on the back and took the glory for myself. Did I ever praise god for such things? Not to my recollection. Mormonism is a works-based system where every effort established my righteousness, not his! Mormonism is a self-centered and self-exalting system that held me captive.

> [21] Because that, when they knew God, **they glorified him not** as God, neither were thankful; but **became vain in their imaginations**, and their foolish heart was darkened. [22] Professing themselves to be wise, they became fools, [23] **And changed the glory of the incorruptible God into an image made like to corruptible man**, and to birds, and four-footed beasts, and creeping things.
> – Romans 1:21-23 (KJV), emphasis added

8.1 The Release

One week later, I taught a second time. In my self-righteous pride, I presumed my performance had been flawless yet again. However, I received a request for a second meeting. I thought, "This can't be good!" I soon learned that I was to be released from that calling. As quickly as this preferred calling began, it was ending!

I was rather upset. After only two weeks, I had developed an attachment to the young people in my class. I had been so encouraged by the first two sessions, and now this ... why? So, I asked and received a flimsy answer. The response gave me one more reason to be upset. One young lady's father complained that I might not be the best choice to teach his daughter.

If I were not serving in this preferred calling, my name would go back into the hat for reassignment elsewhere. The possibility of being pressed into the snotty, goopy, poopy world of ward nursery rose like a specter.

Sitting in my chair, I stared at the floor. I couldn't comprehend what was happening or why. Then a thought came to my mind with absolute clarity,

---
[1] Matthew 22:36-40
[2] Matthew 7:21-23

so I voiced it, "Did you pray to god and get his confirmation before giving me this calling?" The Bishop's counselor knew how the church claimed to work. The premise was that they had prayed, and god had made his will perfectly known. He could give only one answer. His head began to nod solemnly. He affirmed that he and the other leaders had prayed together and received revelatory direction from the Mormon god.

The next thought hit me with power, and my uncertainty became resolve. "Before deciding to have me released, did you pray to know if it was god's will?" For the same reasons, he once again nodded his affirmation. He had no choice. Anything less would have been an admission of failure.

Forcefully I asked, "*Which one screwed up?*" He responded with a look of confusion. So I repeated, "*Which one screwed up?*" This exchange was repeated several times. With each restating, he became more undone. I let him soak in it for a minute or two.

Then I asked, "*Which one of your gods screwed up? Which one got it wrong, your Monday god or your Friday god?*".

He looked as if he had taken a rifle shot to the chest. His eyes became orbs, his face drained, his mouth opened, but He made no sound. Seconds ticked by. It seemed like an eternity. Finally, he muttered, I'll check with the Bishop and get back with you.

8.2 The Investigation

That following Sunday, I was informed there would be an investigation. The Sunday School President visited each class member's home to query the parents. The intent was to uncover some sin or misdeed that might justify my release. The investigation stretched on for weeks while I waited. One father informed me that the questioning was extreme and seemed more like a witch hunt. He was angry; I felt that too. I look back in wonder at these leaders who called me brother while cutting my legs from underneath me. Men of God? Not that I ever noticed.

Grace Notes

I always struggled with "callings". If people were "called of God", I couldn't see it. It always seemed to be the popular or stalwart members who received the elite callings such as Bishop, Relief Society President, Young Women's president, etc. Callings that were less attractive, like nursery leader and tedious record-keeping assignments, went to those who were new, shy, or just different.

It was also true for the youth positions. Children of the elect ward members served in the light. The rest toiled in obscurity.

I saw the same pattern from ward to ward. Callings inspired by God? Not that I could see.

Grace

> ²⁵There is a way that seemeth right unto a man, but the end thereof are the ways of death. ²⁶He that laboureth laboureth for himself; for his mouth craveth it of him. ²⁷An ungodly man diggeth up evil: and in his lips there is as a burning fire. ²⁸A froward man soweth strife: and a whisperer separateth chief friends.
> – Proverbs 16:25-28 (KJV)

After several weeks, the counselor was ready to announce his decision. He informed me that the investigation was complete and he approved me to continue as a Sunday School teacher. Even as a believing Mormon, I found my leader's arrogance very disturbing.

> For they loved the praise of men more than the praise of God.
> – John 12:43 (KJV)

8.3 The Beginning of Understanding

After his announcement, I stared at the floor and once again I ordered my thoughts. I began to speak. I rehearsed how the ward leadership had gone to the Mormon god who personally called me as a Sunday School teacher. Then a week later, church leaders began to worry that their unchangeable god[3] had changed his mind. I reminded him that they had prayed again and discovered their perfect god had dropped the ball. Yup, the Mormon god blew it. One week later, he corrected the screw-up and reversed his previous proclamation. Then, being challenged by me, they relieved god of the decision and placed it in more capable hands. Clearly, this matter was too demanding for the Mormon god, the Bishop, and his counselors. Finally, a kind but oafish middle-aged man settled the issue that baffled the leadership and their bipolar god.

> God is not a man, that he should lie; neither the son of man, that he should repent: hath he said, and shall he not do it? or hath he spoken, and shall he not make it good?
> – Numbers 23:19 (KJV)

I couldn't see it then, but God, the real God, gave me this experience to draw me to Him. This experience and others moved me, little by little, toward the light and to the God of Glory. I look back and see that he was always working in my life, always drawing me out of darkness and to Himself. He is my King, and Him alone do I serve.

I look back on my years in Mormonism and can't help but wonder, how did wolves in sheep's clothing so easily bewitch me?[4] Try as I might, I cannot formulate an answer. I cannot comprehend my willingness to be led in chains. How it could have been, I cannot explain. Nor can I deny.

---

[3] Hebrews 13:8
[4] Galatians 3:1

8.4 When the Wicked Rule

> When the righteous thrive, the people rejoice; but when the wicked rule, the people groan.
> – Proverbs 29:2 (WEB)

Why do the people rejoice when their leaders are righteous? From a worldly perspective, there are many answers. Order replaces chaos; justice will rise while injustice recedes. Righteous rulers serve the people and never exalt themselves. Mormonism's sorry state proves that righteous leaders are scarce indeed.

We live in the world. We hope to live on a spiritual plane above the corruption of natural things. The constant tug-of-war between these opposing forces can be challenging to manage.

Wicked rulers typically exist in two categories. Worldly rulers govern nations, and religious rulers govern souls.

Perhaps no worldly ruler is worse than the Roman Emperor Nero. He came to power after his adopted father died. By murder, he eliminated perceived adversaries, including his mother Agrippina and his first and second wives. He started the "Great Fire of Rome" and blamed the Christians for it. His accusations justified the persecution, torture, and killing of Jesus' followers. Eventually, he took his own life.[5]

There is no shortage of despotic worldly rulers, but these are not the worry. And this brings us to the truly dangerous ruler, the religious ruler.

> I said therefore to you that you will die in your sins; for unless you believe that I am he, you will die in your sins.
> – John 8:24 (WEB)

When these leaders have had their way, tragedy follows. Indoctrinated men and women live inauthentic Christian lives. Being wholly separated from the light, they fail to know the truth.

> [21]Not everyone who says to me, 'Lord, Lord,' will enter into the Kingdom of Heaven; but he who does the will of my Father who is in heaven. [22]Many will tell me in that day, 'Lord, Lord, didn't we prophesy in your name, in your name cast out demons, and in your name do many mighty works?' [23]Then I will tell them, 'I never knew you. Depart from me, you who work iniquity.'
> – Matthew 7:21-23 (WEB)

The Mormon tragedy focuses on false prophets and teachers to the exclusion of God. The promise of laws and ordinances overshadows the wonder of grace.[6] They don't know Jesus or see Him as the only way.

---

[5] Romans 1:28
[6] *Pearl of Great Price*, Article of Faith 3

> Jesus saith unto him, I am the way, and the truth, and the life: no one cometh unto the Father, but by me.
> – John 14:6 (ASV)

The precious Mormon people never see the narrow gate and, consequently, they never trust that He alone is enough.

> [13]Enter ye in at the strait gate: for wide is the gate, and broad is the way, **that leadeth to destruction, and many there be which go in thereat**: [14]Because strait is the gate, and narrow is the way, **which leadeth unto life, and few there be that find it**.
> – Matthew 7:13-14 (KJV), Emphasis added

8.5 Wolves in Sheep's Clothing

The biblical warnings are inescapable. There will be many false prophets, lying teachers, and demonic preachers. Collectively these are wolves in sheep's clothing.[7]

We must never forget that sheep's clothing perfectly disguises the wolf as one of us. That's the whole point! The wolf looks, acts and talks just like one of the flock. Many cannot see the warning signs because wolves move freely among the flock. Because they look like one of us, they mingle with the sheep unquestioned, unopposed and unnoticed. While the sheep nap or have their heads buried in deep grass, they fail to keep watch while the flock is destroyed.

Wolves lure the foolishly naïve from the center's safety to the edge of the flock. On the edge is where the danger lies. God is the center place. That is where His Holy Spirit is living and active. In the center of the church, life is more abundant. In the center, God's people are alert to danger and diligently watching over their brothers and sisters.

> [9]I am the door: by me if any man enter in, he shall be saved, and shall go in and out, and find pasture. [10]The thief cometh not, but for to steal, and to kill, and to destroy: **I am come that they might have life, and that they might have it more abundantly**. [11]I am the good shepherd: the good shepherd giveth his life for the sheep.
> – John 10:9-11 (KJV, emphasis added)

God, knowing of these dangers, lovingly provided patterns we can follow. His perfect formula identifies and excises wolves with the precision of a surgeon's scalpel and a bulldozer's brute force.

To the church in Rome, Paul saw and warned of wolves who, with smooth talk and flattery, moved among the flock. From time to time, they devoured a foolish lamb while deceiving the hearts of the simple.

---

[7]Matthew 7:15

CALLED OF GOD OR MEN

> [17]Now I beg you, brothers, look out for those who are causing the divisions and occasions of stumbling, contrary to the doctrine which you learned, and turn away from them. [18]For those who are such don't serve our Lord, Jesus Christ, but their own belly; and by their smooth and flattering speech, they deceive the hearts of the innocent.
> – Romans 16:17-18 (WEB)

Paul sternly warned the church at Corinth of wolves' ever-present danger.

> [3]But I fear, lest by any means, as the serpent beguiled Eve through his subtilty, so your minds should be corrupted from the simplicity that is in Christ. [4]For if he that cometh preacheth **another Jesus**, whom we have not preached, or if ye receive **another spirit**, which ye have not received, or **another gospel**, which ye have not accepted, ye might well bear with him.
> – 2 Corinthians 11:3-4 (KJV), emphasis added

In this warning, he offered three keys to identify wolves. First, wolves attempt to lead the people after another Jesus because a man who falls for a false god will fall for anything.[8] Second, wolves promote a spirit of deception. Wolves know men's hearts are quick to accept that which they falsely believe to be the Holy Spirit.[9] They falsely perceive a spiritual truth in any experience of emotion, passion, or a burning bosom. Third, wolves point men's depraved hearts to another gospel.[10] People quickly accept false gospels when they acknowledge men who wrongly assume the authority of teachers, rulers, kings, and prophets.[11]

And so, the pieces of the story come together. Wolves deceive the hearts of the simple[12] because they are exceedingly corrupt. Being corrupt and deceived, they put up with evil quickly enough.[13]

As our story comes full circle, we see wolves and sheep. Wolves declare that god speaks through them. Foolish sheep submit willingly on the assumption that the wolves have authority. A wolf, a Mormon leader, told me that a man could decide a matter too complex for the Mormon god. I had every reason to run. I should have run, but unseen chains held me bound to the wolf who was my enemy. I trusted wolves even as they plotted my destruction. Still, I can't decisively tell you why!

---

[8]Psalms 62:4
[9]*Doctrine and Covenants*, 9:8
[10]Galatians 1:6-7
[11]2 Timothy 3:13
[12]Romans 16:17-18
[13]2 Corinthians 11:4

CHAPTER
NINE

THE CHANGING TEMPLE

> We, who are the *body of Christ*, will not be moved!
>
> *Lance*

The longer I remained in the Mormon church, the more I noticed a continuous shift in Mormon doctrine. Key among these were changes in the temple. Answers are elusive when essential ordinances vanish like smoke or morph with chameleon-like ease. In the wake of such modifications, I had no certainty of the reality or credibility of saving ordinances inside the Mormon temple.

9.1   1990 Changes

Before the pivotal revelation of 1990, I had dedicated innumerable hours to temple attendance and the memorization of essential saving ordinances. All I had worked so hard to understand faded to nothing with a single prophetic utterance. I was disconcerted when once necessary ordinances were relegated to the rubbish bin.

Words of the Mormon prophet Brigham Young echo in every temple attendee's ears. His words once motivated me to believe that every aspect of temple service was necessary for salvation. I revered him as a true prophet of the restored gospel. Consequently, I revered his words as eternally significant and salvific, down to the most intricate detail.

> Your endowment is to prepare you to receive all those ordinances in the House of the Lord, which are necessary to enable you to walk back to the presence of the Father, passing the angels who stand as sentinels, being able to give them the key words, the signs, and

tokens, pertaining to the Holy Priesthood, and gain your eternal exaltation.
– "Instruction given in each temple endowment session"

If the things I once learned were once *necessary to enable me to walk back to the presence of the Father*, why have they been modified or deleted? With the stroke of a pen, much of what I once accepted as essential faded away. Like a vapor before the wind, everything I once thought I knew vanished.

Everything once held as holy became a fading memory. So little of my former faith remained, and I struggled to understand where it was going and what was coming as the new-age Mormon replacement.

Gone was the "Pay Lay Ale" Adamic prayer. No longer did I pantomime my own death in a sacred covenant of secrecy. No one demanded that I slit my throat, tear open my chest or spill my bowels. These penalties once required an absolute commitment of secrecy. The removal of crucial temple rituals caused me to ask, were they ever essential, or is it all smoke and mirrors?

For twenty years, I communicated with the lord through the veil upon the "five points of fellowship". That, too, was taken away. Previously, the lord refused to speak until we were united in this heavenly and uncomfortably intimate embrace. After the change, god spoke as casually as two friends in a coffee shop. Everything sacred and revered became base day-to-day chatter.

> *Grace Notes*
>
> I was young, naive, and timid when I first entered the Mormon temple. It blew me away!
>
> No one tells you what to expect. The washing and anointing in the 70s was a distressing invasion of my person. Strange hands on intimate parts of my body made me horribly uncomfortable and embarrassed.
>
> Then came the endowment. I couldn't believe I was mimicking my own death by cutting open my throat, chest, and abdomen.
>
> No one seemed troubled, so I swallowed hard and kept my mouth shut! It always bothered me, though. If this was really God's church, why couldn't I find Him in it?
>
> *Grace*

Another interesting modification to the temple endowment was the removal of a Christian minister in Satan's employ. Mormon leaders simply cut him from the script. I was surprised to see him go because his part perfectly matched Mormon descriptions of Christianity.

I was answered that I must join none of them, **for they were all wrong**; and the Personage who addressed me said that **all their creeds were an abomination** in his sight; that **those professors were all corrupt**; that: "they draw near to me with their lips, but

THE CHANGING TEMPLE

their hearts are far from me, they teach for doctrines the commandments of men, having a form of godliness, but they deny the power thereof."
– *Joseph Smith History*, 1:19, emphasis added

And he said unto me: Behold there are save two churches only; the one is the church of the Lamb of God [Mormonism], and the other is the church of the devil; wherefore, **whoso belongeth not to the church of the Lamb of God belongeth to that great church, which is the mother of abominations; and she is the whore of all the earth.**
– *Book of Mormon*, 1 Nephi 14:10, emphasis added

Brother Taylor has just said that **the religions of the day were hatched in hell**. The eggs were laid in hell, hatched on its borders, and then kicked on to the earth.
– *Journal of Discourses* (N.p.: n.p., n.d.), 6:176, Brigham Young, emphasis added

With a regard to true theology, **a more ignorant people never lived than the present so-called Christian world**.
– *Journal of Discourses* (N.p.: n.p., n.d.), 8:199, Brigham Young, emphasis added

Christianity ... is a perfect pack of nonsense ... **the devil could not invent a better engine to spread his work than the Christianity of the nineteenth century.**
– *Journal of Discourses* (John Taylor, N.p.: n.p., n.d.), 6:167, emphasis added

After *The Church of Jesus Christ of Latter-day Saints* was organized, there were only two churches upon the earth. They were known respectively as the Church of the Lamb of God and Babylon. **The various organizations which are called churches throughout Christendom, though differing in their creeds and organizations, have one common origin. They all belong to Babylon**.
– George Q. Cannon, Jerreld L. Newquist, *Gospel Truth*(Salt Lake City: Deseret Book, 1957) 56, emphasis added

After a lifetime of learning that Christianity is the whore of the earth, created in hell without light, understanding, or truth; I suddenly had to deal with a stark reversal of doctrine. Without success, I struggled to make it compute! The Mormon prophet, Gordon B. Hinckley, was traveling the world and substantially denying every prophet who came before. His every word denied all I had come to know in a lifetime of Mormonism.

> We can respect other religions, and must do so. We must recognize the great good they accomplish. We must teach our children to be tolerant and friendly toward those not of our faith. We are not out to injure other churches. We are not out to hurt other churches. We do not argue with other churches. We do not debate with other churches. We simply say to those who may be of other faiths or of no faith, "You bring with you such truth as you have, and let us see if we can add to it".
>
> – The Church of Jesus Christ of Latter-day Saints, *TEACHINGS OF PRESIDENTS OF THE CHURCH GORDON B. HINCKLEY*(City/Salt Lake City: n.p., n.d.) 277

9.2 2018 Changes

In 2015, while I was still a Mormon in good standing, the church made its first-ever donation to the Utah Pride Center, a Salt Lake City gay support organization. Neither the church nor the center announced the amount, but a local TV station, KTSU, reported it to be $2,500. By 2018, the church was openly working with an LGBTQ support group known as *Affirmation*. Mormon support included a gift of $25,000. In 2019, the church-wide LGBTQ policy was relaxed. In 2020, Brigham Young University welcomed same-sex ballroom dancing for the first time.

None of these represent the Mormon church of my youth. They left me to wonder where the church was going with these many doctrinal reversals. Modifications to the temple endowment would soon answer that question.

When I first began attending the temple, every man and woman covenanted to obey the *law of chastity*. Over the years, this law has morphed to a rather large degree.

> We are instructed to give unto you the law of Chastity; which is, that each of **you shall have no sexual intercourse except with your husband or wife to whom you are legally and lawfully wedded.**
>
> – "Law of Chastity" Mormon Temple Endowment, beginning in January, before 1990, emphasis added

Rumor had it that some temple-going Mormons were engaging in extramarital sex, which they justified since there was no intercourse. Consequently, a clarification of the law became necessary. "Sexual intercourse" was replaced with "sexual relations".

> We are instructed to give unto you the law of Chastity; which is, that each of **you shall have no sexual relations except with your husband or wife to whom you are legally and lawfully wedded.**
> – "Law of Chastity" Mormon Temple Endowment, beginning in January, 1990 through 2018, emphasis added

The next change to the *law of chastity* thoroughly answered my questions regarding the church's reversal of LGBTQ doctrine.

> We are instructed to give unto you the law of Chastity; which is, that the women of God's kingdom and the men of God's kingdom **shall have no sexual relations except with those to whom they are legally and lawfully wedded** according to His law.
> – "Law of Chastity" Mormon Temple Endowment, beginning in January, 2019, emphasis added

Mormon history is a repeating pattern of compromise. When the government brought pressure to bear, the church abandoned polygamy. When pressure was brought to bear, our black brothers and sisters received all the blessings of Mormonism. Today, forces inside and outside the church demand a total acceptance of a practice God has condemned in both biblical testaments. The Mormon leadership will undoubtedly remain true to their past traditions and selectively reject any Bible passages relative to homosexuality.

If history repeats itself, and it always does, the day will come, and it is not far off, when same-sex marriages will be performed in Mormon temples. We will see genetically male children sealed as daughters and girls sealed as sons to Mormon parents. Some will scoff, and others will boldly deny that these things are coming. Every member must concede that the church is already doing what its former membership once thought impossible.

Tragically, the Mormon rank and file will embrace the new doctrine when that day comes. They will accept every lie that comes from Salt Lake. Because they believe church leaders cannot lead them astray, they will relent and follow.[1] In that hour, they will put their heads down and keep marching. They, never having learned the requirement to test every spirit,[2] will trudge on as lambs to the slaughter.

Shortly after leaving Mormonism, I wondered if the Bible actually spoke against homosexuality. I couldn't answer my question. In truth, I had no idea. Try this: Find a Mormon and ask, "Does God speak against homosexuality and if so, where?". I am satisfied that the vast majority will be unable to answer. Having no sure knowledge of God's word on the matter, they will turn to their prophet and blindly fall in line.

---

[1] Galatians 1:8
[2] 1 John 4:1

> If ye were of the world, the world would love its own; but because **ye are not of the world**, but I have chosen you out of the world, on account of this the world hates you.
> – John 15:19 (Darby), emphasis added

9.3 Questions Without Answers

I finally came to a place where I asked hard questions. If God is unchangeable and if the church is true, how are these massive changes possible? Church and family pounded the absolute necessity of temple covenants into my head from my youth. If all these things were ever necessary and important to an unchangeable God, why are they not important still?

> For I know that God is not a partial God, neither a changeable being; but he is unchangeable from ball eternity to all eternity.
> – *Book of Mormon*, Moroni 8:18

The unchangeable god of Mormonism has been rendered weak and changeable before my eyes. I have seen him branded and re-branded so many times. I once believed that the firmness of Mormonism was an immovable rock. Doubts multiplied, and I could not deny them.

9.4 Established on the Rock

Mormonism teaches that the first-century Christian church apostatized from the gospel of Jesus Christ, necessitating a complete restoration.[3] And yet, it appears that the Mormon church is guilty of apostasy. Whatever it was, it is changing, morphing, and in chameleon-like fashion, adapting to every social wind of change. It is guilty of the very weakness it rashly applied to the Christian church. Relative to what the church once was, Mormonism has apostatized from Mormonism.

Do these changes bring the church closer to God or align it with a fallen world? After forty years of faithful temple attendance, I am convinced that all changes have been the fruit of social and political pressures. Changes typically occur to ease the temple goer's discomfort with controversial doctrines or overly intimate rituals.

> **God is not a man**, that he should lie; neither the son of man, **that he should repent**: hath he said, and shall he not do it? or hath he spoken, and shall he not make it good?
> – Numbers 23:19 (KJV)

---

[3] See chapter: Is the Gospel Everlasting?

Does it seem likely that our unchangeable God will change? Of course not! Do the significant changes found in Mormonism seem in keeping with an immutable God? The answer is obvious.

The New Testament writers endured great persecution and unimaginable hardship because they would not renounce the unchanging gospel of Jesus Christ. They went to great lengths to stand boldly before every worldly challenge and quickly condemn any attempt to tamper with truth. Those who taught of other gospels, other gods, or other spirits were boldly rejected. On any occasion when the church began to stray, the people were lovingly corrected and redirected to the true path of faithfulness.

> [3]But I fear, lest by any means, as the serpent beguiled Eve in his craftiness, your minds should be corrupted from the simplicity and the purity that is toward Christ. [4]For if he that cometh preacheth **another Jesus**, whom we did not preach, or if ye receive a **different spirit**, which ye did not receive, or a **different gospel**, which ye did not accept, ye do well to bear with him.
> – 2 Corinthians 11:3-4 (ASV), emphasis added

Instead of changing policy and rewriting doctrine, Peter, James, Paul, and others encouraged the church to stand upon those truths already established and previously accepted.

> **Don't be conformed** to this world, **but be transformed** by the renewing of your mind, so that you may prove what is the good, well-pleasing, and perfect will of God.
> – Romans 12:2 (WEB), emphasis added

> **We must obey God** rather than men.
> – Acts 5:29 (ASV), emphasis added

> ... don't you know that **friendship with the world is hostility toward God**? Whoever therefore wants to be **a friend of the world makes himself an enemy of God**.
> – James 4:4 (WEB), emphasis added

The Bible is clear. The call is for us to stand fast on the Rock that is Jesus Christ. No matter what the world says or does, if we love God, we will plant our flag and make our stand on and for the gospel, which has the power to save.[4]

---

[4] I Corinthians 15:1-4

Any church that builds its doctrine according to society's pressures cannot be true. We cannot trust any who leads such a church. Their house is built on the sand, and indeed it will fall and the inhabitants will be destroyed.[5]

In contrast, the Christian church stands on the Rock that is Jesus. For 2000 years, it has stood through every storm. It will continue to stand, and it will remain unshaken. It, and we who are the *body of Christ*, will not be moved!

> [15]that you may become blameless and harmless, children of God without defect in the midst of a crooked and perverse generation, among whom you are seen as lights in the world, [16]**holding up the word of life**; ...
> – Philippians 2:15-16a (WEB), emphasis added

---

[5] Matthew 7:24-25

Part II

A FALLEN HOUSE

The Collapse of Mormonism

CHAPTER
TEN

A TESTIMONY OF JOSEPH SMITH

> Jesus protected me from Satan's wiles and opened my eyes! For that, I praise His name!
>
> *Grace*

My Mormon testimony was always a bit of a struggle. I loved the church, and I loved my heritage. These things held me bound, captive, immersed, and entangled in a religion to which I was devoted. There was so much to love, yet one thing troubled me continually. This significant and haunting issue was Joseph Smith. Try as I might, I could not gain a testimony that he was God's prophet and mouthpiece. My uncertainty was a source of deep and abiding distress. I saw my inability to testify of Joseph Smith confidently as evidence that I would not receive salvation or exaltation in heaven where god is. My future was in desperate peril. Mormon leaders lined up to confirm my worst fears.

> ... no man or woman in this dispensation will ever enter into the celestial kingdom of God without the consent of Joseph Smith. From the day that the Priesthood was taken from the earth to the winding-up scene of all things, every man and woman must have the certificate of Joseph Smith, junior, as a passport to their entrance into the mansion where God and Christ are—I with you and you with me. I cannot go there without his consent.
> – *Journal of Discourses* (N.p.: n.p., n.d.), 7:289, Brigham Young & Robert L. Millett Ensign, June, 1994

A FALLEN HOUSE

Many have belittled Joseph Smith, but those who have will be forgotten in the remains of mother earth, and the odor of their infamy will ever be with them, but honor, majesty, and fidelity to God, exemplified by Joseph Smith and attached to his name, will never die.
– Harold B. Lee. "Closing Remarks" General Conference, October 1973

...he that confesseth not that Jesus has come in the flesh and sent Joseph Smith with the fulness of the Gospel to this generation, is not of God, but is anti-christ
– *Journal of Discourses* (N.p.: n.p., n.d.), 9:312, Brigham Young

So many times, I leaned on the promises of the Book of Mormon. I trusted god to keep his word and give me the assurance I craved.

> ⁴And when ye shall receive these things, I would exhort you that ye would ask God, the Eternal Father, in the name of Christ, if these things are not true; and if ye shall ask with a sincere heart, with real intent, having faith in Christ, he will manifest the truth of it unto you, by the power of the Holy Ghost. ⁵And by the power of the Holy Ghost ye may know the truth of all things.
> – *Book of Mormon*, Moroni 10:4-5

There are no words to express the sorrow that haunted me. Each attempt to know resulted in the same predictable failure. No amount of prayer, no amount of study, no amount of faith brought an assurance that Joseph Smith was a prophet of God. No amount of strenuous effort brought the sought for confirmation. My deepest desire was to know Joseph was a prophet, and I could not gain

---

Satan's Wiles

Lance and I had traveled to Carthage jail where Joseph Smith died. I thought, surely this will help my unbelief! Near the end of the tour, the guide pointed to the floor. He stated, this is where Hyrum, the brother of Joseph, fell; this is where his blood stained the floor. Wow! Goosebumps! I really felt something!

After returning to our life, the feelings faded and eventually disappeared. Why?

Now that I have found truth in Jesus Christ, I know Satan used my emotions to deceive and lead me away from Jesus Christ. God protected me from Satan's wiles and opened my eyes! For that, I praise His name!

Grace

it for myself. I faced the likelihood, with a broken heart, that exaltation was beyond my reach.

There was a strange and confusing reality amid all this doubt. Though I could not believe in Joseph Smith, I loved many of the words he wrote. I could not reconcile my love and belief in some of his words with my inability to love and believe in him.

The Book of Mormon records many passages that beautifully speak to me still.

> [17] Nevertheless, notwithstanding the great goodness of the Lord, in showing me his great and marvelous works, my heart exclaimeth: O wretched man that I am! Yea, my heart sorroweth because of my flesh; my soul grieveth because of mine iniquities. [18] I am encompassed about, because of the temptations and the sins which do so easily beset me. [19] And when I desire to rejoice, my heart groaneth because of my sins; nevertheless, I know in whom I have trusted.
> – *Book of Mormon*, 2 Nephi 4:17-19

> And behold, I tell you these things that ye may learn wisdom; that ye may learn that when ye are in the service of your fellow beings ye are only in the service of your God
> – *Book of Mormon*, Mosiah 2:17

> And also, ye yourselves will succor those that stand in need of your succor; ye will administer of your substance unto him that standeth in need; and ye will not suffer that the beggar putteth up his petition to you in vain, and turn him out to perish.
> – *Book of Mormon*, Mosiah 4:16

These passages were and are beautiful to me. I believed and still believe they speak truth. Why then, did the same assurance in the prophetic mission of Joseph Smith elude me? Why then, could I not believe?

10.1 A Promise of Hope

From the depths of my despair, a light of hope pushed back the darkness. A prophetic word promised to dispel the gloom that overshadowed my soul. The living prophet of god made a promise. I believed him without doubt or reservation. He challenged me to read the Book of Mormon by the end of the year. He promised that I would receive what I desired most if I would accept and complete this challenge. He promised that my testimony would become all I desired.

Without reservation I promise you that if each of you will observe this simple program, regardless of how many times you previously may have read the Book of Mormon, there will come into your lives and into your homes an added measure of the Spirit of the Lord, a strengthened resolution to walk in obedience to His commandments, and a **stronger testimony** of the living reality of the Son of God.
– Gordon B. Hinckley, "Testimony Vibrant and True", Ensign, August 2005, emphasis added

With unfettered faith, I accepted this challenge with its promise to bring the knowledge that I lacked. How could it fail? I had the seal and promise of the living prophet. In other words, it was a sure and unquestioned word from god to me!

10.2 A Promise Broken

I met every condition of this challenge, but something went terribly wrong. In the end, there was no new assurance that Joseph Smith was a prophet. In fact, I had new reasons to doubt. The validity of a second "so-called prophet" came sharply into question. Heaped before me was undeniable proof that Gordon B. Hinckley was a false prophet, a liar, and a wolf in sheep's clothing.[1] This *"prophet of god"* had prophesied into my life and his prophecy failed.[2] With this, my faith became less and not more.

> [20] But the prophet, which shall presume to speak a word in my name, which I have not commanded him to speak, or that shall speak in the name of other gods, **even that prophet shall die.** [21] And if thou say in thine heart, How shall we know the word which the Lord hath not spoken? [22] **When a prophet speaketh in the name of the Lord, if the thing follow not, nor come to pass, that is the thing which the Lord hath not spoken, but the prophet hath spoken it presumptuously**: thou shalt not be afraid of him.
> – Deuteronomy 18:20-22 (KJV)

> [15] Beware of false prophets, which come to you in sheep's clothing, but inwardly they are ravening wolves. [16] Ye shall know them by their fruits. Do men gather grapes of thorns, or figs of thistles? [17] Even so every good tree bringeth forth good fruit; but a corrupt tree bringeth forth evil fruit. [18] A good tree cannot bring forth evil fruit, neither can a corrupt tree bring forth good fruit. [19] Every tree that bringeth not forth good fruit is hewn down, and cast into the fire. [20] Wherefore

---
[1] Matthew 7:15
[2] Deuteronomy 18:20-22

by their fruits ye shall know them.
— Matthew 7:15 (KJV)

The evil fruit of Gordon B. Hinckley was evident. That his prophesy failed was undeniable. If he was a prophet at all, he was the prophet of a false god. I am equally confident that the same is true of every Mormon prophet and apostle, beginning with Joseph Smith and continuing to the current leadership. All have prophesied similarly, and all were, in my life, false visions and lying divinations.[3]

10.3 Counterfeit Confusion

After several years of living as a born-again Christian, I finally solved the puzzle that confused me those sixty years.

I had loved and believed some of Joseph Smith's writings, but I could not love or believe him. For years, I struggled to understand how this was possible. There seemed to be a logical contradiction, a fallacy I could not resolve. Try as I might, no resolution presented itself. If Smith's words were valid, it followed that he would be a true prophet, but the pieces would not fit, and now I know why.

Satan, the father of lies,[4] the master of counterfeit light had deceived me. He knows moral people will not follow him unless he wraps his lies in beautiful elements of truth. If people find a few things to believe and hold dear, they feel justified in turning a blind eye to the many pieces that just won't fit.

> For if he that cometh preacheth **another Jesus**, whom we have not preached, or if ye receive **another spirit**, which ye have not received, or **another gospel**, which ye have not accepted, ye might well bear with him.
> — 2 Corinthians 11:4

Other gods, other gospels, other spirits? Oh, I had them all! Trying to believe in Joseph Smith is a lot like juggling. I struggled to know and believe in a false god. He is the god I hoped to be, the god I thought Joseph had become, and the god of his dark imagination. Too many balls, too much confusion, and too much contradiction. Try as I might, I could not keep them in the air, and I couldn't understand why.

> No one can serve two masters, for either he will hate the one and love the other; or else he will be devoted to one and despise the other.
> — Matthew 6:24 (WEB)

---

[3] Ezekiel 13:6
[4] John 8:44

And so it was that Satan ruled my world, disguised as an *angel of light*.[5] He bought his apostles and prophets who posed as *ministers of righteousness*.[6] For all those years, I never once noticed that each were clad in *"sheep's clothing"*.[7]

> A sepulchre opened is their throat; with their tongues they used deceit; poison of asps is under their lips.
> – Romans 3:13 (YLT)

---

[5] 2 Corinthians 11:14
[6] 2 Corinthians 11:15
[7] Matthew 7:15

CHAPTER
ELEVEN

THE REAL JOSEPH SMITH

> When people make Joseph Smith their hill to die on, boldly counter, *"show it to me in the Bible!"*
>
> Lance

God's timing is impeccable, perfect, and sometimes, He just blows my mind. According to my timetable, I tend to move forward, trusting myself instead of Him. I suppose I ought to work on that. When I forget essential things, my amazingly patient God powerfully, forcefully, bluntly, and oh, so mercifully brings me back to center. He whispers *"Be still, and know that I am God"*.[1] He reminds me that He fights every battle and that my job is to *"fear not, stand still, and see the salvation of the Lord"*.[2] And in all things, He reminds me that *"His loving kindness is great toward us"*.[3]

I thought I had adequately covered the topic of Joseph Smith until I met with a high-ranking Mormon leader. From 8:30 to midnight, we sat in his living room and spoke of God. This man has not personally initiated an action to harm me, but in the name of *"Mormon priesthood keys"*, he believed, endorsed and enforced a *gag order*,[4] a letter of *false witness*[5] and *prosecution in criminal court*.[6]

Our discussion was largely and mostly cordial and, for that, I praise God. However, there were two minor scrapes.

---

[1] Psalms 46:10
[2] Exodus 14:13
[3] Psalms 117:2
[4] See chapter: The Gag Order
[5] See chapter: Excommunication
[6] See chapter: Given Over to the Courts

The first rough patch was when he indicated that I was never *all in* regarding my Mormon testimony. My automatic response was to challenge his assertion. But that wouldn't be right. You see, I was *all in* with Mormonism except for the single exception to this Joseph Smith thing that I could not resolve.

The second scrape occurred when he became offended, demanding that I *"not muddy the name of Joseph Smith"*. He went on to praise and exalt Smith in a most flowery and respectful manner. I asked, "will you accept the words of Mormon leaders such as John Taylor and even Joseph Smith himself as a fair representation of who and what Smith was?" To this, he was agreeable.

I dedicate the balance of this chapter to the Mormon leader who inspired me to look more closely into the final hours of the Mormon prophet, Joseph Smith.

The apostle, Jeffrey R. Holland, offered a stirring speech about the dying testimony of Joseph and Hyrum Smith. Holland spoke of their unwavering faith as they approached the moment in which they would answer to God:

> In this their greatest–and last–hour of need, I ask you: would these men blaspheme before God by continuing to fix their lives, their honor, and their own search for eternal salvation on a book (and by implication a church and a ministry) they had fictitiously created out of whole cloth?
> – Jeffrey R. Holland. "Safety for the Soul" Talk, General Conference, October 2009

In the words of the most reliable Mormon leaders of Smith's day, we will test him by an examination of his final hours.

Heber C. Kimball's Journal of December 21, 1845, reports that Joseph instructed those of the Quorum who accompanied him to Carthage Jail to remove their *Garments of the Holy Priesthood*. This action stands in direct defiance of the instructions I received in the Mormon temple endowment.

> You have had a Garment placed upon you, which you were informed represents the garment given to Adam and Eve when they were found naked in the Garden of Eden, and which is called the "Garment of the Holy Priesthood." **This you were instructed to wear throughout your life**. You were informed that it will be a shield and a protection to you inasmuch as you do not defile it and if you are true and faithful to your covenants.
> – Bob Witte & Gordon H. Fraser, *What's Going On In There?* (Eugene: Gordon Fraser Publishing, n.d.) 13

On February 27, 1833, according to Doctrine and Covenants, Joseph Smith received a revelation from God concerning the use of wine.

> That inasmuch as any man drinketh wine or strong drink among you, behold it is not good, neither meet in the sight of your Father, only in

> assembling yourselves together to offer up your **sacraments** before him.
> – *Doctrine and Covenants*, 89:5

There was a standing prohibition against the consumption of alcohol in the church. Even so, wine was called for and consumed by the Mormon prophet and his apostles.

> Sometime after dinner we sent for some wine. It has been reported by some that this was taken as a **sacrament**. It was no such thing; our spirits were generally dull and heavy, and it was sent for to revive us. I think it was Captain Jones who went after it, but they would not suffer him to return. I believe we all drank of the wine, and gave some to one or two of the prison guards. We all of us felt unusually dull and languid, with a remarkable depression of spirits. In consonance with those feelings I sang a song, that had lately been introduced into Nauvoo, entitled, 'A Poor Wayfaring Man of Grief', etc.
> – The Church of Jesus Christ of Latter-day Saints, *History of the Church*(Salt Lake City: Deseret Book, n.d.) 7:101

According to current teachings, Joseph Smith placed himself beyond the reach and influence of the Holy Spirit when he partook of an alcoholic beverage.

> You may think that trying alcohol or tobacco one time won't hurt you, but it will. They are harmful substances, and you **cannot feel the Spirit** if you partake of them.
> – The Church of Jesus Christ of Latter-day Saints, "What's the Harm in Trying Alcohol or Tobacco Just Once", Liahona, June, 2008

11.1 Not a Martyr

> Elder Cyrus H. Wheelock came in to see us, and when he was about leaving drew a small pistol, a six-shooter, from his pocket, remarking at the same time. Would any of you like to have this?' Brother Joseph immediately replied, 'Yes, give it to me,' whereupon he took the pistol, and put it in his pantaloons pocket. The pistol was a six-shooting revolver, of Allen's patent . . .
> – The Church of Jesus Christ of Latter-day Saints, *History of the Church*(Salt Lake City: Deseret Book, n.d.) 7:100

Defying the law of the land, Joseph Smith accepted a smuggled pistol while incarcerated. By this, he displayed a total disregard for Mormon doctrine he had written:

> . . . We believe in being subject to kings, presidents, rulers, and magistrates, in obeying, honoring, and sustaining the law.
> – *Articles of Faith*, Twelfth

According to the doctrine he fabricated, the laws of the land bound Joseph Smith. Even so, he drew a smuggled pistol and killed men. All this was a blatant violation of the teachings he forced on the church.

> He [Joseph Smith], however, instantly arose, and with a firm, quick step, and a determined expression of countenance, approached the door, and pulling the six-shooter left by Brother Wheelock from his pocket, opened the door slightly, and snapped the pistol six successive times; only three of the barrels, however, were discharged. I afterwards understood that two or three were wounded by these discharges, two of whom, I am informed, died.
> – The Church of Jesus Christ of Latter-day Saints, *History of the Church* (Salt Lake City: Deseret Book, n.d.) 7:201

Possessing and using that six-shooter in an action prohibited by the law is a crime. Causing the death of others while committing a crime is murder. One can argue that Smith had a right to defend himself, and I don't know that I disagree. However, Smith illegally deployed that handgun and died with blood on his hands.

The Mormon Church claims that Joseph Smith was a martyr. Words have meaning and definitions. The willful misuse of a word is deceitful, at least.

> To seal the testimony of this book and the Book of Mormon, we announce **the martyrdom of Joseph Smith the Prophet**, and Hyrum Smith the Patriarch. They were shot in Carthage jail, on the 27th of June, 1844, about five o'clock p.m., by an armed mob—painted black—of from 150 to 200 persons.
> – *Doctrine and Covenants*, 135:1, emphasis added

> **martyr** noun
> **A person who voluntarily suffers death as the penalty of witnessing to and refusing to renounce a religion**
> – George Merriam & Charles Merriam, *Merriam-Webster* (Springfield: Encyclopedia Britannica, 1831) Number one definition

I will be the first to concede that Joseph Smith's death was violent, brutal, and illegal. Smith did not die voluntarily but instead took lives to avoid being killed. He was murdered, but he was not martyred. His actions disqualify him for the title of "martyr."

11.2 Scales Fall From Our Eyes

In his epistle to the Romans, Paul identified himself as a servant and an apostle to the Lord Jesus Christ. He continued by affirming that we have a specific and profound promise from God.

> ¹Paul, a servant of Jesus Christ, called to be an apostle, separated unto the gospel of God, ²(**Which he had promised afore by his prophets in the holy scriptures**)
> – Romans 1:1-2 (KJV), emphasis added

Paul, who had once hated and persecuted the Christians, came to meet Jesus on the road to Damascus. The light, the power, the spirit, and the word of God flooded Paul, and he became a believer. Paul languished three days in the abyss of absolute darkness because God shut his eyes in total blindness. And yet, I believe he experienced illumination unlike anything formerly known to him. As a Pharisee, Paul knew the Word of God. For three long days, as a new Christian, he had nothing to do but think. So, what do you suppose dominated Paul's thoughts?

I submit, he played and replayed the words of the prophets. Again and again, he reflected on prophecy, and what do you suppose he found? No doubt, he recognized something he had not before noticed. I submit that he came to see Jesus, the Messiah, and the gospel of grace where he had never perceived it before. After three days, God opened his eyes, and he once again saw the world around him. But, there must have been more. He saw, for the first time, the hope and wonder of Jesus, our Lord, and King.

I, like Paul, love to pour over the Bible. What an incredible thing to see what I never saw before. Sixty years in Mormonism and I never comprehended the connective threads that tie both testaments together. They are a tapestry, a perfect picture of Jesus and Him alone. I can't say what Paul may have experienced, but for me, awe, wonder, hope, and peace with God became a sure and binding reality.

We can know Jesus is Messiah because prophets boldly prophesied of his coming. We only need our eyes to be opened, as were Paul's. With open eyes, the Jesus Joseph never knew will find us, lift us, and reveal Himself. By His grace, we are made free.

11.3 Prophesy of Joseph Smith

On Mormonism's official website, a rather interesting article claims the Bible prophesies of Joseph Smith.

> I am sometimes asked if there is any **evidence in the Bible that foretells the divine calling of the Prophet Joseph Smith**. I usually reply that the only sure evidence of the Prophet Joseph Smith's divine calling is a personal witness from the Holy Ghost. Still, **there are many references to the Prophet in the Bible that confirm that testimony.**
> – George A. Horton, Jr, "Prophecies in the Bible about Joseph Smith", Ensign, January 1989, emphasis added

Join me as we work our way through the Bible, examining the passages Horton provided. Together, we will search for Joseph Smith and prophetic evidence of his coming.

> And that seer will I bless, and they that seek to destroy him shall be confounded; for this promise I give unto you; for I will remember you from generation to generation; **and his name shall be called Joseph, and it shall be after the name of his father**; and he shall be like unto you; for the thing which the Lord shall bring forth by his hand [Book of Mormon] shall bring my people unto salvation.
> – Genesis 50:33 (JST)

You may be thinking, but wait, I have read Genesis, and I don't recall that passage. Right you are! Genesis 50 ends with verse 26. This passage only exists in the Joseph Smith translation of the Bible. So yes, this passage does prophesy of the coming of Joseph Smith; but only because he wrote himself in by creating new passages.

The Book of Isaiah provides additional insight. Consider and contrast these passages from the King James Version with their counterparts from the Joseph Smith Translation:

> [20] For the terrible one is brought to nought, and the scorner is consumed, and all that watch for iniquity are cut off: [21] That make a man an offender for a word, and lay a snare for him that reproveth in the gate, and turn aside the just for a thing of nought. [22] Therefore thus saith the Lord, who redeemed Abraham, concerning the house of Jacob, Jacob shall not now be ashamed, neither shall his face now wax pale.
> – Isaiah 29:20-22 (KJV)

> [20] But, behold, it shall come to pass, that the Lord God shall say unto him to whom he shall deliver the book [Book of Mormon], Take these words which are not sealed and deliver them to another, that he may show them unto the learned, saying, Read this, I pray thee. [21] And the learned shall say, Bring hither the book and I will read them; and now because of the glory of the world, and to get gain will they say this, and not for the glory of God. And the man shall say, I cannot bring the book for it is sealed. Then shall the learned say, I cannot read it. [22] Wherefore it shall come to pass, that the Lord God will deliver again the book and the words thereof to him that is not learned [Joseph Smith]; and the man that is not learned shall say, I am not learned. Then shall the Lord God say unto him, The learned shall not read them, for they have rejected them, and I am able to do mine own work; wherefore thou shalt read the words which I shall

give unto thee.
– *Joseph Smith Translation*, Isaiah 29:20-22

How do I begin to address this irrelevant and disjointed rewrite of Isaiah? I boldly demand that *prophecy written after the fact is hardly prophecy.* Again, we see Joseph Smith mentioned in the Bible only because he brashly wrote himself into scripture.

I present one final Bible passage that Horton claimed as a prophecy of the coming Joseph Smith and the Book of Mormon:

> [16] Moreover, thou son of man, take thee one stick, and write upon it, For Judah, and for the children of Israel his companions: then take another stick, and write upon it, For Joseph, the stick of Ephraim, and for all the house of Israel his companions: [17] And join them one to another into one stick; and they shall become one in thine hand.
> – Ezekiel 37:16-17 (KJV)

As a Mormon, I knew this passage well and often used it to defend my faith. I knew this passage because it was frequently quoted in Mormon articles, talks, study manuals, and more. The trouble was, I never read it from the Bible. I readily accepted it as delivered out of an abundance of ignorance and lifelong indoctrination. Horton presented it without context, as the church always does.

> For more than a century, members of the Church have taught that these two 'sticks' represent the Bible (the stick of Judah) and the Book of Mormon (the stick of Joseph or Ephraim). Recent research has revealed that the word stick refers to a wooden, folding writing tablet
> – George A. Horton, Jr, "Prophecies in the Bible about Joseph Smith", Ensign, January 1989, emphasis added

On closer inspection, we discover that the sticks represent the northern and southern kingdoms of Israel. This passage describes the reunification of the two kingdoms into a single kingdom under God.

> [18] And when the children of thy people shall speak unto thee, saying, Wilt thou not shew us **what thou meanest by these?** [19] Say unto them, Thus saith the Lord God; Behold, I will take the stick of Joseph, which is in the hand of Ephraim, and the tribes of Israel his fellows, and will put them with him, even with the stick of Judah, and make them one stick, and they shall be one in mine hand. [20] And the sticks whereon thou writest shall be in thine hand before their eyes. [21] And say unto them, Thus saith the Lord God; Behold, I will take the children of Israel from among the heathen, whither they be gone, and will gather them on every side, and bring them into their own land: [22] And I will make them **one nation** in the land upon

the mountains of Israel; and **one king shall be king to them all**: and they shall be **no more two nations, neither shall they be divided into two kingdoms any more at all**:
– Ezekiel 37:18-22 (KJV), emphasis added

When people present evidence, it is customary to offer the best first. According to Horton, we have just reviewed the best biblical evidence of Joseph Smith. Being the best he can offer, his assertions speak volumes about the Mormon position on the prophet Joseph Smith. The truth exposes the Mormon restoration as a fraud.[7]

Of all the evidences that prove Joseph Smith to be a wolf in sheep's clothing, nothing exposes him as a fraud more than the following:

> I have more to boast of than ever any man had. I am the only man that has ever been able to keep a whole church together since the days of Adam. A large majority of the whole have stood by me. **Neither Paul, John, Peter, nor Jesus ever did it. I boast that no man ever did such a work as I. The followers of Jesus ran away from Him; but the Latter-day Saints never ran away from me yet.**
> – The Church of Jesus Christ of Latter-day Saints, *History of the Church*(Salt Lake City: Deseret Book, n.d.) 6:408, emphasis added

When people make Joseph Smith their hill to die on, boldly counter, "*show it to me in the Bible!*"

---

[7] See chapter: Is the Gospel Everlasting?

CHAPTER
TWELVE

TESTING JOSEPH SMITH

> Because of the great love of God, I was spared shackles, chains, and certain destruction associated with Joseph Smith.
>
> *Lance*

From the beginning of time, false prophets have meant trouble for those who follow God. Students of the Word of God take steps to identify and expose them. Those who do not know God and His word are all too quick to embrace dark doctrines.

> We believe the Bible to be the word of God as far as it is translated correctly; we also believe the Book of Mormon to be the word of God.
> – *Articles of Faith*, Eighth

The warning of Paul is appropriate and applicable in every age. Let all God's people take notice, be vigilant and take a position as watchmen on the wall.[1]

> For if he that cometh preacheth **another Jesus**, whom we have not preached, or if ye receive **another spirit**, which ye have not received, or **another gospel**, which ye have not accepted, **ye might well bear with him**.
> – 2 Corinthians 11:4 (KJV), emphasis added

Through the prophets Jeremiah and Ezekiel, God has spoken regarding false prophets. He condemned men who prophesy from the visions of their minds and hearts.[2] The punishment will be the same for the false prophet and those

---
[1] Isaiah 62:6
[2] Ezekiel 23:16-17

who foolishly follow after him.[3]

This pattern is not unique to the people of ancient Israel. It seems that Mormonism has fallen in line with ancient prophets who prophesied from their hearts and trusted in their minds. A burning bosom is the Mormon measure of truth for all personal and prophetic revelation.[4] Are they not seeking truth according to their hearts and minds? Is that God's prescribed pattern? We shall see.

God never leaves us alone. The truth is readily available to those who seek according to God's word. He has shown us the way. The only question is this, will we follow?

12.1 Testing False Prophets

> [20] But the prophet, which shall presume to speak a word in my name, which I have not commanded him to speak, or that shall speak in the name of other gods, even that prophet shall die. [21] And if thou say in thine heart, How shall we know the word which the Lord hath not spoken? [22] When a prophet speaketh in the name of the Lord, **if the thing follow not, nor come to pass**, that is the thing which the Lord hath not spoken, but the prophet hath spoken it presumptuously: thou shalt not be afraid of him.
>
> – Deuteronomy 18:20-22 (KJV), emphasis added

The Lord has provided a simple test. He equipped us with every necessary thing to discern truth from error, and yet, the Mormon people reject it.[5] It is sobering to know things now that were hidden when I was a zealous member of *The Church of Jesus Christ of Latter-day Saints*. We have not been set adrift on the seas of heresy and abomination. Our loving God provided sail, rudder, charts, and a compass so we can precisely navigate between truth and error. Of most importance, Jesus is our *bright and morning star*[6] by which we navigate. By this sure means of godly navigation, consider two prophesies of Joseph Smith.

> [1] **A revelation of Jesus Christ unto his servant Joseph Smith, Jun.**, and six elders, as they united their hearts and lifted their voices on high. [2] Yea, the word of the Lord concerning his church, established in the last days for the restoration of his people, as he has spoken by the mouth of his prophets, and for the gathering of his saints to stand upon Mount Zion, which shall be the city of New Jerusalem. [3] **Which city shall be built, beginning at the temple lot, which is appointed by the finger of the Lord, in the**

---

[3] Ezekiel 14:10
[4] *Doctrine & Covenants*, 9:8
[5] Matthew 7:13
[6] Revelation 22:16

western boundaries of the State of Missouri, and dedicated by the hand of Joseph Smith, Jun., and others with whom the Lord was well pleased. ⁴Verily this is the word of the Lord, that the city New Jerusalem shall be built by the gathering of the saints, beginning at this place, even the place of the temple, **which temple shall be reared in this generation**. ⁵For verily this generation shall not all pass away until an house shall be built unto the Lord, and a cloud shall rest upon it, which cloud shall be even the glory of the Lord, which shall fill the house. ³¹Therefore, as I said concerning the sons of Moses—for the sons of Moses and also the sons of Aaron shall offer an acceptable offering and sacrifice in **the house of the Lord, which house shall be built unto the Lord in this generation**, upon the consecrated spot as I have appointed
– *Doctrine and Covenants*, 84:1-5, 31, emphasis added

President Smith then stated that the meeting had been called, because God had commanded it; and it was made known to him by vision and by the Holy Spirit. He then gave a relation of some of the circumstances attending while journeying to Zion our trials, sufferings; and said God had not designed all this for nothing, but He had it in remembrance yet; and it was the will of God that those who went Zion, with a determination to lay down their lives, if necessary, should be ordained to the ministry, and go forth to prune the vineyard for the last time, or the coming of the Lord, which was nigh **even fifty-six years should wind up the scene**.
– The Church of Jesus Christ of Latter-day Saints, *History of the Church*(Salt Lake City: Deseret Book, n.d.) 2:182, Joseph Smith, emphasis added

An examination of Smith's prophesies, relative to Deuteronomy 18:20-22, remove all doubt; Smith's prophesies are false. According to the Mormon prophet, the establishment of the New Jerusalem will begin with the erection of a temple in Jackson County, Missouri, before the then living generation's passing. Additionally, Smith prophesied the second coming of Jesus would occur no later than 1891. As of this writing, Jesus has not returned, and the appointed temple lot remains a flat, and grassy void.

12.2 Another Gospel

⁶I marvel that ye are so soon removed from him that called you into the grace of Christ unto another gospel: ⁷ Which is not another; but there be some that trouble you, and would pervert the gospel of Christ. ⁸**But though we, or an angel from heaven, preach any other gospel unto you than that which we have preached**

> **unto you, let him be accursed.** ⁹As we said before, so say I now again, If any man preach any other gospel unto you than that ye have received, let him be accursed.
> – Galatians 1:6-9 (KJF), emphasis added

Joseph Smith and the *The Church of Jesus Christ of Latter-day Saints* defined and redefined the pure gospel of Jesus Christ.[7] This matter is covered with exacting detail in the chapter entitled, *Is the Gospel Everlasting?*.

12.3 Other Gods

> ¹If there arise among you a prophet, or a dreamer of dreams, and giveth thee a sign or a wonder, ²And the sign or the wonder come to pass, whereof he spake unto thee, saying, **Let us go after other gods**, which thou hast not known, and let us serve them; ³Thou shalt not hearken unto the words of that prophet, or that dreamer of dreams: for the **Lord your God proveth you, to know whether ye love the Lord your God with all your heart and with all your soul**. ⁴Ye shall walk after the Lord your God, and fear him, and keep his commandments, and obey his voice, and ye shall serve him, and cleave unto him. ⁵And that prophet, or that dreamer of dreams, shall be put to death; because he hath spoken to turn you away from the Lord your God, which brought you out of the land of Egypt, and redeemed you out of the house of bondage, to thrust thee out of the way which the Lord thy God commanded thee to walk in. So shalt thou put the evil away from the midst of thee. ⁶If thy brother, the son of thy mother, or thy son, or thy daughter, or the wife of thy bosom, or thy friend, which is as thine own soul, entice thee secretly, saying, **Let us go and serve other gods**, which thou hast not known, thou, nor thy fathers;
> – Deuteronomy 13:1-6 (KJV), emphasis added

Paul's direction is simple enough. Anyone who teaches the people to go after and serve other gods is a liar. Not only is this a test of those who claim to be prophets or teachers, but it is also a test for us. We love God when we faithfully apply this test to every gospel question. Conversely, if we fail to use this test, our failure confirms a lack of love for God. Let us, therefore, prove our love by applying this test to the Mormon prophet, Joseph Smith.

> ¹⁸ For I know that God is not a partial God, neither a changeable being; but he is **unchangeable from all eternity to all eternity**.
> – *Book of Mormon*, Moroni 8:18, emphasis added

---

[7] 1 Corinthians 15:1-4

God himself was once as we are now, and is an **exalted man**, and sits enthroned in yonder heavens! ... **We have imagined and supposed that God was God from all eternity**. I will refute that idea, and take away the veil, so that you may see. ... and that **He was once a man like us**; yea, that God himself, the Father of us all, dwelt on an earth, the same as Jesus Christ Himself did; and I will show it from the Bible.
- The Church of Jesus Christ of Latter-day Saints, *History of the Church*(Salt Lake City: Deseret Book, n.d.) 6:305, Joseph Smith, emphasis added

The Father has a **body of flesh and bones as tangible as man's** ...
- *Doctrine and Covenants*, 130:22a, emphasis added

The Father being a **personage of spirit**, glory and power: possessing all perfection and fulness ...
- *Doctrine & Covenants*, Lectures on Faith, Lecture Fifth, The Godhead, 1835 until 1921 editions

Joseph Smith presents multiple and contradictory definitions of God. Joseph Smith is a false prophet, even without turning to the Bible. The many descriptions of Smith's god are so diverse that they cannot be reconciled. Who is God according to Joseph Smith?

1. A being who is and is not eternally god.
2. A being who has and has not a body of flesh and bone as tangible as yours and mine.
3. A being who never changes except for when he does.

In testing Joseph Smith according to Deuteronomy 13:1-4, we need not look far. He is a false prophet based on a single Bible passage.

> [8]**Jesus Christ is the same** yesterday, today, and forever. [9]Don't be carried away by various and strange teachings ...
> - Hebrews 13:8-9a (WEB), emphasis added

12.4 Pinnacle of Heresy

I reserved one final topic for particular and peculiar examination. Joseph Smith modified many parts of the Bible and called his work the Joseph Smith Translation. Among his modifications, *unsupported by manuscript evidence*, one passage exceeds every heresy and dwarfs every blasphemy. With the insertion of a single word, "*not*", Smith denied every reason Jesus came in the flesh and died as my substitute and yours. These are fighting words that ought to cause every true disciple to rise up in righteous fury.

Every soul who lived and died believing this blasphemy will tremble in stark terror under the weight of God's furious wrath. Joseph Smith, a child of the father of lies,[8] blatantly and willfully deceived untold millions, including my family, living and dead. These people, blinded and unprepared, followed Smith on the broad way, through the wide gate, and on to eternal destruction.[9] The cost of this travesty leaves me in deep, incomprehensible sorrow.

> But to him that worketh not, but believeth on him that **justifieth the ungodly**, his faith is counted for righteousness.
> – Romans 4:5 (KJV), emphasis added

> But to him that seeketh not to be justified by the law of works, but believeth on him who **justifieth *not* the ungodly**, his faith is counted for righteousness.
> – *Joseph Smith Translation*, Romans 4:5, emphasis added

If this alone is the evidence against Joseph Smith, it is more than ample. It establishes him as a wolf masquerading as a *minister of righteousness*.[10]

12.5 In Christ Alone

I often recall wasted years when I desperately sought a testimony of Joseph Smith. I thought it would save me. Try as I might, I could not obtain what I most desired, and I could not comprehend why. I didn't recognize that I was an enemy to God. I couldn't see that all my best efforts were filthy rags[11] and rubbish[12] before my Holy God.

Instead of trusting in Jesus, a foreign concept to me at the time, I followed the prophets of Mormonism, and I was lost!

> ... and he that confesseth not that Jesus has come in the flesh and **sent Joseph Smith with the fullness of the Gospel** to this generation, is not of God, but is Antichrist, ...
> – *Journal of Discourses* (N.p.: n.p., n.d.), 9:312, Brigham Young, emphasis added

Over time, true repentance[13] brought me more and more into the protective arms of Jesus. As He drew me ever closer, His word penetrated the clutter of lies. His truth set me free.[14] The corruption uttered by wolves in sheep's

---

[8] John 8:44
[9] Matthew 7:13
[10] 2 Corinthians 11:14
[11] Isaiah 64:6
[12] Philippians 3:8
[13] See chapter, How do I Repent?
[14] John 8:32

clothing,[15] faded. The light of Christ overwhelmed and overwrote Mormon fables as new hope pushed back the lies.

> and every spirit who doesn't confess that Jesus Christ has come in the flesh is not of God, and this is the spirit of the Antichrist, ...
> – 1 John 4:3a (WEB)

The Church of Jesus Christ of Latter-day Saints, controlled by Satan, desired that I place all my trust in another false prophet, Joseph Smith. God, in His mercy, used the plan of the Devil for my good.[16] Try as I might, God held me back and prevented the testimony of Joseph Smith from sprouting and maturing in my heart. Had it grown, it would have certainly bound me over to destruction.

What a curious thing. The dark plan of Mormon leaders became the catalyst that led me to Jesus and salvation. In a weird and warped sort of way, I owe them my gratitude.

> And as for you, ye meant evil against me; but God meant it for good...
> – Genesis 50:20a (ASV)

Looking back, I see the salvation of the Lord.[17] At every step, He held me back from destruction[18] and prepared me for the day when I would finally incline my eye toward God[19] and desire Him with all my heart. On that day, I became a recipient of the boundless love of God.[20]

> See how great a love the Father has given to us, that we should be called children of God! For this cause the world doesn't know us, because it didn't know him.
> – 1 John 3:1 (WEB)

Because of the great love of God, I was spared shackles, chains, and certain destruction associated with Joseph Smith. Because of God's great love, I did not have to choose between Joseph or Jesus. I never had to grapple with the conflict that grips all who try to believe in them both.[21] Because Jesus spared me from that awful lie, I was free to fall into His arms with full, unwavering faith.

---

[15] Matthew 7:15
[16] Genesis 50:20
[17] 2 Chronicles 20:17
[18] Proverbs 24:11
[19] Hebrews 12:2
[20] John 15:9
[21] Matthew 6:24

CHAPTER
THIRTEEN

THE GAG ORDER

> My Mormon beliefs were crumbling before my eyes, and I was shaken to the core.
>
> *Lance*

My final years of Mormonism were years of political activism. More than once, I ran for political office on a unapologetic Constitutional platform. Some efforts succeeded, while others ended in defeat. The most visible of these ended in an unsuccessful bid for a seat in the Idaho House of Representatives.

I was and still am an advocate of the United States Constitution. I am quick to accept every opportunity to defend freedom's principles as enumerated in the Constitution, Declaration of Independence, and related liberty documents, including the Bible. Only by the defense of liberty will it be preserved.

In those years, I wrote a weekly column for a Pocatello, Idaho newspaper, the Idaho State Journal. Additionally, I published my work on a personal blog.

My political efforts focused on the idea that we must preserve inalienable rights,[1] or surely we will soon lose religious freedoms.[2] The link between general liberty and religious freedom is essential and must remain permanently affixed. Break the link, and you lose both. We live in a culture that increasingly defends liberty and justice while rejecting God. History tells the sad story of nations that desired freedom without God, only to lose both. Such is our inevitable future if we stay the current course.

In the summer of 2015, I wrote a column entitled *"CRP, the Criminal Restoration Policy?"*. CRP stands for "Conservation Reserve Program". It is a lawless policy where the government forcefully takes money from every

---

[1] Declaration of Independence
[2] First Amendment of the Constitution of the United States

taxpayer and gives it to landowners who promise not to farm their land. This flawed government policy promotes a lack of industry and an absence of production. The government and participating landowners call this program, "good for America". Generally, those compelled to pay for such programs have a different perspective.

I live in Southeastern Idaho, where the land is rich but largely unproductive due to CRP. Consequently, this government waste was a touchy topic for my column. Many with flawed scruples are drawn to promise of *free money*. Of course, there is no free money. Before the government can give dollars to one, they must be taken, forcefully from another.

In this column, I called out an Idaho senator and representative from my legislative district who had land enrolled in CRP. I called out my predominantly Mormon community of 300 people for receiving 25.7 million dollars of stolen money in the few years leading up to my column. To complicate matters, my Mormon Bishop had received nearly half a million dollars of *free* government money. Lastly, the Stake President processed farm loans in an industry where CRP was frequently used to generate easy cash-flow.

CRP has produced a shameless generation of landowners who never intend to make the land productive again. Instead, they have secured employment outside the farming industry while enrolling vast tracts of acreage in an unending series of decade-long CRP contracts.

I quoted the Mormon church's former prophet, Ezra Taft Benson, in support of my position. He declared CRP and all similar programs to be *Legal Plunder*.[3] Legal because a corrupt law said so and plunder because programs such as these are ultimately theft.

13.1 The Gag Order

Upon publication of "*CRP, the Criminal Restoration Policy?*", My Bishop summoned me to his office. He demanded, "You may never again speak publicly of the church!" After a moment's reflection, I began to ask clarifying questions. Does this restriction apply to my newspaper column? He answered, yes! My blog? Yes! Public speaking? Yes! Constitution classes? Yes! In short, the church was issuing a gag order that applied to all forms of communication. He indicated that failure to comply would result in the loss of my temple recommend.

Indicating that I understood the gag order, I left the Bishop's office deeply troubled. In verbal and written communication that followed, I spoke to the Bishop about guarantees provided by the First Amendment to the Constitution of the United States. That amendment guarantees freedom of speech, freedom of the press, and freedom of religion. He aggressively attempted to restrict each of these God-given and Constitutionally guaranteed rights.

---

[3] Ezra Taft Benson, *The Proper Role of Government*(N.p.: n.p., 1968)

I pointed to the Mormon principle of *Free Agency* which grants to every man the right to move, do, speak and act according to the dictates of his conscience.[4] I opened the Doctrine & Covenants to him and read a commandment to honor and uphold the Constitution of the United States.[5] I reminded him of the 12th Mormon Article of Faith that demands he "*obey, honor, and sustain the law*". No argument was persuasive, and the gag order ultimately stood.

In the days and weeks that followed, I continued to go about my business as before. After all, the law of the land, the law of God, and the law according to Mormonism were clear. Apparently, law and doctrine were not a priority for this Mormon Bishop. A few weeks later, I wrote a column in violation of the gag order. Again, the Bishop called me to his office, where things became massively oppressive. He took my temple recommend.[6]

13.2 Put the Wise to Shame

After my second appointment with the Bishop, I stopped by my daughter's home. Her husband was the son-in-law I initially loved to hate. When we first met, he was inked, pierced, and worst of all, a "godless Christian." The last thing I wanted was this man as the husband of my daughter and the father of my grandchildren. My pharisaical, Mormon judgment was so ugly in those early years. I praise God that he fixes broken things like me.

That evening, as I sat in his living room, he was the only voice of reason. Without condemnation, he questioned why I allowed men so much authority over my life. There was a crazy kind of conflict in my mind. He was a Christian and, in my view, deluded by false theology. On the other hand, my Bishop, Stake President, friends, and family encouraged me to walk a path leading straight to hell. Everything I thought I knew to be true and everyone I believed to be wise were neither true nor wise. Conversely, the "heathen" Christian offered *words of life*. Only in his remarks did I find counsel in keeping with my convictions and god, as I understood him then.

Sometimes God puts the most unlikely people in our lives to save us from the hell of our own making.

> but God chose the foolish things of the world, that he might put to shame them that are wise; and God chose the weak things of the world, that he might put to shame the things that are strong;
> – 1 Corinthians 1:27 (ASV)

---

[4] *Doctrine and Covenants*, 101:78
[5] *Doctrine and Covenants*, 101:77
[6] See chapter: Taking The Temple

13.3 Peter and John

I didn't realize that religious, legalistic zealots had done the same to Christians of the past. I had no understanding that the Sanhedrin of Jesus' day was still alive and well. They re-named, and re-branded old evils in shiny, new Mormon packaging.

A year or so after receiving the gag order, I read Acts 4 and 5. I was blown away! Being annoyed by Peter and John's teaching, the council brought them in to answer for imagined wrongdoings.

> And they called them, and commanded them not to speak at all nor teach in the name of Jesus.
> – Acts 4:18 (KJV)

I couldn't believe my eyes! Peter and John's story is my story! The Bible laid it out as it happened to them and as it was happening to me. Peter and John's response amazed me further still.

> [19]But Peter and John answered and said unto them, Whether it be right in the sight of God to hearken unto you more than unto God, judge ye. [20]For we cannot but speak the things which we have seen and heard.
> – Acts 4:19-20 (KJV)

In those days, I was dumber than a box of Mormon rocks. At that time, I knew nothing. Since then, God has opened my mind to know and love his word. My answer, in substance, matched the response of the Apostles. I know God gave me a response even in my ignorance and rebellion. He was drawing me then, and I praise his name above all names.[7]

When Peter and John refused to comply with a godless mandate, they were imprisoned, brought before the council a second time, beaten, and sent away. After all that, the gag order against them remained in place.

The Church of Jesus Christ of Latter-day Saints brought legal charges against me, sought significant fines and a lengthy jail term. Every Sunday, they place guards at the church house doors and tell the people that guards are necessary to protect them from me. The church has banned me from attending important events such as weddings, baby blessings, and funerals when held on Mormon properties. With Peter and John, I rejoice!

> And they departed from the presence of the council, rejoicing that they were counted worthy to suffer shame for his name.
> – Acts 5:41 (KJV)

Like Peter and John, I have been privileged to go house to house in my largely Mormon community to teach and preach Jesus Christ.

> And daily in the temple, and in every house, they ceased not to teach and preach Jesus Christ.
> – Acts 5:42 (KJV)

---

[7]Philippians 2:9

THE GAG ORDER

I have learned that no struggle is too large when God and His angels fight for me.

> And he said, Fear not, for they that are with us are more than they that are with them.
> – 2 Kings 6:16 (Darby)

CHAPTER
FOURTEEN

TAKING THE TEMPLE

> If I turned away from every good thing and became evil, the church would certify me as "good." Or, if I stood on principle and honor, the church would label me as "bad."
>
> — *Lance*

The weeks following the receipt of the gag order[1] were immensely challenging. The Mormon directive was to "cease and desist" all public expressions of my faith and all public mention of my church. Everything I knew and everything I believed cried out, this is wrong!

I was a columnist, I was a blogger, I was a public speaker, I was a political activist, I was a constitutional instructor, and I was a Mormon. Everything I knew demanded that I open my mouth and share a testimony of these things boldly and freely.

> This term [property] in its particular application means "**that dominion which one man claims and exercises over the external things of the world, in exclusion of every other individual.**"
> – James Madison, "Property" (Published in the National Gazette) March 29, 1792, emphasis added

⁷⁷According to the laws and **constitution** [Constitution of the United States] of the people, which I have suffered to be established,

---
[1] See chapter: The Gag Order

> and **should be maintained for the rights and protection of all flesh,** according to just and holy principles; ⁷⁸**That every man may act in doctrine and principle pertaining to futurity, according to the moral agency which I have given unto him**...
> – *Doctrine & Covenants*, 101:77-78a, emphasis added

Everything I knew, and all I had been taught, demanded that I share the message of Mormonism with the world. If I honored the gag order, I would renounce everything I held dear. So I continued to act according to my conscience. Consequently, the Bishop met with me and took away my temple recommend. The Mormon temple recommend is a small piece of paper that certifies the holder is temple worthy. Its loss may seem inconsequential to those outside the Mormon church. For those on the inside, it is everything.

> Every foundation stone that is laid for a Temple, and every Temple completed according to the order the Lord has revealed for his holy Priesthood, lessens the power of Satan on the earth, and increases the power of God and Godliness, moves the heavens in mighty power in our behalf, **invokes and calls down upon us the blessings of the Eternal Gods**, and those who reside in their presence
> – George Q. Cannon *Millennial Star*, November 12, 1877, emphasis added

Only by becoming and remaining *temple worthy* could I expect to receive the best blessings of the Mormon god. Joseph Smith said, *"Here, then, is eternal life—to know the only wise and true God; and you have got to learn how to be gods yourselves ..."*.[2] Every Mormon strives for the day when he or she will become a god or goddess. This exalted state was my endgame and the only acceptable outcome. The Mormon god grants exaltation to only worthy Mormons, and my worthiness had been taken.

I was given two unacceptable choices and told to choose one. If I turned away from every good thing and became evil, the church would certify me as "good." Or, if I stood on principle and honor, the church would label me as "bad." But, if I did wrong to be pronounced right, I could keep my temple recommend, and maintain my temple worthiness with a lie. But if I lied to be saved, God would know it! How does that work?

> But the fearful, and unbelieving, and the abominable, and murderers, and whoremongers, and sorcerers, and idolaters, and all **liars**, shall have their part in the lake which burneth with fire and brimstone: which is the second death.
> – Revelation 21:8 (KJV), emphasis added

My Mormon leadership removed all hope of salvation and exaltation. I didn't know then that their authority sprang from the blasphemous imaginations of Joseph Smith.[3] I believed Mormonism held the promise of the only

---
[2] Joseph Smith. "King Follett Discourse" Sermon, Nauvoo, April 7, 1844
[3] See chapter: A Cursed Church

true church on the face of the earth. I couldn't comprehend why the "true church of god" would do this. How could they deny everything to a devout and zealous believer such as I? Consequently, I struggled with the possibility that *The Church of Jesus Christ of Latter-day Saints* was a false religion.

Thus, I struggled with Mormon doctrines that stood in stark contradiction. There was a standard of truth I always believed, and there was Mormonism where that standard became lost. I struggled to balance Mormon scriptures that boldly contradicted Mormon leaders.

The loss of my temple recommend and ever mounting contradiction plunged me into two terrible years that we collectively call *the Dark Years*.

CHAPTER
FIFTEEN

THE DARK YEARS

> I didn't want to lose my best friend, but in a way, I already had. "God, please help him!"
>
> *Grace*

All was death. Everyone and everything to which I once anchored my soul fractured, crumbled, and fell away. With it, I fell. I was falling ... falling. My heart, my soul, my mind cried out. My hands searched frantically for something, anything to cling to, but there was nothing. In the empty darkness, I lost everything. Like a vapor driven before the wind, all I once knew and loved vanished. All was void, empty, and a cloak of impenetrable darkness.

Friends, ward members, and family turned away. Some turned in silence, some in accusation, some to open hatred. Leaders of the church, who I once believed were called of God, became *Sanhedrin*. From the top floor of the church office building to the Mormon trenches of my small rural town, all were *Sanhedrin*. These men were as vessels, outwardly presentable but full of corruption;[1] whitewashed tombs, deceptively beautiful but filled with death.[2] They were as vipers at my feet.[3]

According to those I loved most, I was Korihor (the Book of Mormon Antichrist), servant of Satan, idol worshiper, apostate, weak, hateful, liar, pornography addict, abuser of children, and utterly shunned. This shift, was for me, an overnight and instantaneous transition. In an instant, I who had once been a noble, righteous, worthy man became the height of sin. The shift in my reality from white to black was shattering.

---

[1] Matthew 23:25-26
[2] Matthew 23:27-28
[3] Matthew 23:33

15.1 A Silent Cry

It began in those fuzzy moments between sleep and wakefulness. My mind cried out "BISHOP!" The silent cry echoed inside my skull, reverberated, and faded to an empty, lonely silence. Only an unseen void remained. My cries were the beginning of a desperate petition to be heard, a plea for justice, a plea for Mormon leaders to do the righteous thing. Though my voice was silent, my mind was shrieking and clamoring to be recognized. These involuntary cries grew in frequency until they filled and dominated the first thoughts of morning to the last conscious thoughts of an endless night. Yes, those nights were endless and haunted. Before long, I repeated my pointless pleas hundreds of times every day. Like a specter, they haunted me with relentless torment. I couldn't free my mind. The cries played and replayed like a chant from hell. The world around me never heard and never knew of the unsolvable conflict, and endless noise in my head: "BISHOP!" "BISHOP!" "BISHOP!".

Each desperate cry for help died in the silent void of nothingness. After all, how do you seek love from those who never knew it? Where do you find nobility in wretchedness or light in the darkness? How do you request justice of those without godly bounds who are a law unto themselves? Each pleading, broken cry began as hope and faded into empty and undeniable hopelessness.

I began grinding my teeth. I ground them until they became loose, and my jaw ached. No amount of trying and no quantity of concentration stopped the endless, pointless activity of the damned. This habit has faded but not completely vanished. For me, it is a frequent reminder of a time when I lived under the demonic power of hell's master.

Doing anything was just too hard. My business suffered, construction on our house slowed. Yard work ground to a dead stop. Worst of all, our marriage suffered. It didn't become ugly or angry, only sad ... so very, very sad and lonely.

Thoughts of ending it all came from time to time. With a quick tug of a trigger, it would all end. These ideas were not frequent, and I did not take them too seriously. Still, they did visit from time to time, and I allowed them to linger because they temporarily silenced the relentless cries of the damned.

In Grace's eyes, I saw the worry. I wondered if I needed professional help but couldn't bring myself to ask. I reasoned that only a crazy person needs help. So, as long as I don't ask, that might prove me to be okay, right? I just kept moving forward and hoping for the best. But, I had to admit that I was falling apart and getting worse. I never admitted to anyone but myself that I was losing my grip. I was terrified!

The only therapy I could afford was through LDS Social Services. Each available counselor would be in the employ of the church. I knew they would serve the Mormonism first, church leadership second, and me last of all. Of more importance, my Stake President, an evil man whose only desire was to satisfy his lust for absolute control, would be involved in my treatment, and that was unthinkable.

15.2 The Dragon

Slowly, I came to see the true face of Mormonism. That cursed church was, for me, the massive red, seven-headed Dragon from the twelfth chapter of Revelation.[4] It had taken nearly everything from me. Of the little that remained ... it wanted that, too! As I contended with one lying tongue, six more launched newly manufactured false accusations. When I cut the head off one criminal act, six more heads had six more crimes waiting in the wings. When I fended off one attack from gaping jaws and tearing teeth, six more circled to attack from behind.

I fought the Dragon with all my strength. Occasionally, I wounded the beast. Yet, I suffered many tearing bites to body and soul for every blow I landed. I was fighting, and I was losing ... badly!

The Dragon hates Christmas because the Dragon Slayer was born on that day. Even as a tiny baby, squirming in a manger, He had power and authority that struck fear in the heart of the Dragon.

> And I will put enmity between thee and the woman, and between thy seed and her seed; it shall bruise thy head, and thou shalt bruise his heel.
> – Genesis 3:15 (KJV)

He waited to devour the child as soon as he was born.[5] When death came to every boy child in Bethlehem, the Dragon Slayer was already on his way to Egypt.

Grace Notes

Those were such dark years! Lance struggled between his love of Mormonism and a growing Mormon evil that he could not deny. He had been falsely accused, his temple recommend taken, and he was devastated.

Most days, Lance would call me at work. When he didn't, I was petrified. I wondered, did Mormon leaders accuse or attack him again? What would I find when I returned home? These days were truly haunting.

Lance was slipping away, and I didn't know how to help! "Please God, end this torture!" I didn't want to lose my best friend but in a way, I already had. "God, please help him!"

I had turned away from Mormonism in my heart and mind. Privately, I listened to worship music. I shared a few songs with Lance hoping beyond hope that he would hear the message. He wasn't getting it!

Finally, I saw something change in him. Darkness was lifting. God heard my prayers and stopped the evil that was killing my sweet Lance. God truly heard and healed.

Grace

---

[4] Revelation 12:3
[5] Revelation 14:4

The Dragon hates the Crucifixion. On the cross, the Dragon Slayer conquered sin. Three days later, rising from the tomb, the Dragon Slayer conquered death. The final blows struck the Dragon with infinite power. The Dragon's days were numbered. Mortally injured, he lashed out with new anger and ferocity. His time was limited, and he knew it!

My fight continued as a futile battle, a battle where defeat was the only possible outcome. I would absolutely, in time, be utterly destroyed. I could only delay death, but I could not avoid it. I could hold off destruction for a time, but I could not prevent its arrival. Strength faded, resolve weakened. The taste of my own death rose like bile in my throat. The stench of it filled my nostrils.

15.3   Counsel From the Pit of Hell

The "incredibly bizarre" punctuated these challenging times. A longtime friend and Mormon high priest gave me this bit of counsel. He reminded me that when a Mormon leader, *"tells you to do something wrong, and you do it, the Lord will bless you for it."*[6] The Stake President, who had directed the Bishop in all his actions, soon gave me the same counsel. It didn't take long for the same advice to come from my own family. They were actually telling me that I must do wrong to be seen as right by the Mormon church and its unholy god. Those I loved and respected were demanding that I walk a dark path leading straight to hell! They assured me that all hope of again being numbered among the *good Mormons* hinged on embracing and doing evil.

I had been taught this doctrine all my life and accepted it without hesitation. Deep down, I believed those who hold priesthood keys, including Stake Presidents and Bishops, were incapable of leading me astray.

> If I were to attempt that, the Lord would remove me out of my place, and so He will any other man who attempts to lead the children of men astray from the oracles of God and from their duty.
> – *Doctrine & Covenants*, Official Declaration 1, Wilford Woodruff

> But the voice of the First Presidency and the united voice of those others who hold with them the keys of the kingdom shall always guide the Saints and the world in those paths where the Lord wants them to be.
> – Joseph Fielding Smith. "Eternal Keys and the Right to Preside" General priesthood meeting, April 8, 1972

Well-meaning among friends and family begged, "stop fighting, surrender and do the Dragon's will!" They thought they were saying, surrender to the

---

[6]ChristHeber J. Grant as quoted by Marion G Romney, *The Covenant of the Priesthood* Ensign, April 1972

church leaders who only desire your well-being. What they were actually saying was far different; Surrender your integrity, abandon your honesty, sacrifice your conscience, turn from God, and surrender your salvation for the sake of blind guides.

> Let them alone: they are blind guides. **And if the blind guide the blind, both shall fall into a pit.**
> – Matthew 15:14 (ASV), emphasis added

Those who should have had my back betrayed me. They promised the Mormon god would count my sin as righteousness in the end. This advice seemed foolish, even blasphemous to me. I could only reject this dark counsel first imagined by the father of lies.[7]

All I believed became an illusion. I desperately needed the church to be true. I desperately needed the Mormon leaders to be men of God as I once believed they were. My Mormon beliefs were crumbling before my eyes, and it shook me to the core. Family, friends, and church leaders actively and aggressively encouraged me to do evil for the cause of good. Is that even possible? Can evil be done to accomplish good? I concluded that it could not. I decided that I will not and, in the end, I did not follow them! I fought on.

15.4 Pointless Pleas for Resolution

Those years were punctuated with endless phone calls, letters, and face-to-face meetings with church leaders from every level of Mormonism. My petitions began with local leaders and moved up to regional and then area leaders.

Finally, my petition arrived on the top floor of the church office building in Salt Lake City. Three times, high-ranking leaders reviewed all relevant documentation and returned with an assurance that I had done nothing wrong. They indicated that a quick and easy resolution was in the works. Upon running their decision past upper levels of Mormon management, these men quietly faded away. Mormonism is such that even the best men will cower, lose resolve, and willingly do wrong when Salt Lake speaks.

I will never forget the meeting when Grace and I sat before the Stake President and his first counselor. Again and again, the Stake President accused me of using my newspaper column to speak as one having authority in the church. I lost track of the number of times I denied his baseless accusations. Finally, I said, "Show me the column, and if I acted inappropriately, I will take the hit." He responded, "I have it, but it's not here; it's at my home." I answered, "Good, go get it; I'll wait." He never did produce the offending column. He could not because of the many columns I had written; none supported his false accusations. None of this was about doctrinally inappropriate columns I may have written. All of this was about his disagreement with my opinions and his

---
[7] John 8:44

determination to silence my voice. A resolution with this man was impossible because total domination was his only objective.

I didn't know Grace had already shaken the dust of Mormonism off her feet. That is why her actions shocked me so completely. She sprang to her feet, looked the accusatory Stake President straight in the eye, gave him a sharply pointed piece of her mind, and marched out the door. I watched her back as she went through the door. I was stunned!

Grace is a peaceful and gentle soul. She is not one to show anyone disrespect. I had never before seen her pushed to this point in forty years of marriage! My shock turned to livid anger. By what authority did this arrogant and accusatory Stake President provoke her so? **Don't mess with my Grace!** Her courage gave purpose to my resolve. I rose to my feet, stuck a finger in his face, and barked, "**SHAME ON YOU!**"

Turning on my heel, I followed Grace through the door. This was the day I stopped believing, stopped caring, stopped searching for a resolution with the church. After that terrible day, I took my first steps on a journey that ultimately brought me to Jesus.

> Ask, and it shall be given to you; seek, and ye shall find; knock, and it shall be opened to you;
> – Matthew 7:7-8 (YLT)

15.5 The Dragon Slayer Comes

As I struggled on, devoid of hope, the Dragon Slayer approached. He knows all, has all understanding, and he alone has the power to vanquish the evil one.[8] The Dragon has seven heads, each fierce and lethal. But, only one heart ... small, black, and hard as any stone. The heart is difficult to hit and harder yet to hurt, but therein lies the weakness. The Dragon Slayer drove his spear through scales of steel, past ribs of iron, and to the very center with a mighty thrust. The Dragon roared in anger and defiance. No matter, the black heart was pierced.

> [14]Yahweh God said to the serpent, Because you have done this, you are cursed above all livestock, and above every animal of the field. You shall go on your belly and you shall eat dust all the days of your life. [15]I will put hostility between you and the woman, and between your offspring and her offspring. He will bruise your head, and you will bruise his heel.
> – Genesis 3:14-15 (WEB)

The beast, in the form of Mormonism, fell to the earth still and dead. Likewise, I fell, utterly spent. Looking up, my eyes searched the face of Love. It was Jesus, my God! I struggled to my knees and, with great effort, lifted

---
[8]Colossians 2:15

THE DARK YEARS

heavy hands. Once again, I cried out. This time, my words were new, "Jesus, save me!". Finally, thankfully, mercifully, my plea was heard, and healing began.

The season of despair drew to a close. My fall into the abyss slowed, stopped, and reversed. Light gathered, driving all darkness back into the pit from whence it came. Death vanished, and abundant life settled over me like a warm blanket.

> The thief cometh not, but for to steal, and to kill, and to destroy: **I am come that they might have life, and that they might have it more abundantly**.
> – John 10:10 (KJV) , emphasis added

Under my feet, I discovered a foundation, sure and firm. It is on the unmovable rock of my God that I stand now and forever, having been made a new creation in Christ Jesus.

> Therefore if anyone is in Christ, he is a new creation. The old things have passed away. Behold, **all things have become new**.
> – 2 Corinthians 5:17 (WEB), emphasis added

Part III

SIFTING THROUGH THE RUBBLE

Testing Every Spirit

Part III

SIFTING THROUGH THE RUBBLE

CHAPTER
SIXTEEN

IS THE GOSPEL EVERLASTING?

> ...how in blue blazes will anyone ever live the gospel? How could I, as a Mormon, possibly satisfy the unnamed list of demands required by the ever-changing god of Mormonism?
>
> *Lance Earl*

The necessity of living the Mormon gospel is a topic that fills the head of every member of the church. It is the subject of endless discussions. It is the purpose of classroom lessons and the topic of innumerable Sacrament meeting talks. Bishop's worthiness interviews, which occur at least annually, will focus on how well the gospel standards are being satisfied. How well I remember the futility of pretending to be a faithful adherent to the gospel.

I never slowed down long enough to realize, I didn't know what it meant to live the gospel. I raised five children; one fine son, and four beautiful daughters. I made sure they knew of the necessity of living the gospel while I never once taught them what the demands of gospel living entailed. I couldn't teach what I did not know.

There was, however, one definition of the gospel that seemed to be universally accepted. This was the gospel I knew and accepted as the truth.

In its fulness, the gospel includes **all the doctrines, principles, laws, ordinances, and covenants** necessary for us to be exalted in the celestial kingdom.
 – The Church of Jesus Christ of Latter-day Saints, *True to the Faith* (Salt Lake City: n.p., n.d.) 76

I had heard this definition from the mouths of many high-level Mormon leaders. I read it in teacher's manuals, student study manuals, and church magazines. Oh, I heard it a lot, but I never knew what it meant. I had the definition with no understanding of its underlying meaning. Regrettably, I dutifully passed this confusion to the next generation. Many of them are now teaching the same to my grandchildren.

If the gospel includes all the doctrines, principles, laws, ordinances, and covenants necessary to be exalted in the celestial kingdom, it seems wise to know what they are. Is there a list that defines them? No! Is there a scripture that lists them? No! Has a Mormon leader ever taken an opportunity to enumerate them? No! How then, in blue blazes, will anyone ever live the gospel? If none can live the gospel, who will be saved?

The gospel became this constant source of discouragement. I knew I had to live it, whatever it was. Because I couldn't define it, I could never know my standing before God. I was falling short in the parts of the gospel I knew. I had no clue or assurance regarding the totality of an unknowable gospel. How could I have confidence in salvation without a clear picture of the required works?

Mormon salvation is only possible as a condition of completing or fulfilling a list of unlisted requirements. It is ultimately an impossible gospel!

No Confidence in the Book of Mormon

The first paragraph on the introduction page of my old and well used Book of Mormon reads;

> The Book of Mormon is a volume of holy scripture comparable to the Bible. It is a record of God's dealings with the ancient inhabitants of the Americas and contains, **as does the Bible**, the fulness of the everlasting gospel.
> – The Church of Jesus Christ of Latter-day Saints, *Book of Mormon*(Salt Lake City: The Church of Jesus Christ of Latter-day Saints, 1981 edition) Introduction, emphasis added

This introduction should cause Mormon eyebrows, in every nation, to knit together in consternation. The first premise of Mormonism is that the church and Bible were corrupted sometime after the death of Jesus and His original apostles.

> One example is the Great Apostasy, which occurred after the Savior established His Church. After the deaths of the Savior and His Apostles, men corrupted the principles of the gospel and made unauthorized changes in Church organization and priesthood ordinances. Because of this widespread wickedness, the Lord withdrew the authority of the priesthood from the earth.
> – The Church of Jesus Christ of Latter-day Saints, *True to the Faith*(Salt Lake City: n.p., n.d.) 13

The Mormon church claims that many plain and precious truths have been removed from the Bible. Therefore, the only true and living church had to be restored by the Mormon prophet Joseph Smith. However, this version of the Book of Mormon introduction clearly indicates that the gospel was and is fully preserved in the Bible. Why then was a restoration necessary? Instead of answering the question, leaders of the Mormon church changed the Book of Mormon.

> The Book of Mormon is a volume of holy scripture comparable to the Bible. It is a record of God's dealings with ancient inhabitants of the Americas and contains the fulness of the everlasting gospel.
> – The Church of Jesus Christ of Latter-day Saints, *Book of Mormon*(Salt Lake City: The Church of Jesus Christ of Latter-day Saints, 2004 & 2006 editions) Introduction, emphasis added

Removed are the words, "as does the Bible." With the removal of four simple words, the Book of Mormon's introduction renounced the Bible. With this significant contradiction scrubbed from the collective memory of the Mormon people, the church was free to continue with the theory that the gospel was lost and later restored by Joseph Smith. The Mormon church has held fast to this belief, filling their official publications to overflowing with heresy.

16.1 The Gospel Wherein We Stand

I will never forget the day I found and comprehended the Everlasting Gospel of Jesus Christ.

> [1]Moreover, brethren, **I declare** unto you the gospel which I preached unto you, which also ye have received, and **wherein ye stand**; [2]**By which also ye are saved**, if ye keep in memory what I preached unto you, unless ye have believed in vain. [3]For I delivered unto you first of all that which I also received, how that **Christ died for our sins** according to the scriptures; [4]And that **he was buried**, and that **he rose again the third day** according to the scriptures:
> – I Corinthians 15:1-4 (KJV)

It was as if God pulled a heavy curtain back and flooded my darkened mind with brilliant white light.

This gospel is the doctrine and founding principles upon which we who follow Christ stand. On this hill, we plant our flag. Here we earnestly contend for the faith which *was once delivered unto the saints*.[1] And here we defend and die with Jesus.

Paul seems to be saying that this is the center place of our faith. What we are as Christians hinges on this central truth.

---

[1] Jude 3

The real Everlasting Gospel of Jesus Christ is such a blessing to the true follower of Jesus. The gospel is short, enumerated, understandable, doable. Above all, I praise God because this discovery has made me free.

CHAPTER
SEVENTEEN

WHITE AND DELIGHTSOME

> O God, heal me of this evil, of this disease, purge my heart of this poison!
>
> *Lance*

We are uniquely different and equally loved by God. What joy we would have in this world if we loved as He loves!

17.1 A Culture of Hate

According to Mormon doctrine, I learned who and what I truly was while sitting in a Mormon priesthood meeting. I was about fourteen years of age and was a teacher in the Aaronic priesthood. My instructor explained that we all lived in a pre-mortal world as spirit sons and daughters of our Heavenly Father and one of his goddess wives. In that forgotten world, the Mormon Jesus and Lucifer, our elder brothers, got in a bit of a scrap over who would rule the yet uncreated Earth.

The conflict between these two "would-be rulers" spread to us, the other spirit children of our Heavenly Father. One by one, every brother and sister made a choice, some aligning with Lucifer and others with Jesus. In the end, Lucifer lost the battle. God cast him and his followers down from heaven to become the Devil and his demons.

My priesthood instructor impressed upon us; we can know something of our performance in the war in heaven. Based solely on the color of our skin and the place of our birth, we can know who was noble and who was not. Because of these factors, God numbered us among His most valiant spirit sons and daughters. With that understanding, pride became a curse more damning than all others.

Those born with black skin were the shirkers and ne'er-do-wells who followed Jesus, but just barely. Because they were *not valiant*, God sent them here and placed a permanent curse of black skin on each one.

> **Now, my young friends of the Aaronic Priesthood, you are these valiant and noble sons of our Father!** You are the strength of the Lord's house, His warriors! You are those who chose good over evil and who exhibited "exceedingly great faith" and "good works." **And because of your personal history, you were entrusted to come to the earth in these last days to do again what you did before** –to once again choose good over evil, exercise exceedingly great faith, and perform good works –and to do so in behalf of the kingdom of God on the earth and your fellowman!
> – James J. Hamula, "Winning the War against Evil", Ensign, November 2008, emphasis added

17.2   Hate From the Beginning

Racist hate sprang up in the infancy of the church. It quickly became a primary theological pillar of Mormonism.

> I do not believe that the people of the North have any more right to say that the South shall not hold slaves, than the South have to say the North shall.... the first mention we have of slavery is found in the Holy Bible.... And so far from that prediction being averse to the mind of God, it [slavery] remains as a lasting monument of the decree of Jehovah, to the shame and confusion of all who have cried out against the South, in consequence of their holding the sons of Ham in servitude.
> – Joseph Smith, "Letter to Oliver Cowdery", the Messenger and Advocate, Vol. II, No. 7, April 1836

> **The moment we consent to mingle with the seed of Cain the Church must go to destruction**, – we should receive the curse which has been placed upon the seed of Cain, and never more be numbered with the children of Adam who are heirs to the priesthood until that curse be removed.
> – Fred C. Collier, *The Teachings of President Bigham Young*(Salt Lake City: Collier's Publishing, 1987) 46, emphasis added

For behold, the Lord shall curse the land with much heat, and the bareness thereof shall go forth forever; and there was a blackness came upon all the children of Canaan, that they were despised among all people.
– *Pearl of Great Price*, Moses 7:8

17.3 Hate in My Lifetime

As a young boy, I sat on the living room rug and watched endless sessions of General Conference. The following quotes are from prophets and apostles familiar to me. Awe filled me each time they spoke, despite their endless monotone droning. They were, in my eyes, the Lord's anointed. Many of these men remained alive until my late teens and early adulthood. They shaped my thinking and molded my closely held religious views. I must now expose the racist and poisonous indoctrination of my youth. Here, I attempt to describe and condemn the caustic seed planted in me. This seed sprang up, and its roots sank deep into my vulnerable and trusting heart. This Mormon poison is one thing I bitterly resent above every other injustice.

> I know of no scriptural basis for denying the Priesthood to Negroes other than one verse in the Book of Abraham (1:26); however, I believe, as you suggest that the real reason dates back to our pre-existent life.
> – Llewelyn R. McKay, *Home Memories of President David O. McKay*(N.p.: n.p., 1956) 226-231

> It is true that the negro race is barred from holding the Priesthood, and this has always been the case. **The Prophet Joseph Smith taught this doctrine**, and it was made known to him, although we know of no such statement in any revelation in the Doctrine and Covenants, Book of Mormon, or the Bible.
> – General Board Y. M. M. I. A,, *The Improvement Era, Vol 27, 1923-1924*(Salt Lake City: n.p., n.d.) 565, Joseph Fielding Smith, emphasis added

> Negroes in this life are denied the priesthood; under no circumstances can they hold this delegation of authority from the Almighty. The gospel message of salvation is not carried affirmatively to them.... **Negroes are not equal with other races** where the receipt of certain spiritual blessings are concerned...
> – Bruce R. McConkie, *Mormon Doctrine*(Salt Lake City: Bookcraft, 1958) 477, emphasis added

> There were no neutrals in the war in heaven. All took sides either with Christ or with Satan. Every man had his agency there, and men receive rewards here based upon their actions there, just as they will receive rewards hereafter for deeds done in the body. The Negro, evidently, is receiving the reward he merits.
> – Joseph Fielding Smith, *Doctrines of Salvation*(Salt Lake City: Bookcraft, 1954-56) 65-66

Others, god saw as better than black people, but just barely. These include native Americans, Hispanics, Asians, and all others with skin darker than my own. The underlying principle, we were taught, is that god curses wicked people with dark skin. The curse can be the result of evil deeds in the pre-existent world or this world. Unlike black people, who presumably sinned before they were born, others sinned after their births and were cursed. In the Book of Mormon, Lamanites fall into the second category. Today, we know them as native Americans.

> ⁶And the skins of the Lamanites were dark, according to the mark which was set upon their fathers, which was a curse upon them because of their transgression and their rebellion against their brethren, who consisted of Nephi, Jacob, and Joseph, and Sam, who were just and holy men. ⁷And their brethren sought to destroy them, therefore they were cursed; and the Lord God set a mark upon them, yea, upon Laman and Lemuel, and also the sons of Ishmael, and Ishmaelitish women. ⁸**And this was done that their seed might be distinguished from the seed of their brethren, that thereby the Lord God might preserve his people, that they might not mix and believe in incorrect traditions which would prove their destruction. ⁹And it came to pass that whosoever did mingle his seed with that of the Lamanites did bring the same curse upon his seed.**
> – *Book of Mormon*, Alma 3:6-9, emphasis added

Doctrinally, not much is known about the sins of other brown-skinned peoples. However, we have this unquestioned pattern in Mormonism, dark-skinned people, in some way, came off the godly rails, and the Mormon god responded.

> Is there reason then why the type of birth we receive in this life is not a reflection of our worthiness or lack of it in the pre-existent life? ... can we account in any other way for the birth of some of the children of God in darkest Africa, or in flood-ridden China, or among the starving hordes of India, while some of the rest of us are born here in the United States? **We cannot escape the conclusion that because of performance in our pre-existence some of us**

are born as Chinese, some as Japanese, some as Latter-day Saints. There are rewards and punishments, fully in harmony with His established policy in dealing with sinners and saints, rewarding all according to their deeds.
– Mark E. Peterson. "Race Problems – As They Effect the Church" Talk, BYU, August 27, 1954, emphasis added

The Mormon god, I was taught, also had a problem with white people born to non-Mormon families. They fought on the Mormon god's side in the war in heaven with strength and courage. However, in some way only known to God, their performance had been somewhat of a disappointment.

My Mormon instructor explained, God sent the most valiant spirits to live in active, righteous, white Mormon homes. He informed us that we were literally the best of the best, saved for these last days because we were the more noble and most loved by God. By such teaching, pride in myself and contempt for others flourished.

17.4 A Burning Hatred

Tragically, I carried a perverted disdain for people of color for most of my life. I never admitted it. I hid it well, but ugly judgment and hatred were always with me. If ever I was served by a black waiter or waitress, I was careful to note where his or her hands touched my plate. Covertly, I rotated the plate until the perceived contamination was furthest from me. Then, I carefully slid my food to the near side, where I was more confident it would not be polluted.

The Olympics were always a strange and awkward affair. When a black American competed against a white athlete from any other nation, you guessed it ... I was white first and American second.

One year after we were saved, Grace said, "You have got to see this video!" I cued it up to see a boy about ten years old, passionately, emotionally, lovingly, and with incredible expression, signing a favorite worship song. I don't know from where or how it came, but the first words from my mouth were a negative, **"Oh, he's black!"**.

I cannot describe the anger, disgust, and shame that filled me. I thought such things were dead in me. Even so, there was no denying the poison that poured freely from my cursed mouth. Cancer sinks deep in a man's heart and can be challenging to eradicate. I still had the sickness ... *O God, heal me of this evil, of this disease, purge my heart of this poison!*

FORGIVE ME!

These things are embarrassing and difficult to admit, but it is important to come clean. I received my most compelling and lasting racist training from the *The Church of Jesus Christ of Latter-day Saints*.

Is there a curse of black skin? Of course not. Is there a curse of a hard heart charred black by unjustified hatred? Yes there is and I received that curse by the hands of evil men. Is there a great physician who replaces charred hearts of stone with hearts of flesh? Oh, you better believe it!

> I will also give you a new heart, and I will put a new spirit within you; and I will take away the stony heart out of your flesh, and I will give you a heart of flesh.
> – Ezekiel 36:26 (WEB)

CHAPTER
EIGHTEEN

NOT QUITE WHITE

> A profound apology is all I have to offer. An earnest request for undeserved forgiveness is my plea.
>
> *Lance*

Characters from the Book of Mormon are provably black? And modern-day Mormons? The majority are black men and women! Canonized scripture and prophetic Mormon teaching establish these claims beyond doubt. What does that mean for the Mormon priesthood? Buckle up; this ride is a bit bumpy.

18.1 The Egyptians were Black Men

This is the story of the first black men, according to Mormonism.

> ... after the flood we are told that the curse that had been pronounced upon Cain was continued through Ham's wife, as he had married a wife of the seed. And why did it pass through the flood? **Because it was necessary that the devil should have representation upon the earth as well as God;** ...
>
> – *Journal of Discourses* (N.p.: n.p., n.d.), 22:304, John Taylor, emphasis added

From Ham and his black wife, the nation of Egypt sprang up. Biblically, Egypt is commonly used to represent the world, sin, bondage, and idolatry. Mormonism adds greater dimension and depth to the symbolism of the Bible. Egypt and all of its people fall under God's anathema and into disfavor with deity due to Cain's curse, which manifests with a skin of blackness.

[21] Now this king of Egypt was a descendant from the loins of Ham, and was a partaker of the blood of the Canaanites by birth. [22] **From this descent sprang all the Egyptians**, and thus the blood of the Canaanites was preserved in the land.
– *Pearl of Great Price*, Abraham 1:21-22, emphasis added

Now, Pharaoh being of that lineage **by which he could not have the right of Priesthood** ...
– *Pearl of Great Price*, Abraham 1:27a

18.2 Ephraim and Manasseh were Black Men

If we accept the Mormon position that all Egyptians were descendants of Ham and his black wife, we must also come to grips with a plethora of new doctrine relative to the nation of Israel.

After being sold into Egypt, we know that Joseph took an Egyptian wife who bore him two sons.[1]

And Pharaoh called Joseph's name Zaphnath–paaneah; and he gave him to wife Asenath the daughter of Poti–pherah priest of On ...
– Genesis 41:45 (KJV)

[51] And Joseph called the name of the firstborn Manasseh: For God, said he, hath made me forget all my toil, and all my father's house. [52] And the name of the second called he Ephraim: For God hath caused me to be fruitful in the land of my affliction.
– Genesis 41:51-52 (KJV)

Ephraim and Manasseh are a bit problematic for the Mormon church. They were born to Joseph and his Egyptian wife. Since *all Egyptians* were under the curse, so then was the wife of Joseph and every child she bore.[2] Consequently, they fell under the curse of black skin and became subject to all associated limitations and restrictions. Like Pharaoh, Ephraim and Manasseh had no right to the priesthood. Why then did God make them fathers of two tribes of Israel that bore their names?

18.3 The Nephites were Black Men

The Book of Mormon people, Nephites, and Lamanites are the descendants of the prophet Lehi or the man Ishmael. Let us turn our attention to these two fathers of the Book of Mormon.

---
[1] Genesis 41:50-52
[2] *Pearl of Great Price*, Abraham 1:22

It is true that **Lehi was a descendant of Manasseh** (Alma 10:3), but the Nephites were just as much the descendants of Ephraim, for we know that **Ishmael, who was the other founder of the colony, was a descendant of Ephraim**. This we learn from the Prophet Joseph Smith, but it is not so stated in the Book of Mormon. This information was contained in the 116 pages of lost manuscript which was not re-translated into the Book of Mormon.
- Joseph Fielding Smith, *Answers to Gospel Questions*(Salt Lake City: Deseret Book, n.d.) 3:197–198

And Abinadi was a descendant of Nephi, who was the son of Lehi, who came out of the land of Jerusalem, who was a descendant of Manasseh, who was the son of Joseph who was sold into Egypt by the hands of his brethren.
- *Book of Mormon*, Alma 10:3

18.4   Joseph Smith was a Black Man

The Book of Mormon claims to include quotes from Joseph of Egypt. He reportedly prophesied of the coming of the modern-day Joseph Smith who would bear his name. Joseph Smith claimed to be of the seed of Joseph of Egypt, the husband of a black woman.

> 15 And his name shall be called after me; and it shall be after the name of his father. And he shall be like unto me; for the thing, which the Lord shall bring forth by his hand, by the power of the Lord shall bring my people unto salvation.
> - *Book of Mormon*, Second Nephi 3:15

Brigham Young confirmed Joseph Smith's claim that he was of the tribe of Ephraim.

> The Book of Mormon came to Ephraim, **for Joseph Smith was a pure Ephraimite**, and the Book of Mormon was revealed to him.
> - *Journal of Discourses* (N.p.: n.p., n.d.), 2:268–269, Brigham Young & Daniel H. Ludlow, "Of the House of Israel", Ensign, January 1991, emphasis added

18.5   I Am a Black Man

I received my patriarchal blessing under the hand of a Mormon patriarch. In the name of Jesus Christ, he laid his hands on my head and declared that I, like Joseph Smith, am of the tribe of Ephraim. Apparently, we are not alone. The church claims that the majority of all church members are of Ephraim.

A patriarchal blessing includes a declaration of lineage, stating that the person is of the house of Israel -a descendant of Abraham, belonging to a specific tribe of Jacob. Many Latter-day Saints are of the tribe of Ephraim, the tribe given the primary responsibility to lead the latter-day work of the Lord.
– The Church of Jesus Christ of Latter-day Saints, "Patriarchal Blessings", www.churchofjesuschrist.org

If we were to examine the patriarchal blessings of every living member of *The Church of Jesus Christ of Latter-day Saints*, all or most would point to Ephraim or Manasseh. In a few instances, we may find people from other tribes. However, if we were to examine every patriarchal blessing in those people's family trees, I am confident we would discover Ephraim, Manasseh, or both. Consequently, every living member of the church, per Mormon doctrine, has black blood in their veins. Therefore, when a Mormon man marries a Mormon woman, the mixed blood of the man will mix with the mixed blood of the woman and condemn them all.

18.6 What of Abraham

If Mormon scripture is true, the foundations of Judaism and Christianity are forever and irreparably damaged. In that case, everything we hold sacred and dear must be bulldozed to the ground and replaced with the creeds of Mormonism.

According to the Book of Abraham, the Mormon god cursed Cain and all of his descendants with a skin of blackness. This curse was preserved through the flood by Ham's wife, a descendant of Cain. Finally, *all Egyptians* are descendants of Ham's wife and received the curse of Cain.[3]

Acting as a self-declared prophet of God, Brigham Young taught,

> Shall I tell you the law of God in regard to the African race? If the white man who belongs to the chosen seed mixes his blood with the seed of Cain, the penalty, under the law of God, is death on the spot. This will always be so.
> – *Journal of Discourses* (N.p.: n.p., n.d.), 6:110, Brigham Young

[1]Now Sarai Abram's wife bare him no children: and she had an handmaid, an **Egyptian**, whose name was Hagar. [2]And Sarai said unto Abram, Behold now, the Lord hath restrained me from bearing: I pray thee, go in unto my maid; it may be that I may obtain children by her. And Abram hearkened to the voice of Sarai. [3]And Sarai Abram's wife took Hagar her maid the **Egyptian**, after Abram had

---
[3]*Pearl of Great Price*, Abraham 1:21-22

dwelt ten years in the land of Canaan, and gave her to her husband Abram to be his wife.

– Genesis 16:1-3 (KJV), emphasis added

If Brigham Young truly spoke for God and if he revealed the unchanging law of God, how was Abraham not *put to death on the spot* when he laid with Hagar? If Brigham Young spoke the truth, I have many questions. If the Mormon god killed Abraham, who took Isaac to the mount and there prepared to sacrifice him? If the Mormon god killed Abraham, who told Isaac, "My son, God will provide himself a lamb for a burnt offering?" If god killed Abraham, how could there be a people of Israel? If god killed Abraham and there never was a people of Israel, from whence sprang Jesus?

18.7 Deepest Regret

When I reflect on these things, my heart is distraught. I carried an ugliness for most of my life that clouded and darkened all that I was. As a Mormon, I believed all I ever heard without question. I never thought to challenge or test the lies. I allowed them to sink deeply into my heart of stone and fester there.

Second, only to my deep shame of presuming to be a high priest like my Lord and King,[4] my bigotry is my greatest regret. My humiliation for this great evil, I cannot begin to describe. Through it all, I remain in awe that Jesus, who knew no sin, bore my pain, shame, and sorrow on the cross! If this is not perfect love, then I must ask ... what is it?

I am profoundly troubled that I was a part of this open hatred against my dark-skinned brothers and sisters. My heart aches for generations of good people who suffered needlessly under unjustifiable oppression. I am sorrowful for those millions who I, and my white Mormon brothers, hated without cause.

I regret teaching this evil doctrine to others who, in some cases, taught it again. I regret the offense I caused toward God when I rejected those He created. I am ashamed that Satan's destructive power was allowed to grow and thrive in my heart. A profound apology is all I have to offer. An earnest request for undeserved forgiveness is my plea.

But, there is hope. Cancer grows little by little, building upon itself until it affects the whole body. Likewise, a healthy body by the power of the *Great Healer* can purge itself and be made whole. I now accept all people, regardless of color, with joy and love. They, like me, are created in the image of God. I praise God for this tender mercy, by which He shook lose the chains of hate and bigotry.

> Holy Father, Thy wisdom excites our admiration, Thy power fills us with fear, Thy omnipresence turns every spot of earth into holy ground; but how shall we thank Thee enough for Thy mercy which

---

[4] See chapter: High Priest

comes down to the lowest part of our need to give us beauty for ashes, the oil of joy for mourning, and for the spirit of heaviness a garment of praise? We bless and magnify Thy mercy, through Jesus Christ our Lord. *Amen*

– A. W. Tozer, *Three Spiritual Classics*(Chicago: Moody Publishers, 2018) 155

CHAPTER
NINETEEN

A CURSED CHURCH

> The Word of God does not change. The gospel of the Lord does not change. The nature of God does not change. God, Himself does not change.
>
> — *Lance*

Nothing happens, nothing moves, nothing is authorized, and nothing is binding in *The Church of Jesus Christ of Latter-day Saints* without the priesthood.

> The General Authorities are representatives of the Savior. They hold the priesthood and the keys to direct the work of the Lord's Church. As we follow their counsel and sustain them with our faith, obedience, and prayers, we will receive great blessings.
> – The Church of Jesus Christ of Latter-day Saints, *DUTIES AND BLESSINGS OF THE PRIESTHOOD*(Salt Lake City: n.p., n.d.) 83

19.1   No Priesthood

Mormon priesthood holders love to trace their *priesthood line of authority* back to Smith, through Peter, James, and John, and ultimately to Jesus Christ. This priesthood lineage provides a sense of legitimacy and authority for such men. I remember the excitement of men when they discovered their priesthood line traced through famous characters in Mormon history.

> I am wondering how many of you are able to trace your priesthood genealogy back to Jesus Christ? ... Isn't it exciting that we are that near to the Lord Jesus Christ in this most important element? And

isn't it exciting that whenever you lay your hands upon a person to ordain him it is the same as if the Lord himself did it?
– The Church of Jesus Christ of Latter-day Saints, "Members Can Request Priesthood Line of Authority", www.churchofjesuschrist.org

We have established that the fathers of ancient and modern Mormonism, Lehi, Ishmael, and Joseph Smith, are descendants of Ephraim or Manasseh. We have further demonstrated that these Mormon elites received the curse of Cain through the wife of Ham, a "black" woman.

We must not inter-marry with the Negro. Why? If I were to marry a Negro woman and have children by her, my children would all be cursed as to the priesthood. Do I want my children cursed as to the priesthood? **If there is one drop of Negro blood in my children, as I have read to you, they receive the curse**. There isn't any argument, therefore, as to inter-marriage with the Negro, is there?
– Mark E. Peterson. "Race Problems – As They Affect the Church" Talk, BYU, August 27, 1954, emphasis added

The Mormon narrative indicates that Peter, James, and John appeared to Joseph Smith and conferred upon him the same priesthood they received under the hand of Jesus. They could not because Smith was born under the curse of Cain. Consequently, all priesthood blessings were prohibited. Smith did not pass that priesthood to other men because he never had that power within himself.

Joseph Smith is the spring from which all modern Mormon priesthood flows. Looming over the church is clear evidence that this spring must be considered dry! The same is unavoidably true of the Book of Mormon patriarchs. Thus, the fathers of Mormonism, ancient and modern, are dry and dust-filled wells!

The priesthood ban, before 1978, denied the priesthood to any with even *one drop* of black blood. Even now, after removing the ban, the curse still haunts the church. All Mormon priesthood traces through cursed men because drops of black blood flowed in them before 1978. Church doctrine establishes that no priesthood authority exists or ever existed in *The Church of Jesus Christ of Latter-day Saints*, ancient or modern.

19.2 No Ordinances

From birth to death, priesthood ordinances punctuate Mormon lives. These serve as essential way-points on the road leading to exaltation and eventual godhood. Ordinances can only be performed by men who hold the priesthood. If no priesthood exists in the church, of what value are priesthood ordinances?

Shortly after birth, Mormon children receive a name and a blessing. At age eight, each child gets baptized and receives the gift of the Holy Ghost. The

Aaronic priesthood and ordination to the office of Deacon happens automatically for every twelve-year-old boy. Additional ordinations occur as the boy advances to the office of Teacher and then Priest. Mormon teens frequent the temple to be baptized and receive the Holy Ghost on behalf of deceased persons. At around age eighteen, young men receive the Melchizedek priesthood and ordination to the office of Elder. Before serving a mission or being married, young men and women enter the temple to be washed, anointed, and receive their endowment. Couples kneel at the temple altar where they are married for time and all eternity. With every assignment in the church, the called person is set apart for that work. Weekly in sacrament meetings, members receive the ordinance of the sacrament. Finally, most church members receive many blessings for spiritual or physical healing.

I was also ordained to the office of Seventy and High Priest. These last ordinations are no longer routine for Mormon men, but at one time, they were.

Even in death, a man claiming to hold the priesthood will dedicate a grave to protect the body until it comes forth in the resurrection.

> Ordinances and blessings are to be performed with faith in Heavenly Father and Jesus Christ and according to the guidance of the Holy Ghost. Leaders ensure that they are performed with proper approval (where necessary), with the required priesthood authority, in the proper way, and by worthy participants.
> – The Church of Jesus Christ of Latter-day Saints, "General Handbook", Priesthood Ordinances and Blessings

If the canonized scripture of *The Church of Jesus Christ of Latter-day Saints* is true, no priesthood has been or is now present in the church. Every baptism, marriage, blessing, ordination, and all other Mormon priesthood manifestations are void without the priesthood. Of more importance, if no priesthood exists, every action taken in the name of God by the power of that false priesthood is blasphemy.

> Therefore, son of man, speak unto the house of Israel, and say unto them, Thus saith the Lord God; Yet in this your fathers have blasphemed me, in that they have committed a trespass against me.
> – Ezekiel 20:27 (KJV)

In light of these many false "works of righteousness", I think it is best to let Jesus respond, as only He can.

> [21] Not every one that saith unto me, Lord, Lord, shall enter into the kingdom of heaven; but he that doeth the will of my Father which is in heaven. [22] Many will say to me in that day, **Lord, Lord, have we not prophesied in thy name? and in thy name have cast out devils? and in thy name done many wonderful works?** [23] And then will I profess unto them, I never knew you: depart from me, ye that work iniquity.
> – Matthew 7:21-23 (KJV), emphasis added

19.3 A Culture of Denial

Throughout the church's history, church leaders have affirmed racist practices as official Mormon doctrine. Current leaders attempt to erase the words of Mormon prophets now dead. If Mormonism's prophets genuinely speak for God, how can they be divided on this or any point of doctrine?

The Mormon people are intimately familiar with a Book of Mormon passage prophesying that God will lift the curse on the Native American people. With the curse's lifting, they will be blessed with white and delightsome skin.

> ...their scales of darkness shall begin to fall from their eyes; and many generations shall not pass away among them, save they shall be a **white and a delightsome** people.
> – *Book of Mormon*, 2 Nephi 30:6, All editions prior to 1981

In 1981, the church changed what Joseph Smith called "the most correct of any book on earth". The word "*white*" was replaced with the word "*pure*". Today, many insist that this was a clarification since "white" does not refer to a person's actual skin color; rather, it describes a person's state of heart.

FairMormon is an organization dedicated to providing answers to criticisms of the doctrine, practice, and history of *The Church of Jesus Christ of Latter-day Saints*.

> Furthermore, "white" was a synonym for "pure" at the time Joseph translated the Book of Mormon:
> – FairMormon, "'White and delightsome' changed to 'pure and delightsome'", https://www.fairmormon.org

However, the Book of Mormon clearly attaches skin color to sin.

> And he had caused the cursing to come upon them, yea, even a sore cursing, because of their iniquity. For behold, they had hardened their hearts against him, and they had become like unto a flint; wherefore, as they were white, and exceedingly fair and delightsome, that they might not be enticing unto my people the Lord God did cause a skin of blackness to come upon them.
> – *Book of Mormon*, 2 Nephi 5:21

> [14] And it came to pass that those Lamanites who had united with the Nephites were numbered among the Nephites; [15] And their curse was taken from them, and their skin became white like unto the Nephites; [16] And their young men and their daughters became exceedingly fair, and they were numbered among the Nephites, and were called Nephites. ...
> – *Book of Mormon*, 3 Nephi 2:14-16

Mormon leaders have taught that "white and delightsome" is a reference to skin pigmentation and does not reflect purity of the heart.

> You may inquire of the intelligent of the world whether they can tell why the aborigines of this country are dark, loathsome, ignorant, and sunken into the depths of degradation ... When the Lord has a people, he makes covenants with them and gives unto them promises: then, if they transgress his law, change his ordinances, and break his covenants he has made with them, he will put a mark upon them, as in the case of the Lamanites and other portions of the house of Israel; but by-and-by they will become a white and delightsome people.
> – *Journal of Discourses* (N.p.: n.p., n.d.), 7:336, Brigham Young

Spencer W. Kimball referenced 2 Nephi 30:6 and declared, the Indians "are fast becoming a white and delightsome people", indicating that:

> The [Indian] children in the home placement program in Utah are often lighter than their brothers and sisters in the hogans on the reservation
> – Spencer W. Kimball. Talk, General Conference, October 1960

The church's first presidency is set apart as prophets, seers, and revelators. For over one hundred years, they have spoken clearly about people of color, especially American Indians and Blacks. During that entire time, the Mormon people considered their words to be literally the Word of God.

19.4 Inquiries and Justification

Dr. Lowry Nelson was an internationally respected LDS sociologist working at the *Utah State Agricultural College* which is now *Utah State University*. In 1947, he made an inquiry of the First Presidency under the Prophet George Albert Smith. The Mormon practice of denying priesthood and temple blessings to Black people was the topic. The official response follows:

> Dr. Lowry Nelson
> Utah State Agricultural College
> Logan, Utah
>
> Dear Brother Nelson:
>
> ... The basic element of your ideas and concepts seems to be that all God's children stand in equal positions before Him in all things.
>
> Your knowledge of the Gospel will indicate to you that this is contrary to the very fundamentals of God*s dealings with Israel dating from the time of His promise to Abraham regarding Abraham 1 s seed and their position vis-a vis God Himself* Indeed, some of God*s children were assigned to superior positions before the world was formed. We

are aware that some Higher Critics do not accept this, but the Church does.

Your position seems to lose sight of the revelations of the Lord touching the preexistence of our spirits , the rebellion in heaven, and the doctrines that our birth into this life and the advantages under which we may be born have a relationship in the life heretofore.

From the days of the Prophet Joseph even until now, it has been the doctrine of the Church, never questioned by any of the Church leaders, that the Negroes are not entitled to the full blessings of the Gospel.

Furthermore, your ideas, as we understand them, appear to contemplate the intermarriage of the Negro and White races, a concept which has heretofore **been most repugnant** to most normal-minded people from the ancient patriarchs till now. God's rule for Israel, His Chosen People, has been endogenous. Modern Israel has been similarly directed.

We are not unmindful of the fact that there is a growing tendency, particularly among some educators, as it manifests itself in this area, toward the breaking down of race barriers in the matter of intermarriage between whites and blacks, but it does not have the sanction of the Church and is contrary to Church doctrine.

Faithfully yours,
(signed) Geo, Albert Smith
J. Reuben Clark, Jr.
David 0, McKay

– The Church of Jesus Christ of Latter-day Saints, "A letter to Dr. Lowry Nelson Utah State Agricultural College" (Signatories: Geo Albert Smith, J. Reuben Clark, Jr. and David 0, McKay) 1947, emphasis added

Stewart Udall was a multi-generational Mormon. He was elected to Congress in 1954 and served for three terms. President John F Kennedy appointed Udall to serve in his cabinet as Secretary of the Interior in 1961.

As a civil servant, Udall worked for racial integration and equal rights in professional sports. While working toward that end, he received a troubling letter that motivated him to question church policy.

Now as a member of the most segregated organization on earth, how can you tell a man who to hire on a ball club? Is it Constitutional? Please don't be victimized by the seed of Cain.

– "An letter to Stewart Udall" (From anomalous) archive.org

Honorable Stewart L. Udall
Secretary of the Interior
Washington, D. C.

Dear Secretary Udall: We appreciate very much your thoughtfulness in advising us of the growing criticism of the Church with regard to the issues of racial equality and the rights of minority groups.

We agree with you that it is a matter of great concern to the Church, and that it deserves our wise attention. We hasten to assure you that this is a matter which has received the closest, the wisest and, we hope, the most inspired attention of which the brethren are capable.

In considering this question in the past, practically every president of the Church has made some statement in reference thereto. When we read the three letters which you enclosed to President McKay, his immediate comment was, "We admit negroes to the Church by baptism, but we do not let them receive the Priesthood."

We have always felt that we could do more for the Negro than any other church. We know that through baptism the door to the celestial kingdom of God is opened. In 1949 the First Presidency, after discussion with the Council of the Twelve, wrote the following:

"The attitude of the Church with reference to negroes remains as it has always stood. **It is not a matter of the declaration of a policy but of direct commandment from the Lord, on which is founded the doctrine of the Church from the days of its organization, to the effect that negroes may become members of the Church but that they are not entitled to the priesthood at the present time**. The prophets of the Lord have made several statements as to the operation of the principle. President Brigham Young said: 'Why are so many of the inhabitants of the earth cursed with a skin of blackness? **It comes in consequence of their fathers rejecting the power of the holy priesthood, and the law of God**. They will go down to death. **And when all the rest of the children have received their blessings in the holy priesthood, then that curse will be removed from the seed of Cain, and they will then come up and possess the priesthood, and receive all the blessings which we are now entitled to.**'

President Wilford Woodruff made the following statement: 'The Day will come when all that race will be redeemed and possess all the blessings which we now have.'

The position of the Church regarding the negro may be understood when another doctrine of the Church is kept in mind, namely, that **the conduct of spirits in the pre-mortal existence has some determining effect upon the conditions and circumstances under which these spirits take on mortality**, and that while the details of this principle have not been made known, the principle itself indicates that the coming to this earth and taking on mortality is a privilege that is given to those who maintained their first estate; and that the worth of the privilege is so great that spirits are willing to come to earth and take on bodies no matter what the handicap may be as to the kind of bodies they are to secure; and that among the handicaps failure of the right to enjoy in mortality the blessings of the priesthood, is a handicap which spirits are willing to assume in order that they might come to earth. Under this principle there is no injustice whatsoever involved in this deprivation as to the holding of the priesthood by the negroes."

... **You will see that President McKay's remarks at the moment are in keeping with the statements of his predecessors.**
...

Thanking you very kindly for your interest once again, we are Faithfully, your brethren

Henry D. Moyle

Hugh B. Brown

– The Church of Jesus Christ of Latter-day Saints, "A letter to Stewart L. Udall Secretary of the Interior" (Signatories: Henry D. Moyle and Hugh B. Brown) 1961, emphasis added

Current Mormon leaders have thrown all who came before under the proverbial bus. They have denied their words and in-so-doing, have declared these former leaders to be unfaithful servants. They have taken what the entire church once considered to be official doctrine and trampled it under their feet.

Over time, Church leaders and members advanced many theories to explain the priesthood and temple restrictions. **None of these explanations is accepted today as the official doctrine of the Church.**
– The Church of Jesus Christ of Latter-day Saints, "Race and the Priesthood", www.churchofjesuschrist.org/study/manual/gospel-topics-essays/race-and-the-priesthood

None renounced the past prophets of Mormonism more forcefully than the apostle Jeffrey R. Holland. His words forever changed the once accepted doctrine of the curse of Cain.

From the mid-1800s, the Church did not ordain men of black African descent to the priesthood or allow black men or women to participate in temple endowment or sealing ordinances. Over the years, a variety of theories were advanced to justify the restriction. Elder Jeffrey R. Holland of the Quorum of the Twelve Apostles has emphasized that those theories given in an attempt to explain the restrictions are "**folklore**" that must never be perpetuated: "However well-intended the explanations were, I think almost all of them were **inadequate**

and/or wrong. ... We simply do not know why that practice ... was in place."
– Jeffrey R. Holland, "Extending the Blessings of the Priesthood", Liahona & Ensign, June 2018, emphasis added

An official denial cannot erase long and well documented history. It cannot eradicate this official practice of exclusion and hate.

19.5 Peace At Last

For sixty years, I lived in this complex and contradictory world. In all that time, I saw the church reverse itself on many things, including the topic of race. I often struggled and failed to understand the shifting sands of Mormon doctrine. In all that time, I never found satisfactory answers to complex questions. Time and again, my spiritual house fell, and great was the fall of it. Each time, I rebuilt on the sands of shifting and shaking doctrine without comprehending the futility.

> [26] And every one that heareth these sayings of mine, and doeth them not, shall be likened unto a foolish man, which built his house upon the sand: [27] And the rain descended, and the floods came, and the winds blew, and beat upon that house; and it fell: and great was the fall of it.
> – Matthew 7:26-27 (KJV)

Today, I live in a different world. The Word of God does not change. The gospel of the Lord does not change. The nature of God does not change.[1] God, Himself does not change. On the stability of the Rock, I stand for He is my cornerstone.[2]

> [24] Therefore whosoever heareth these sayings of mine, and doeth them, I will liken him unto a wise man, which built his house upon a rock: [25] And the rain descended, and the floods came, and the winds blew, and beat upon that house; and it fell not: for it was founded upon a rock.
> – Matthew 7:24-25 (KJV)

In this new world, I finally have peace and solidarity with God![3]

---

[1] Hebrews 13:8
[2] Acts 4:11
[3] Romans 5:1

CHAPTER
TWENTY

HOW DO I REPENT?

> Our vision, our direction, our love, our praise, our adoration, and our devotion turn from the world and become directed toward Jesus only, and we become new.
>
> *Lance*

Per my training, Mormon repentance is the only way to be approved by God. I understood the concept and the necessity. However, I couldn't figure it out. No matter how diligently I tried, I couldn't get it done.

As a Mormon boy, I lied to avoid trouble. When Mom cooked a meal I didn't much like, I waited for the kitchen to empty. When it was safe, I lifted the heat register out of the floor and dumped the foul rations in the vent. In those tender years, my sinful nature found a place in my life, and it hung on.

In time, I desired forgiveness and a right standing with god. I had once justified sin by saying, *it is a small thing*. Rationalization offered no release from my growing guilt. A thousand little things cluttered my mind, heart, and memory. I just kept sinning and sinning. Each new sin I tossed into the growing heaps of condemning clutter. They became mountains I could never climb.

A well-meaning Bishop gave me *The Miracle of Forgiveness* by the Mormon apostle, Spencer W. Kimball. The following are a few memorable excerpts:

> Eternal life hangs in the balance **awaiting the works of men**. This progress toward eternal life is a matter of achieving perfection. ... **Perfection therefore is an achievable goal**.
> – Spencer W. Kimball, *The Miracle of Forgiveness*(Salt Lake City: Bookcraft, 1969) 208-209, emphasis added

There must be **works - many works** - and an all-out, total surrender, with a great humility and "a broken heart and a contrite spirit."
– Spencer W. Kimball, *The Miracle of Forgiveness*(Salt Lake City: Bookcraft, 1969) 325, emphasis added

It depends upon you whether or not you are forgiven, and when. It could be weeks, it could be years, it could be centuries before that happy day when you have the positive assurance that the Lord has forgiven you. **That depends on your humility, your sincerity, your works, your attitudes**.
– Spencer W. Kimball, *The Miracle of Forgiveness*(Salt Lake City: Bookcraft, 1969) 325, emphasis added

To "try" is weak. To "do the best I can" is not strong. **We must always do better than we can**. This is true in every walk of life.
– Spencer W. Kimball, *The Miracle of Forgiveness*(Salt Lake City: Bookcraft, 1969) 165, emphasis added

Better than I can! What am I suppose to do with this?

Passages such as these weighed heavily on my mind. Perfection, by *works, many works* and doing *better than I can* seemed beyond my reach. Even now, it is more than I can ever do. I simply could not meet such a high standard. On top of that, I was still sinning and could not seem to stop.

> And now, verily I say unto you, I, the Lord, will not lay any sin to your charge; go your ways and sin no more; **but unto that soul who sinneth shall the former sins return**, saith the Lord your God.
> – *Doctrine and Covenants*, 82:7, emphasis added

I wanted eternal life. I wanted to achieve Mormon godhood and its promise of endless celestial sex. In moments of sober honesty, the stark truth weighed me down. I had not scaled the mountain of works. From where I stood, I had not yet even glimpsed the summit. I reluctantly concluded that if Mormon repentance and personal perfection are the standards for eternal life, I would gain nothing.

> [42]Behold, he who has repented of his sins, the same is forgiven, and I, the Lord, remember them no more. [43] By this ye may know if a man repenteth of his sins—behold, **he will confess them and forsake them**.
> – *Doctrine and Covenants*, 58:42,43, emphasis added

Not only was I continuing day to day in sin, but I also was not creative enough to consistently find new and original sins. Instead, I returned, like a dog to his vomit, eagerly lapping up what I had previously cast away.[1]

Instead of anxiously awaiting the return of the Lord, I feared him. I hoped for enough time and strength to become perfect according to my persistent righteous living.

20.1   Mormon Definition of Repent

Gospel Principles is an instruction manual published by *The Church of Jesus Christ of Latter-day Saints*. Chapter 19, entitled *Repentance*, lists seven essential steps by which a person must repent. Until every step is successfully completed, no forgiveness will be granted.

Step 1: We Must Recognize Our Sins

Is this even possible? It seems likely that we will miss something unless our understanding of sin is equal to God's. Because our hearts are hard and our eyes blind, it is highly doubtful that we will ever recognize all our sins. I wondered, does this leave me marked for destruction?

Worse yet, we make excuses and justify certain sins. Imagine that you live a fully perfect life except for one little sin which you foolishly consider minor and insignificant. Further, your indulgences in that sin are so infrequent that they seem hardly worth mentioning. Will that single, occasional failing keep you from heaven? Let's take a look from God's perspective:

> For whosoever shall keep the whole law, and yet offend in one point,
> he is guilty of all.
> – James 2:10 (KJV)

God sees our "insignificant sin" as no more and no less than breaking every law and commandment. God sees every sin as rebellion, which makes the small things we justify enormously destructive!

Step 2: We Must Feel Sorrow for Our Sins

Instead of sorrow, it is easy to make excuses and invent justifications.

God is love, but is that all? Does He hate? Let me put this in terms we can understand. We love children, so we hate abortion and child abuse. Because we love the Jews, so we hate the Holocaust. Having black friends and neighbors, so we hate slavery.

If fallen folks like us hate these works of evil, how much more will a perfectly holy God hate such things?

---

[1] 2 Peter 2:22

> The foolish shall not stand in thy sight: thou hatest all workers of iniquity.
> – Psalms 5:5 (KJV)

It is right to feel sorrow for our sins. It seems better to tremble in fear, for nothing is more terrible than the wrath of God. Fearful trembling must also accompany sorrow. It is a terrible and terrifying thing to be subject to God's wrath and fiery anger.

> Let no man deceive you with vain words: for because of these things cometh the wrath of God upon the children of disobedience.
> – Ephesians 5:6 (KJV)

Step 3: We Must Forsake Our Sins

Some think this step is possible, and I wonder, are they deluded? Do they honestly believe they can live without sin? We exist on a plane infinitely separated and significantly below God. Can we see or understand our desperate condition from our low vantage point? We are unable to recognize every sin, large or small. How can our lives not be a constant and a direct assault against the glory of almighty God? Sin is our common enemy. We are guilty. On our own, by our strength, how will we ever right ourselves?

> [10] As it is written, there is none righteous, no, not one: [11] There is none that understandeth, there is none that seeketh after God. [12] They are all gone out of the way, they are together become unprofitable; there is none that doeth good, no, not one.
> – Romans 3:10-12 (KJV)

The apostle Paul viewed the weakness of his flesh this way:

> For I don't know what I am doing. For I don't practice what I desire to do; but what I hate, that I do.
> – Romans 7:15 (WEB)

Mormonism tells a different story. The doctrine requires a total and unfailing effort before God can grant forgiveness.

> And what is repentance? **The forsaking of sin.** The man who repents, if he be a swearer, swears no more; or a thief, steals no more; **he turns away from all former sins and commits them no more.** It is not repentance to say, I repent today, and then steal tomorrow; that is the repentance of the world, which is displeasing in the sight of God.
> – The Church of Jesus Christ of Latter-day Saints, *Teachings of the Presidents of the Church Wilford Woodruff* (Salt Lake City: n.p., n.d.) 71-72, emphasis added

HOW DO I REPENT?

> The miracle of forgiveness is available to all of those who **turn from their evil doings and return no more**, because the Lord has said in a revelation to us in our day: "Go your ways and sin no more; but unto that soul who sinneth [meaning again] shall the former sins return, saith the Lord your God"
> – Harold B. Lee. "Stand Ye in Holy Places" Talk, General Conference, April 1973, emphasis added

> Those who receive forgiveness and then repeat the sin are held accountable for their former sins.
> – The Church of Jesus Christ of Latter-day Saints, *Gospel Principles* (Salt Lake City: n.p, n.d) 253

How can anyone attempt to live up to this standard without falling into utter, soul-wrenching despair? In my struggle for perfection, these demands crushed me!

Step 4: We Must Confess Our Sins

I do not argue against this step, but should our confession be to men or God? When we sin against a brother or sister, it is right to confess to the person we harmed. Beyond that, is there a biblical requirement to confess to men? *Gospel Principles* insists that confession to men is necessary, "... *we must confess serious sins—such as adultery, fornication, homosexual relations, spouse or child abuse, and the sale or use of illegal drugs to the proper priesthood authority.*"

Is God so weak that He requires the assistance of men to forgive the more serious sins? Is His blood too watered down, thinned, and anemic to cover egregious sins? Will God require the assistance of some Mormon leader? If the answer is yes, the Mormon god is very, very small.

> If we confess our sins, he is faithful and just to forgive us our sins, and to cleanse us from **all** unrighteousness.
> – 1 John 1:9 (KJV), emphasis added

God does not divide sin into major and minor categories. All sin is rebellion and an assault against the glory of God. According to James, any sin is equivalent to committing every sin.[2] It appears that God does not view the law as individual parts. Instead, He sees it as a whole that is either fully kept or completely broken.[3]

---

[2] James 2:10
[3] Galatians 5:3

Step 5: We Must Make Restitution

Since every sin is rebellion and an assault against the glory of the God who made us and granted every breath, how can we make restitution? Since we are decidedly below almighty God, with what can we repay?

Isaiah represented his most righteous doings in an interesting way:

> But we are all as an unclean thing, and all our righteousnesses are as **filthy rags**; and we all do fade as a leaf; and our iniquities, like the wind, have taken us away.
> – Isaiah 64:6 (KJV), emphasis added

A Strong's Concordance translation for filthy is *ed*, pronounced, *ayd*. The term refers to a woman's *menstrual flux*.

In his letter to the Philippians, Paul rehearsed his impressive resume to show the value of his best qualifications. Then, viewing his best against the standard of God, he wrote:

> ⁴Though I might also have confidence in the flesh. If any other man thinketh that he hath whereof he might trust in the flesh, I more: ⁵**Circumcised the eighth day**, of the stock of Israel, **of the tribe of Benjamin**, an Hebrew of the Hebrews; **as touching the law, a Pharisee**; ⁶Concerning zeal, persecuting the church; **touching the righteousness which is in the law, blameless**. ⁷But what things were gain to me, those I counted loss for Christ. ⁸Yea doubtless, and I count all things but loss for the excellency of the knowledge of Christ Jesus my Lord: for whom I have suffered the loss of all things, and **do count them but *dung***, that I may win Christ, ⁹And be found in him, **not having mine own righteousness**, which is of the law, but that which is through the faith of Christ, **the righteousness which is of God by faith**:
> – Phillipians 3:4-9 (KJV), emphasis added

Turning to Strong's Concordance, we discover the Greek translation for *dung* is *skubalon*, pronounced *skoo'-bal-on*. The translation speaks of excrement.

Isaiah and Paul held a similar opinion of their ability to impress God with their many accomplishments and good works. Imagine going before a holy God to make atonement for your sins with nothing more than a box of filthy menstrual rags and steaming mounds of your own excrement.

We possess nothing worthy of repayment for evil deeds. Remember, filthy rags and dung represent our best efforts, not our failings. Sin is our common problem, and we cannot work our way clear. Mormonism resists God and tells the members that their good works will be enough.

> We believe that through the Atonement of Christ, all mankind may be saved, by obedience to the laws and ordinances of the Gospel.
> – *Articles of Faith*, Third

HOW DO I REPENT?

Is salvation attainable by combining our works and the atonement of Jesus? Paul knew better. Jesus is our all in all. He alone is enough. Any attempt to save ourselves by any combination of our effort and Jesus' contribution is a recipe for hell.

> **Christ is become of no effect unto you**, whosoever of you are justified by the law; ye are **fallen from grace**
> – Galatians 5:4 (KJV), emphasis added

> ⁸For by grace are ye saved through faith; and that not of yourselves: it is the gift of God: ⁹**Not of works**, lest any man should boast.
> – Ephesians 2:8-9 (KJV), emphasis added

Step 6: We Must Forgive Others

I fully agree.

Step 7: We Must Keep the Commandments of God

We have established that none of us are good, that *all have sinned, and come short of the glory of God.*⁴ We know that a lifetime of keeping the commandments produces nothing but *filthy rags* and *dung*. In step 1, we established that we cannot recognize every sin. That being the case, how will we ever be able to keep steps 2-7? Nevertheless, Mormonism affirms that no salvation is possible unless we perfectly complete each step of repentance and follow all the commandments!

> **Keep my commandments continually**, and a crown of righteousness thou shalt receive. And except thou do this, **where I am you cannot come**.
> – *Doctrine and Covenants*, 25:15, emphasis added

The Mormon people are required to keep every commandment? If so, there must be a list of these demands. Where can they find it? How can they know what their god requires? No list? There is no list! Why is there no list? Can anything be more unjust than demanding perfect compliance when there is no declaration of what that means? This is what the Mormon god did to Grace and me and is still doing to millions under his control.

20.2 Biblical Repentance

Our merciful and loving God knows that we will never measure up to the law. He fully understands that a single and relatively minor misstep will make us

---
⁴Romans 3:10-18

enemies to God. Consequently, any sin guarantees condemnation and eternal destruction.[5] The law, being beyond the capabilities of Isaiah and Paul, leaves each of us without hope. Mormons will be under a double condemnation. How much more unattainable perfection will be with the addition of enhanced Mormon repentance, laws, and ordinances. The LDS solution decisively sentences each adherent to an eternity in the lake of fire,[6] which is the second death,[7] where they will be tormented day and night forever and ever.[8]

God is good[9] and rich in mercy.[10] He has not abandoned us,[11] but has instead provided a way we can be reconciled with him unto endless life.[12]

> Who is made, not after the law of a carnal commandment, but after the power of an endless life.
> – Hebrews 7:16 (KJV)

If we desire to repent, we should begin with an understanding of what *repent* means. In Hebrew, the word for repent is *nacham*, pronounced, *nä-kham*. According to Strong's Concordance, it means to "make a strong turning to a new course of action". The Greek equivalent is *metanoia*, pronounced *met-an'-oy-ah*. Returning to Strong's, we discover the meaning, "change of mind".

When considering together the Hebrew and Greek, we see a common thread. It is a change of mind, direction, purpose, and focus. We see no requirement to turn from a specific sin, forsake all sin, or keep every commandment. In the original languages, we see nothing of Mormonism's seven steps.

Please do not misunderstand, I am not suggesting we have a license to sin. Instead, I join Paul in declaring, despite our best efforts, the sins of the flesh will be ever present in us.

> [18]For I know that in me (that is, in my flesh,) dwelleth no good thing: for to will is present with me; but how to perform that which is good I find not. [19]For the good that I would I do not: but the evil which I would not, that I do. [20]Now if I do that I would not, it is no more I that do it, but sin that dwelleth in me. [21]I find then a law, that, when I would do good, evil is present with me. [22]For I delight in the law of God after the inward man: [23]But I see another law in my members, warring against the law of my mind, and bringing me into captivity to the law of sin which is in my members. [24]O wretched man that I am! who shall deliver me from the body of this death?
> – Romans 7:18-24 (KJV)

---

[5] James 2:10
[6] Revelation 20:15
[7] Revelation 20:14
[8] Revelation 20:10
[9] Psalms 73:1
[10] Ephesians 2:4
[11] Isaiah 41:10
[12] John 3:16

HOW DO I REPENT?

In Exodus 32, the Lord was angry with the people of Israel. He saw that they deserved the fullness of His destructive wrath. God is two things: He is just, so His fearful wrath is deserved and appropriate for all who sin. God is also love. He will extend mercy to save undeserving sinners under certain conditions. Moses, acting as a shadow of Messiah who was to come, prayed for mercy and grace. God granted the request,

> And the Lord **repented** of the evil which he thought to do unto his people.
> – Exodus 32:14 (KJV), emphasis added

In this example, we see that repentance is not a cessation of sin but a change of mind and a turning to a new course. The Mormon version of repentance only makes sense if God sinned! As Moses interceded for the people in a relatively minor way, Jesus is the mediator with a reach that spans all eternity. Jesus is the reason God will turn from the destruction we deserve and extend the grace we cannot earn.

> But God commendeth his love toward us, in that, while we were yet sinners, Christ died for us.
> – Romans 5:8 (KJV)

To be forgiven by God, what then must we do? When asked how a man may do the works of God, Jesus answered in simple clarity and redemptive beauty.

> Jesus answered and said unto them, This is the work of God, that ye **believe on him whom he hath sent**.
> – John 6:29 (KJV), emphasis added

Can we repent by turning to Mormonism's pattern for repentance? This method requires that we trust our own ability to turn from sin and keep every commandment. It demands that we approach God with our *filthy rags* and stinking *dung* to turn Him from His wrath. Mormon repentance demands that we do not trust fully in Jesus. It insists we must make His work complete by adding our strength, power, and good deeds. How is this not adding the sin of non-belief to the original sin?

What if we turn to Jesus and trust Him alone? In doing this, we automatically turn away from everything else. With this simple action, we turn away from the world. We turn from our lust and the evil yearning of the flesh. The pride of our eyes fades away because there can be no arrogance in the presence of a holy God. Our vision, direction, love, praise, adoration, and devotion turn from the world and focus on Jesus alone.

> Therefore **if any man be in Christ, he is a new creature**: old things are passed away; behold, all things are become new.
> – 2 Corinthians 5:17 (KJV), emphasis added

In turning toward Jesus, we find rest in His sure promise:

> There is therefore now **no condemnation to them which are in Christ Jesus**, who walk not after the flesh, but after the Spirit.
> – Romans 8: (KJV), emphasis added

CHAPTER
TWENTYONE

FIG LEAF APRON

> These scales made not seeing as natural as dying.
>
> — Lance

In the temple endowment movie, Satan appears to Adam and Eve, in human form, and entices them to eat the forbidden fruit. After eating, an interesting exchange occurs:

> **Adam:** What is that apron you are wearing?
> **Satan:** It is an emblem of my power and priesthoods.
> **Adam:** Priesthoods?
> **Satan:** Yes, priesthoods.
> **Elohim [God the Father]:** Jehovah, let us go down and see the man Adam in the Garden of Eden.
> **Jehovah [Jesus]:** We will go down, Elohim.
> **Adam:** I hear them coming.
> **Satan:** See, you are naked. Take some fig leaves and make you aprons. Father will see your nakedness. Quick, hide.
> **Narrator:** Brethren and Sisters, put on your aprons.
> – "Temple Endowment presentation", excerpt, prior to 1990

From the day we married until we were saved, Grace and I wandered precisely forty years in the wilderness of Mormonism. We spent much of that time in the Mormon temple. I dutifully donned my green apron in strict obedience to Satan and never once stopped to ask, why? Why are we following the Devil? It never crossed my mind. Equally troubling is this, Satan wore an apron which he said was an emblem of his power and priesthoods. Immediately following his announcement, he instructed me to wear a similar apron. The church identifies the apron as a vital part of the robes of the *holy priesthood*. I was too blind to see and so completely controlled that I never thought to question even the absurd.

Before his conversion, Paul was as blind as I had been. His healing from spiritual blindness is a personal and beautiful reminder of my day of seeing.

> And immediately there fell from his eyes as it had been scales: and
> he received sight forthwith, and arose, and was baptized.
> – Acts 9:18 (KJV)

Now, enjoying the miracle of sight, I often look back and wonder, why did I so willingly follow Satan? This question seemingly has no logical or rational answer. I can only conclude that I was afflicted with scales of darkness that covered my eyes and darkened my mind. These scales were the fruit of intense, lifelong indoctrination. So closed was my mind that I never thought to question or reason or test a thing.[1]

Like a mechanized part in the Mormon machine, I moved each time the church threw a switch, pulled a lever, or engaged a gear. No thought, no recognition, only blind obedience drove me in every action.

According to the temple endowment, Satan commanded Adam and Eve to put on an apron to cover their nakedness. With biblical understanding, we know that Adam and Eve used fig leaves to hide their sin, rebellion, guilt, and shame. Having recognized their sin, they felt naked and utterly exposed before God.

> And he said, I heard thy voice in the garden, and I was afraid, because
> I was naked; and I hid myself.
> – Genesis 3:10 (KJV)

Not only did Adam and Eve sin when they ate the fruit, but they also sinned when they tried to cover their guilt with a silly apron. They sinned again when they failed to take responsibility for their rebellion. The man blamed the woman, and the woman blamed the serpent. By the actions of Adam and Eve, sin entered the world.

> [12] And the man said, The woman whom thou gavest to be with me,
> she gave me of the tree, and I did eat. [13] And the Lord God said unto
> the woman, What is this that thou hast done? And the woman said,
> The serpent beguiled me, and I did eat.
> – Genesus 3:12-13 (KJV)

We are all as Adam and Eve and willingly partake of forbidden fruit. My idolatry in the Mormon temple is a case in point. In that brick and mortar temple, I pretended to worship God with signs and tokens; all made with my hands.

---

[1] I John 4:1

> [24] God that made the world and all things therein, seeing that he is Lord of heaven and earth, dwelleth not in temples made with hands; [25] Neither is worshipped with men's hands...
> – Acts 17:24-25a (KJV)

Many of us try to cover our sin, guilt, and rebellion. In my case, and that of the Mormon people, sin is covered with an outer illusion of righteousness.[2] This false covering caused me to become Pharisee-like in my judgment of others. In measuring myself against another man's weakness, I saw myself as good and hoped God would be *wise enough to see the same*.

> [10] Two men went up into the temple to pray; one was a Pharisee, and the other was a tax collector. [11] The Pharisee stood and prayed by himself like this: '**God, I thank you that I am not like the rest of men**: extortionists, unrighteous, adulterers, or even like this tax collector. [12] I fast twice a week. I give tithes of all that I get.'
> – Luke 18:10-12 (WEB), emphasis added

Try as we might; we cannot hide our true nature from God. We cannot cover or cleanse ourselves. We need a redeemer. God rejected the fig leaf aprons because Adam and Eve used them to deceive Him. My every attempt to mask my true and fallen nature was with the same intent and the same result.

> There is no creature that is hidden from his sight, but **all things are naked and laid open before the eyes of him to whom we must give an account**.
> – Hebrews 4:13 (WEB), emphasis added

God rejected the fig leaf apron and made them coats of skins.[3] In this, we see a thread of truth that runs through the entire Bible. The only covering for sin is the shed blood of the perfect lamb, Jesus our Lord. Never, in sixty years of Mormonism, did I imagine such a thing could be true. Evident is the reality that no effort, on our part, will cover or cleanse us from any level of sin. The best we have to offer God is filthy rags and dung.[4]

> Therefore we conclude that a man is justified by faith without the deeds of the law.
> – Romans 3:28 (KJV)

Nevertheless, in the Mormon temple, I donned my green apron in blind obedience to Satan, the father of lies. We all did, and we left it on for the balance of the temple experience. We went to the temple veil, representing a separation between the physical world and heaven. At the veil, we went through

---

[2] See chapter: Of Blue, Beards, and Blasphemy
[3] Genesis 3:21
[4] See chapter: How do I Repent?

a process to establish our righteousness before God. We passed through the veil and into the Celestial Room, representing heaven. Even in the Celestial room, we continued wearing the apron that represented our weak attempt to hide from God. I, and they, proudly wore the apron that Satan loved and God hated. With scales over our eyes, we ignorantly served darkness. Those scales of blindness made acts of evil as natural as breathing.

21.1 By Their Works You Shall Know Them

This temple experience is a perfect illustration of the Mormon gospel. The LDS devout work to exhaustion to establish the outward appearance of righteousness. They seek to establish their righteousness by good works, professions of worthiness, charitable deeds, and endless priesthood ordinances. Where such things are emphasized, the precious blood of Jesus is thinned, weakened, and washed away. In the place of salvation by grace through the blood of Christ, the Mormon people apply man-made coverings for sin.

In my personal experience, I worked to make God indebted to me. I labored to compel God to give me the justice I demanded and the rich blessings I foolishly thought I deserved. If I had taken the time to think it through, I might have realized that the wages of sin is death.[5] Death, yes death, was the reward I foolishly demanded.

> [20]There is a law, irrevocably decreed in heaven before the foundations of this world, upon which all blessings are predicated- [21]**And when we obtain any blessing from God, it is by obedience to that law upon which it is predicated.**
> – *Doctrine and Covenants*, 130:20-21, emphasis added

> *I, the Lord, am bound* when ye do what I say; but when ye do not what I say, ye have no promise.
> – *Doctrine & Covenants*, 82:10, emphasis added

I never dreamed that my plan to compel God might be flawed. My hope hinged on my ability to be a worthy priesthood holder and perform many good works. I planned to impress God with a lifetime collection of good works. I never imagined my works to be what Isaiah and Paul called filthy rags and dung.[6] I never took the time to understand how God sees the real wretched me.

> [20]Wherefore by their fruits ye shall know them. [21]Not every one that saith unto me, Lord, Lord, shall enter into the kingdom of heaven;

---
[5] Romans 6:23
[6] See chapter: How do I Repent?

but he that doeth the will of my Father which is in heaven. [22]Many will say to me in that day, Lord, Lord, have we not prophesied in thy name? and in thy name have cast out devils? and in thy name done many wonderful works? [23]And then will I profess unto them, **I never knew you: depart from me, ye that work iniquity**.
– Matthew 7:20-23 (KJV), emphasis added

This passage applies directly to the Mormon people and, tragically, they cannot see.

21.2 Temple Recommend

The Mormon people must regularly pass two temple recommend worthiness interviews before entering the Mormon temple. The first is conducted by the Bishop or one of his counselors—the second by a member of the stake presidency. For me, it was a simple thing to answer every worthiness question in the affirmative until the dreaded final question. I knew in advance how I would answer and why my answer would be a blatant, intentional lie.

Do you consider yourself worthy to enter the Lord's house and participate in temple ordinances?
– Last temple recommend interview question.

Each time this question was asked, my mind raced over three passages of Mormon scripture. These passages haunted me. Guilt rose like bile in my throat as my mind reached for an absolution I never found.

... for the Lord cannot look upon sin with the least degree of allowance.
– *Book of Mormon*, Alma 45:16b

And no unclean thing can enter ...
– *Book of Mormon*, 3 Nephi 27:19a

[42]Behold, he who has repented of his sins, the same is forgiven, and I, the Lord, remember them no more. [43]By this ye may know if a man repenteth of his sins—behold, **he will confess them and forsake them**.
– *Doctrine and Covenants*, 58:42-43, emphasis added

I had then, and still have, many sins which I have not forsaken. I knew it then as I assuredly know it today. Because I had sin in my life, the Mormon god could not look on me with the least degree of allowance. Sin made me unclean; consequently, I had no right to enter what I considered to be the Temple of the lord. In each interview, my mind raced over the undeniable wretchedness that made me unworthy. Simultaneously, I nodded my head and claimed a worthiness that was never mine.

Immediately following my blatantly false affirmation of worthiness, the interviewer solemnly signed my temple recommend. His signature was an authoritative confirmation that I had been examined and found clean. We, the interviewer and interviewee, took these actions fully aware that neither he nor I met the Mormon worthiness requirements. According to the harsh demands of Mormon scripture, we did not measure up. He lied, I lied, we lied, and God knew it!

This duly authorized temple recommend was my certificate of worthiness. It went in my wallet to be carried with me always. With it, I boldly and falsely proclaimed my holy standing before God.

The temple recommend was my Mormonized substitute for the fig leaf apron. With this paper apron, I appeared worthy even though I had partaken of forbidden fruit. With it, I foolishly attempted to hide my nakedness precisely as Adam and Eve once did. With a lie and a paper apron, I gained access to the temple. A man sat at the temple door who was equally aware that he did not measure up. He checked my recommend with pomp and solemnity while pretending to verify my worthiness. All this ceremony was a mock effort to guard against an unclean thing entering the temple of his god.

A harsh reality presses down on every temple recommend holder. Each carries a burden that brings them so low in times of honest reflection. In such moments, everyone must confront their inability to measure up to the legalistic demands of ritualized Mormonism. Worse yet, none comprehend that they cannot do it.[7] Endlessly, they try just a little harder. Predictably, every new effort leads to a new failure in an endless cycle of hopeless despair.[8] Struggling under the yoke of sin and failure, none have an assurance of salvation, and that is the great tragedy.[9]

21.3 A Better Covenant

Something indescribable happens when a zealous Mormon gives everything to Jesus. A weight lifts, peace descends, and hope rolls in like the tide.

> But now hath he obtained a more excellent ministry, by how much also he is the mediator of a **better covenant**, which was established upon **better promises**.
> – Hebrews 8:6 (KJV), emphasis added

---

[7] Acts 15:10
[8] Romans 7:10
[9] 1 John 5:13

Thank you, dear God, for removing my apron, exposing my nakedness, and washing me in the blood of the Lamb. I praise your name for doing for me what I could never do alone.

CHAPTER
TWENTYTWO

HIGH PRIEST

> I rejoice in the knowledge that God gave me the gift of all I never deserved and could not earn.
>
> *Lance*

When I reached the appropriate age, I was automatically ordained to the office of High Priest. It happened, and I never gave it a second thought. My ordination was simply a matter of doing what was done before in the way it had always been done. It was just another chapter of Mormonism and a rite of passage for the Mormon male.

As a saved Christian, I came across a surprising Bible passage. It outlines the job description for a High Priest. Reflecting on my years as a Mormon High priest, I failed to see how I satisfied even one job requirement.

> For every high priest taken from among men is ordained for men in things pertaining to God, **that he may offer both gifts and sacrifices for sins:**
> – Hebrews 5:1 (KJV), emphasis added

As a High Priest, I was to act for men offering gifts and sacrifices for sins. As a Mormon High Priest, I should have done these things. In truth, I did none of them, but Jesus did.

> ⁸For by grace are ye saved through faith; and that not of yourselves: **it is the gift of God**: ⁹Not of works, lest any man should boast.
> – Ephesians 2:8-9 (KJV), emphasis added

For the wages of sin is death; but **the gift of God is eternal life** through Jesus Christ our Lord.
— Romans 6:23 (KJV), emphasis added

But God commendeth his love toward us, in that, while we were yet sinners, **Christ died for us**.
— Romans 5:8 (KJV), emphasis added

How much more shall the blood of Christ, who through the eternal Spirit offered himself without spot to God, **purge your conscience from dead works** to serve the living God?
— Hebrews 9:14 (KJV), emphasis added

For even the Son of man came not to be ministered unto, but to minister, and to **give his life a ransom for many**.
— Mark 10:45 (KJV), emphasis added

When the new covenant, the better covenant, was enacted, the job description for a High Priest became forever amended. No man can hold the office of High Priest unless he can save men and women to the uttermost. I can't, but Jesus can!

> Therefore he is also able to save to the uttermost those who draw near to God through him, seeing that he lives forever to make intercession for them.
> — Hebrews 7:25 (WEB)

What man among all Mormon priesthood holders can do such a thing? Who among the greatest of all men is equal to this job requirement?

Those Old Testament High Priests were nothing but a shadow of Jesus. These men were a similitude of Jesus, the last great High Priest who was to come. None but Jesus Christ, our *Messiah*, our *Savior*, and our *Lord* will ever satisfy the totality of his mission.

Was I a legitimate High Priest? No, I was not. I was a fraud, a counterfeit. As a phony, I possessed nothing of my great and glorious King's qualities or abilities!

I had wrongfully assumed I had power as a High Priest. Blasphemously, I protected the gates of heaven at the temple veil. It was heresy to believe that my Mormon priesthood could save and exalt me or anyone.

A few years before Jesus rescued me, I attended a High Priest quorum meeting. The instructor explained that it is not Jesus Christ who judges the human heart, but Joseph Smith. I was surprised but accepted this revelation as a matter of course. After all, that is the way of the indoctrinated!

HIGH PRIEST

> ... no man or woman in this dispensation will ever enter into the celestial kingdom of God without the consent of Joseph Smith. From the day that the Priesthood was taken from the earth to the winding-up scene of all things, **every man and woman must have the certificate of Joseph Smith, junior, as a passport to their entrance into the mansion where God and Christ are**—I with you and you with me. I cannot go there without his consent.
> – *Journal of Discourses* (N.p.: n.p., n.d.), 7:289, Brigham Young & Robert L. Millet Ensign, June 1994, emphasis added

What once seemed right in my Mormon heart of stone was darkness in the light of Christ. God gave me a heart of flesh[1], and I began to see. It was like a scroll of hell's best-kept secrets slowly unrolled to reveal evil on an unprecedented scale. As a Born Again Christian, the immensity of this great evil crystallized in my mind. Shocking recognition drove me to my knees in shame, conviction, and tears. I love the Word of God, and the more I learn of God, the more my heart is broken because of my personal blasphemy.

I had sought God in a temple built with hands. Had I taken time to read the Word of God, I would have known that He was not there.

> God that made the world and all things therein, seeing that he is Lord of heaven and earth, dwelleth not in temples made with hands;
> – Acts 17:24 (KJV)

On the spire just over my head, when I served in the temple, was the image of a Mormon angel. Had I troubled myself to read the Word of God, I would have discovered the horror of idolatry.

> Thou shalt not make unto thee any graven image, or any likeness of any thing that is in heaven above, or that is in the earth beneath, or that is in the water under the earth:
> – Deuteronomy 5:8 (KJV)

I claimed the power of Jesus Christ for myself. Had I read the Word of God, I would have known with absolute certainty that Jesus alone is our final High Priest. I would have recognized that I was exalting myself with glory that belonged to God and none else.

> he who opposes and exalts himself against all that is called God or that is worshiped; so that he sits as God in the temple of God, setting himself up as God.
> – 2 Thessalonians 2:4 (WEB)

In a place where God said he would never be, I pretended to find Him. Joining the likes of Joseph and Brigham, I shouldered Jesus aside, utterly rejecting

---
[1] Ezekiel 11:19

Him as the way, the truth, and the life.[2] Boldly, I represented the Mormon prophet Joseph Smith, as a temple veil worker, and declared that he and I have God's power to save and exalt. Reaching up to heaven, I pulled down the power, the glory, and the perfection of Jesus. I claimed for myself His faithfulness, goodness, and every Godly attribute. In arrogance, pride, and abject evil, I pulled these things from God and attempted to place them on myself, to claim them as my own.

As the Bible and the Holy Spirit revealed the depths of my sin, I melted before the radiant power of God. Peter and I share a common pain.

> When Simon Peter saw it, he fell down at Jesus' knees, saying, Depart from me; for **I am a sinful man**, O Lord.
> – Luke 5:8 (KJV), emphasis added

I was shattered by the evil thing I had done. I was beyond broken for the abomination I had become. Falling on my face, I could only plead for mercy, for a tender mercy to which I had no right.

Oh God, Forgive Me!

Amid my pain, there was hope. I joyously recalled the many ways Jesus used Peter for His glory and in His kingdom. We are never so far removed from God that He will not welcome us into the body of Christ and adopt us as sons and daughters.[3]

I am evil beyond measure and unworthy of your love, oh God. I have chased after my glory and gone after other gods in arrogance and stupidity. I sought to impress and make you a debtor to me by my own efforts.[4] All I have to show is the shame of filthy rags and dung.[5]

I have nothing, I am nothing, and I deserve only God's mighty wrath unto destruction. In a fair world, I would have received exactly that. I would have died a fiery and brutal death. I should have been cast off into exquisite suffering for eternity.

> [9] Know ye not that the unrighteous shall not inherit the kingdom of God? Be not deceived: neither fornicators, nor idolaters, nor adulterers, nor effeminate, nor abusers of themselves with mankind, [10] Nor thieves, nor covetous, nor drunkards, nor revilers, nor extortioners, shall inherit the kingdom of God.
> – 1 Corinthians 6:9-0 (KJV)

I was all this and so much more. Mercifully, this world is not fair according to the reckoning of men. It is lovely and perfect according to the love of God. What a joy it is to be so loved by God that He would willingly set aside every offense and heap grace upon grace to cover my sin.

---

[2] John 14:6
[3] John 1:12
[4] *Doctrine & Covenants*, 82:10
[5] See chapter: How do I Repent?

[11] And such were some of you: but ye are washed, but ye are sanctified, but ye are justified in the name of the Lord Jesus, and by the Spirit of our God.
– 1 Corinthians 6:11 (KJV)

All that remains in me is awe and worship. In my place, Jesus suffered under the weight of all my sin. I rejoice in the knowledge that God gave me the gift of all I never deserved and could not earn.

CHAPTER
TWENTYTHREE

MAKING OTHER GODS

> He suffered and was crushed in
> my place and yours.
>
> *Lance*

My boyhood family did not read the Bible. Volumes of Mormon scripture, which we esteemed above the Bible, were thoughtlessly cast aside and seldom considered. I had no passion for learning the things of god. Mormonism? I knew only those verbal traditions and stories passed down. Such stories played on my emotions. These bound me to the church with sentiment only. To assume I had any measure of provable truth was the height of rabid, religious insanity.

Trusted adults taught me that Mormonism is the restored gospel of Jesus Christ. Some would claim that plain and precious truths went missing from the Bible. We had prophets, seers, and revelators who never bothered to show us which Bible verses were corrupt, and I never thought to question why! This blind faith was the foundation upon which I rejected God and embraced false gods.

23.1   The Great Apostasy

It is easy for those who trust the Bible to expose the Mormon priesthood as foolish folklore. The Mormon priesthood rests on the lie of biblical corruption, which assumes the erasure of plain and precious truths relative to the priesthood. The Mormon position demands that God cannot keep his holy promises.[1]

---

[1] Isaiah 40:8, Psalm 102:26, Matthew 16:18, Matthew 24:35, Mark 13:31, Luke 21:33, 1 Peter 1:25

For some time after Jesus ascended to heaven, the Church continued to teach the truth, and thousands of people from many cities joined the Church. However, in time some who had joined the Church refused to obey the laws and ordinances of the gospel and changed them to suit their own ways of thinking. Many members, including the Apostles and other priesthood leaders, were persecuted and killed. As these men were killed and others fell away from the truth, the Church lost the authority of the priesthood. Eventually, the priesthood no longer remained in the Church.
– The Church of Jesus Christ of Latter-day Saints, *DUTIES AND BLESSINGS OF THE PRIESTHOOD*(Salt Lake City: n.p., n.d.) 12

As biblical Christians, we rest in God's promise to preserve His word and the gospel it contains. We have His word on it.

... upon this rock I will build my church; and the gates of hell shall not prevail against it.
– Matthew 16:18b (KJV)

23.2 The Making of Other Gods

The Church of Jesus Christ of Latter-day Saints does not believe God can keep His promise and preserve His word. Consequently, Mormon leaders quickly create and disseminate strange doctrine and false gods to the people.

For Heavenly Father's purposes to be accomplished, **Christ's atoning power needs to be made available to God's children** ... Through the priesthood, the power of godliness is manifest in the lives of all who make and keep gospel covenants and receive the associated ordinances.
– Dale G. Renlund. The Priesthood and the Savior's Atoning Power, General Conference, October 2017 & The Church of Jesus Christ of Latter-day Saints, *Foundations of the Restoration Teacher Material*(Salt Lake City: n.p., n.d.) 57, emphasis added

The atoning power of God needs to be made available to *mere, mortal, Mormon men?* Do you comprehend the height of blasphemy in this single statement? If this claim is accurate, Jesus had no reason to go to the cross. And, we would not need Him to pay the price for our sins. Why should He go if men have the power to work it out for themselves? With a single blasphemes statement, Jesus, the way, the truth, and the life and the only way to the Father, became unnecessary. Why would any man need a Savior when he possesses the power within himself to ascend to heaven unaided?

When I remember back to the time when I believed such lies, my heart breaks. That such evil once resided in me is difficult to accept and impossible to deny. Jesus said, "... except ye believe that I am he, ye shall die in your sins."[2] Whatever the Mormon god is, that thing, that invention of false prophets is not He!

Jesus is God, and as such, He can heal, cleanse and save anyone He desires. He can work through men and women of His choosing. Renlund went far beyond that mark and ventured into the realm of heresy. He assumes for himself and all Mormon priesthood holders the atoning power that is Christ's alone. He gives men Jesus' singular ability to save. By his statement, Renlund removes Jesus as the only way by which men will be saved.[3] Worse yet, it establishes sinners on the throne of God!

> [1] If there arise among you **a prophet**, or a dreamer of dreams, and giveth thee a sign or a wonder, [2] And the sign or the wonder come to pass, whereof he spake unto thee, saying, **Let us go after other gods, which thou hast not known, and let us serve them**; [3] Thou shalt not hearken unto the words of that prophet, or that dreamer of dreams ...
> – Deuteronomy 13:1-3a (KJV), emphasis added

In claiming the saving power of God for himself and other Mormon priesthood holders, Renlund identifies himself as a prophet who says, *Let us go after other gods, which thou hast not known.*[4] Point of fact, Renlund is creating other gods, false gods, which we have not known.

Who, then, is the god we have known? The Bible tells us that no God was formed after our God.[5] Yet, Renlund and *The Church of Jesus Christ of Latter-day Saints* exalts and empowers millions of other gods. The Bible quotes God who says, beside me, there is no other God.[6] Renlund establishes Mormon priesthood holders as a group of "other gods" standing beside my holy God. Jesus alone is the way, the truth and the life,[7] and there is no other name under heaven by which men will be saved.[8] Renlund says, Jesus Christ and Mormon priesthood holders share in that godly atoning power. In so doing, he has become an enemy of God who masquerades as a minister of righteousness,[9] a wolf in sheep's clothing,[10] and a lying prophet who will perish with those who believe his lies.[11]

> [9] But thou shalt surely kill him; thine hand shall be first upon him to put him to death, and afterwards the hand of all the people. [10] And

---

[2] John 8:24b
[3] John 14:6
[4] Deuteronomy 13:2
[5] Isaiah 43:10
[6] Isaiah 44:6
[7] John 14:6
[8] Acts 4:12
[9] 2 Corinthians 11:15
[10] Matthew 7:15
[11] Jeremiah 27:15

thou shalt stone him with stones, that he die; **because he hath sought to thrust thee away from the Lord thy God**...
– Deuteronomy 13:9-10a (KJV), emphasis added

Mormonism's presumptive overreach establishes God's power within themselves as follows:

> Speaking to all priesthood bearers, President Joseph Fielding Smith said: "We are the Lord's agents; we represent him; he has given us authority which empowers us to do all that is necessary **to save and exalt ourselves as well as his other children in the world** ... We are ambassadors of the Lord Jesus Christ. Our commission is to represent him. We are directed ... **to do what he would do if he were personally present**"
> – Joseph Fielding Smith. Talk, Conference Report, April 1971 & The Church of Jesus Christ of Latter-day Saints, *DUTIES AND BLESSINGS OF THE PRIESTHOOD* (Salt Lake City: n.p., n.d.) 3, emphasis added

And thus, we have established the Mormon position that by the power of this priesthood, men share in *power to save and exalt themselves and others*. What is required to save a sinner? What is necessary to save a saint? Here's your clue: sinners or saints all need a perfect redeemer!

> [13]You were dead through your trespasses and the uncircumcision of your flesh. He made you alive together with him, having forgiven us all our trespasses, [14]**wiping out the handwriting in ordinances which was against us. He has taken it out of the way, nailing it to the cross.**
> – Colossians 2:13-14 (WEB), emphasis added

For **him who knew no sin** he made to be sin on our behalf, so that in him we might become the righteousness of God.
– 2 Corinthians 5:21 (WEB), emphasis added

I am fully aware of my failings, my inattention to detail, and the weakness of my understanding. Can you imagine me as your god? Can you imagine the world I might manage? The Monday morning gravity outages would be murder. Grace always complains that I tend to be tunnel-visioned in my work. I can see it now; my focus would be only on restoring gravity. Once I discovered the problem, I would turn it back on, never stopping to think that one-third of my people are floating at thirty-thousand feet. Oh yea, my people would flat love me ...

Lance

Jesus didn't just take a list of our sins to the cross. He became sin. Jesus took our sins on Himself and in Himself and nailed each one to the cross, through his flesh. In Him, the list of my sins was nailed to the cross. Before He could do this for me, he had to be one who knew no sin.[12] If, therefore, the Mormon priesthood has that same power, they must be without sin. Can such a man be found?

> Yet it pleased the Lord to bruise [crush in modern translations] him; he hath put him to grief: when thou shalt make his soul an offering for sin, he shall see his seed, he shall prolong his days, and the pleasure of the Lord shall prosper in his hand.
> – Isaiah 53:10 (KJV), emphasis added

For you and I, all the Father's vengeful wrath pressed down and brought Jesus low, even to death. He suffered and was crushed in my place and yours. In ignorance, we cry out in an unfair world, "give me justice"! What fools we are! If we receive justice, each of us must go to the cross and suffer death while the terror of God's wrath, without measure, inflicts us. Even as He did this for each of us individually, even as our shortsightedness crushed Him, He cried, "Father forgive"![13]

Think of every Mormon you have ever heard of or known. From Joseph Smith to the last born Mormon infant, who among these many millions was or is without sin? Who among all of these carried our sin to the cross, wiped out our debt, and nailed it there? Who among the inhabitants of the whole earth from Adam until today loved us this much? Who but Jesus alone!

> [17]That Christ may dwell in your hearts by faith; that ye, being rooted and grounded in love,[18]May be able to comprehend with all saints what is the breadth, and length, and depth, and height; [19]And to know the love of Christ, which passeth knowledge, that ye might be filled with all the fulness of God.
> – Ephesians 3:17-19 (KJV)

---

[12]2 Corinthians 5:21
[13]Luke 23:34

Part IV

LEANING ON THE ROCK

Learning to Trust Jesus

CHAPTER
TWENTYFOUR

THE WORDS

> As surely as night passes into day, as winter gives way to spring, our *darkest years* faded in the light of a new day.
>
> — *Lance*

There are paths that a man must walk. Many are steep and strewn with danger. Oftentimes, a difficult climb leads to a place of still waters and green pastures ... a place of rest.

> [1]The Lord is my shepherd; I shall not want. [2]He maketh me to lie down in green pastures: he leadeth me beside the still waters. [3]He restoreth my soul: he leadeth me in the paths of righteousness for his name's sake.
> – Psalms 23:1-3 (KJV)

24.1   Some Words are Harder to Say

It had been months since I made the decision. I knew what I had to do, but I couldn't bring myself to tell Grace. I had to tell her; there was no escaping that. The doing was much more challenging than knowing. Urgency compelled me to move. Fear held me back.

The last months of my darkest years took on a new complexion. I was no longer conflicted. Doctrinal contradiction and evil edicts of Mormon leaders no longer held me bound. In many ways, this was the easiest part because the chains of legalism had fallen away. I was set free, but one hurdle remained.

I had to tell my Mormon wife that I no longer believed, but how? Every time I thought of it, I almost became sick. This news could potentially fracture what had been a wonderful marriage. News like this has meant disaster for many marriages. The possibility terrified me because ours had been nearly perfect from the start. As I weighed the possibility of conflict and marital discord, one truth was unmistakable; Grace had the right to know.

I found her in the kitchen, seated at the bar. I took her hand in mine, "Can we talk?" She looked at me. I swallowed hard and murmured, *"I don't think I can be Mormon anymore"*. My heart stopped while I waited. Her answer most likely came in seconds, but the wait was eternal for me. "I'll need a few days to think about it".

For several long days, I waited and worried and worried and waited. I ached to shake the answer out of her. I could not! Her response was too important to rush, so I waited some more and ... tried not to die!

It had taken a long time and much in the way of personal agony to come to this point. Anxious as I was to see it done, I had no right to push her to a quick decision. It was Grace's turn to find her own answers.

The weight of my decision was tremendous to bear. It didn't affect only me. It could be devastating for my sweet wife. It had the potential of having a lasting and hurtful impact on my children and grandchildren. My dear mother, a life-long Mormon and a temple worker, would indeed be shattered. It would break her heart, and that broke mine.

My family would see my decision as an intentional shredding and unraveling of our eternal family. The weight was heavy, and I was troubled. Yet, I could not deny the release from oppression that came with my decision. In the clatter and tumble of chaotic thought, there was peace I could not understand.

I had tried to remain faithful to Mormonism and its leaders. I longed to have and know the truth. Having both together was impossible.[1] I learned that truth and Mormonism are, and will always be, mutually exclusive. Mormonism is the nemesis of truth. Both cannot exist together in harmony.

24.2 A New Beginning

I was confident in my decision to leave Mormonism. Grace was the unknown. Would my decision add a new level of conflict in her life? I waited on her answer, and not knowing was torment to me.

Finally, her answer came, *"I'm with you, let's do this"*. Every day since has been the best day of my life. Together, we began our journey. We were free from the legalistic burdens of Mormonism. No longer were we subject to the dictates of the devil. Gone were those days of measuring what we knew to be good and right and proper against a corporate church's contradictory demands. We were set free from corrupt leaders who professed righteousness while acting otherwise.

---

[1] Matthew 6:24

None is able to serve two lords, for either he will hate the one and love the other, or he will hold to the one, and despise the other; ye are not able to serve God and Mammon.
– Matthew 6:24 (YLT)

24.3 A New Day

Jesus promised that the truth would make us free. Before we could be fully set free, one thing remained. Hand in hand, we turned our backs on the lie of Mormonism and its oppressive tyrants in sheep's clothing.[2] We distanced ourselves from a false gospel that oppresses. Above all, we rejected the false Mormon Jesus who cannot save.[3]

Together, we turned to face the eastern horizon. Behind us, the sunset of Mormonism faded to an appropriate blackness. We watched the horizon for the gathering light that would herald the rising of the Son, the Son of God! Our last breath as slaves was drawn in and released with a shudder. We tasted the heavy, damp, musty air of captivity for the last time.

As surely as night passes into day, as winter gives way to spring, our *darkest years* vanished in the light of a new day. The Light came and washed over us, carrying away an ocean of pain. It covered us like a warm blanket, and for the first time in a very long time, we had peace. In the light of the rising Son, we saw color and beauty never before perceived. We drew our first sweet breaths as disciples of the Lord Jesus Christ. The Son[4]

> *Grace Notes*
>
> Things were getting desperate. I could see Lance was warring within himself.
>
> And then, it happened. He asked, "Can we talk?" Hmm, I thought, this sounds serious! He then said, *"I don't think I can be Mormon anymore."* I wondered what might have happened to bring him to this point. Was he upset about some additional accusation, or was this real?
>
> I told him that I needed time to think about it. I wanted to make sure he wasn't making this decision on the rebound from some hurt.
>
> My heart cried, "Wow! Oh, praise God! Are my secret prayers being answered?" He wandered the house for a couple of days, looking at me with concern. Soon enough, I could see that he was serious. I let him know that I felt the same about leaving the church. What joy! What freedom!
>
> *Grace*

---
[2] Matthew 7:15
[3] Matthew 7:15
[4] Luke 1:32

rose, the Light[5] illuminated, the Word[6] beckoned *"come follow me"*,[7] and we did!

> The night is far gone, and the day is near. Let's therefore **throw off the works of darkness**, and let's **put on the armor of light**.
> – Romans 13:12 (WEB), emphasis added

---

[5] John 8:12
[6] John 1:1
[7] Luke 9:23

CHAPTER
TWENTYFIVE

RED LETTERS

> Along the way, God did crazy good things in our hearts.
>
> *Lance*

We were like two starry-eyed kids on Christmas morning.

25.1 New Bibles

The large brown panel van pulled into the yard. We had been anxiously waiting when the anticipated day finally arrived. We were so excited!

My Mormon learning led me to believe all Bible translations were corrupted, and hated by God. I accepted the King James as the best of the bunch even though I regarded it as flawed and untrustworthy.

I remember a day some twenty years earlier when I had occasion to be alone in the sanctuary of a Christian church. Resting on the pulpit was one of those, "other translations". I carefully opened the cover and thumbed through the pages. Totally missing were passages such as, *"Ye silly Mormon, knowest thee not that thees, thys and thous endoweth not thine Holy Bible with the power of thy God?"* As I scanned the pages, my eye was drawn to translation differences. I noted the absence of Elizabethan English and the presence of a more understandable rendering. I closed the book and backed away. Somehow, looking at the pages and reading the passages seemed to be ... sinful!

It was only years after leaving Mormonism that I understood why the King James translation was held in such high esteem by the Mormon church. Joseph Smith plagiarized many passages of the King James Bible and inserted them, word for word, into his signature religious book. Plagiarized quotes in the Book of Mormon match only the King James. Therefore, any translation with minor variances will undermine canonized LDS scripture and invalidate the Book of Mormon.

> The problem of what to retain or omit in translation is not as crucial for the Latter-day Saint. **Much of the KJV text-particularly many chapters of Isaiah and the Sermon on the Mount-is contained in the Book of Mormon** or verified in the Pearl of Great Price or in the Doctrine and Covenants ...
> – The Church of Jesus Christ of Latter-day Saints, "Why does the Church still use the King James Version?", www.churchofjesuschrist.org/study/ensign/1987/06/i-have-a-question/why-does-the-church-still-use-the-king-james-version , emphasis added

The brakes squealed quietly as the truck came to a stop. The brown door slid open, a man in matching attire exited with a box that bore my name. Like silly kids, Grace and I ripped and tore at the packaging until two new Bibles rested on the table before us. One was a rich brown, not unlike dark chocolate; the other was a lighter saddle brown. I gave Grace the first choice. She has always loved dark chocolate, so she scooped up the darker Bible. Her selection was perfect because I prefer milk chocolate.

We thumbed the pages in anticipation. Our fears of biblical corruption had long since melted. We wanted to know God and were excited to hear His word ... from Him!

25.2 Everything to God

The question before us was how do we find God? We only knew the Mormon way and had no one to direct us. We knew for sure that our forty-year journey in Mormonism was a dead end. We needed something new and authentic. We had no real idea where to begin.

When I reflect on our desperate need to know God, I remember a talk show. A Mormon guest on the show said the strangest thing.

> We approach God from the rear, coming first to the "D", and then the "O". Only after doing the "DO" of Mormon works are we able to approach the "G" and know God.
> – Unknown

For sixty years, I worked to do the "DO" of Mormon works. Despite all that effort, I never found God. I now know, my constant attempt to please God by my works is the backward way. We cannot sneak up on God from behind. When I abandoned the constant striving to impress God, things changed. When I approached Him in humility, surrender, and fear, He found me!

Having been redeemed, I joyfully share the good news because God justified me while I was ungodly.[1] Light drives me to share the story of His grace in my life.

On the day our new Bibles arrived, we knelt together at the kitchen table. We prayed like we had never prayed before. We told God of our weariness caused by endless half-truths and outright lies. "Oh God" we prayed, "show us your truth!" So great was our need that we held nothing back, "If there is a cost God, we will gladly pay". The next words spoken were new for us, "If you need our jobs, our home, our land, God, everything we freely offer". What came next surprised me even as the words fell from my lips, "Take everything we know and think we know. Take those people we cherish as friends and associates, God, take our children if that is the cost of knowing you".

That evening, we sat side by side in bed and began to read. We started in Matthew and poured over every word. Along the way, God did crazy good things in our hearts.

What happened next cannot be described in words. It was like switching on a light or opening a door. Just that quick, I knew the truth. I would never dare compare myself to Paul except in this one thing. It was as if I had fallen, and the instant I rose again, I just knew. In many ways, it was my Damascus road.

> Immediately something like scales fell from his eyes, **and he received his sight**. He arose and was baptized.
> – Acts 9:18 (WEB), emphasis added

I had been walking in the blackest darkness for sixty years. Scales covered my spiritual eyes for such a long, long time. I had been utterly blind, and I never knew it. In an instant, I could see, and my new vision was ... a miracle!

Coming to know God's truth was not a line upon line, precept upon precept kind of thing. It came as a

Grace Notes

Receiving our new bibles was so exciting! I wanted to dig in and learn everything about Jesus. Finally! Before opening our bibles, we prayed, asking God for his truth. We laid everything at the foot of the cross; literally everything!

As we read, we discovered things we had never seen before. So many times, we stopped, looked at each other, and said, "Who put that in the bible?" Then we would laugh together and read on.

I think one of the most amazing things about reading a red-letter bible is to know that those are the actual words of Jesus Himself. As new Christians, it meant a lot to see those extraordinary words.

Our eyes were truly and finally opened! What joy filled my heart!

Grace

---
[1] Romans 4:5

flash of light, understanding, and certainty. This experience has had a profound and lasting effect on everything I am.

A pastor once asked, "what Bible passage saved you?" I replied, "Matthew chapter one." His response was comical, and it brings a smile still. He shot back, "That's just a genealogy. No one gets saved by reading a genealogy!" He is a good pastor and a good friend, but he was so wrong in this case. What is it about a genealogy that can save? For me, the answer is straightforward. We had sincerely surrendered everything to Jesus. In total and unrestrained surrender, we turned to Him. We didn't know it then, but we repented in the form and fashion the Bible defines.[2] So, having turned to the Lord, only one thing remained, and that was His Word. When we opened and read the word of God, He kept a great promise.

> So then faith cometh by hearing, and hearing by the word of God.
> – Romans 10:17 (KJV)

So you see, it didn't matter what we read so long as it was the Word of God. There is power unto salvation in every utterance of God's Word. We read through the long list of names beginning with Abraham and ending with Jesus. I had no understanding of these people's importance, and I failed to see the prophecy. I couldn't pronounce many names and utterly failed to understand their significance. That didn't matter! God only wanted me to understand one key thing.

> Ask, and it shall be given to you. Seek, and ye shall find. Knock, and it shall be opened to you.
> – Matthew 7:7 (Darby)

25.3 Be Reconciled to Your Brother

Grace and I continued devouring the Bible at every opportunity. We couldn't get enough, and we couldn't get it fast enough. Even so, one passage stopped me cold. The first time I read it, I knew that I couldn't continue in the Lord until I first set one thing right.

> [23]If therefore you are offering your gift at the altar, and there remember **that your brother has anything against you**, [24]leave your gift there before the altar, and go your way. **First be reconciled to your brother, and then come and offer your gift.**
> – Matthew 5:23-25 (WEB), emphasis added

I read those words and instantly saw the face of my Mormon Bishop. The dark years[3] had been very difficult for both him and me. He was the father of

---
[2] See chapter: How do I Repent?
[3] See chapter: The Dark Years

the ward according to Mormon tradition. If he was the father, he undoubtedly regarded me as the rebellious and disrespectful son.

He demanded what I could not give. Because I felt his demands to be evil, I refused. When he couldn't defend himself against my onslaught of unbending arguments, he felt disrespected, twice telling me, "I am no longer your friend." We were at an impasse.

This Bishop had much against me. I struggled with lingering anger as well. I read and reread this passage and knew, without question or reservation, that God was speaking to me. Before I could move on in my relationship with Jesus, this thing, whatever it was, had to be laid to rest.

Every attempt to speak with him, by whatever means, was rejected. I reasoned, "If he won't speak with me, then it is his problem." Feeling justified, I moved on and tried to forget about this Bishop. Sometimes, we see things one way, and God views them from a different perspective. I had no peace and no rest in my justification. God kept pushing, nudging, and bumping me to keep going. One cold winter night, I saw the Bishop pulling out of the local Mormon church parking lot. I stopped my car in my lane, stepped out, and stood in the middle of his. He came to a stop.

As I approached, his window came down. After a brief greeting, I assured him that personal issues could and should be resolved even if we could never agree on some things. He stared at me. I continued, "I hope you can forgive me, and I do forgive you." I expressed my desire to be neighbors, friends, and brothers. He continued to stare, saying nothing. I wished him a good night and walked away.

I don't know if anything changed in my Bishop that night. But, something dark and valueless fell from my heart. God had changed and made me new according to his will and purpose. So ended my first experience of hearing God direct me through His word. It was awesome!

> For which cause we faint not; but though our outward man perish, **yet the inward man is renewed day by day**;
> – 2 Corinthians 4:16 (KJV), emphasis added

25.4 Mormon Conspiracy

Our first venture through the Bible had its share of comedy. We were sitting up in bed when we began the book of Acts. I intently listened while Grace read, *And when the day of Pentecost was fully come, they were all with one accord in one place.*[4] I said, "Wait, wait, wait! Before you continue, tell me all you know about Pentecost." Grace was so cute. How can anyone not love her to death? She responded, "Ummm ... I've heard of it. Ummm ... I think it's something the Catholics do." This funny story presented me with a grand opportunity to give Grace a hard time. There was, however, a problem; I knew nothing more!

---
[4] Acts 2:1 (KJV)

One of the most unbelievable parts of this story is that I had been a Gospel Doctrine instructor. I spent an entire year teaching the New Testament to Mormon adults. The direction to instructors is to only teach what is in the manual. Consequently, I did not teach the New Testament from the New Testament. Instead, I led the class from a sanitized manual. I never read the entirety of any bible chapter I was teaching. The class expected nothing more and had no interest beyond the passages preapproved by the Mormon elite.

I still had my old Gospel Doctrine manual, so I turned to the lesson covering Acts 2. I was shocked by what it did not teach. Twice, the manual pointedly declared that the Holy Ghost filled the twelve apostles alone. There was no mention of the 120 who were also there. Likewise, there was no mention of the 3000 in Jerusalem who were born again.

Why did the Mormon church sanitize this story? Why did they hide the biblical truth that over 3,000 people, in addition to the twelve, received the Holy Spirit? In Mormonism, all authority is centralized in the first presidency and twelve apostles. The leaders cannot afford to have it leak out that God is not partial, that God will empower whom He chooses, that all are equal in His eyes. If that message is ever heard and believed, it will shatter every Mormon leader's standing.

A short time later, we read of a people called the Bereans. That name was foreign to us. The Bible told us that these people were "more noble" than others. It seemed strange that these "more noble" Christians were unknown to us. Why would any follower of Jesus not know about these noble people? How can any Christian not ask what made these people noble and how do we follow their example?

Again, I turned to my Gospel Doctrine teacher's manual to see what it had to say. It made mention that Paul and Silas taught in Berea. The Mormon church scrubbed every detail about these people's nobility and what acts made them noble.

From the foundation of Mormonism, the church taught that its leaders could not lead the people astray. This teaching is essentially the chains, stocks, and shackles that bind and enslave. Paul was pleased that the Bereans tested every word he spoke against what God had previously revealed. The Mormon leaders know that the church will fall when its members do the same.

Since my salvation, I have asked innumerable Mormons, "What do you think of Pentecost and the Bereans?" I have been unable to find even one who is familiar with the coming of the Holy Spirit or these "more noble" people. This reality is a heartbreaking justification for weeping!

It is inconceivable that professing followers of Jesus will intentionally erase God's to hide the truth. To delete the Lord only to retain earthly power is a horrific and unthinkable practice. Yet, the conspiracy of church leaders against God and the Mormon people is undeniable. The church hid the truth and misled the people with depraved indifference and premeditation. The eternal cost is incalculable.

> For what shall it profit a man, if he shall gain the whole world, and lose his own soul?
> – Mark 8:36 (KJV)

25.5 Joy in the Word

Our reading was with such joy. As we uncovered truth upon truth, long hidden by the Mormon church. We were thunderstruck at every turn of the page. We gaped in wonder and astonishment at the birth of the church. We could barely comprehend the miracle of grace. The simplicity of repentance was marvelous.[5] Above all, we fell hopelessly in love with Jesus. We saw prophecy after prophecy fulfilled before our eyes. We saw the power, glory, wonder, and splendor of our God for the first time in our lives. It took our breaths away.

Forty long years we, as a couple, wandered in the wilderness of Mormonism. As we symbolically crossed the Jordan and set foot on the land of promise, we fell to our knees, lifted our hands, and gave thanks to God from whom all blessings flow. In our daily walk with the Lord, we shout loud praises continuously to our God, and He has heard. Time and again, we have watched God fight for us. Again and again, we have watched walls that seemed impenetrable turn to rubble and fall.[6]

> So the people shouted when the priests blew with the trumpets: and it came to pass, when the people heard the sound of the trumpet, and the people shouted with a great shout, that the wall fell down flat, so that the people went up into the city, every man straight before him, and they took the city.
> – Joshua 6:20 (KJV)

That's us; we have our own Jericho!

---

[5] See chapter: How do I Repent?
[6] See chapters: The Dark Years, Excommunication, Given Over to the Courts

CHAPTER TWENTYSIX

EXCOMMUNICATION

> I have planted and watered the best I am able. Dear God, I pray, bring the increase.
>
> *Lance*

I had been Christian for about six months when the strangest thought flooded my mind. I believe it was God doing what God does so well. There are sixteen men in a Mormon Stake Presidency and High Council. The Holy Spirit persistently nudged until a thought crystallized in my mind. One or more of these men had questions that could not be asked or answered. These men dared not ask because such questions are perceived to be inappropriate and faithless doubting. Believable answers to essential gospel questions are elusive. Confusion mounts when the living prophet refutes the teachings of dead prophets and Mormon scripture denies Mormon scripture. Therefore, the search for Mormon-approved answers leads to a multiplication of troubling questions.

Church leaders insist that its members trust only media published by the church. Material from a source other than official Mormon literature is regarded as anti-Mormon and evil. Furthermore, seeking answers to difficult gospel questions is typically seen as a lack of faith and the likely result of grave sin. Consequently, these men could not seek answers by looking outside of Mormonism and found no reliable truth by looking in.

President Oaks acknowledged that some Latter-Day Saint couples face conflicts over essential values and priorities. Matters of Church history and doctrinal issues have led some to a crisis of faith. Oaks acknowledged that they often wonder how to best go about researching and responding to such matters. In answer, Oaks made a shocking revelation. His response exposes the absolute power Mormonism has over the hearts and minds of the members.

> **I suggest that research is not the answer.**
> – Dallin H. Oaks. Devotional, to young married couples at Chicago, February 2, 2019

The more I puzzled on the irreconcilable predicament of the American Falls, Idaho Stake Presidency, and High Council, the more I was convinced that I must act. The Holy Spirit drove me to stand before them and bear a witness of Jesus. Each man needed to know what Jesus had done for me and would do for them. Along with their families, these men fiercely needed the assurance only Jesus can provide. Without the good news of Jesus, they are destitute and without hope. Without the light of God, they could not recognize the vacancy of their empty existence. An excommunication hearing appeared to be the best opportunity to speak before these sixteen men.

I placed several telephone calls and sent multiple emails to the Stake President, wherein I requested the hearing. He responded to none of my inquiries. After several weeks of fruitless attempts, I thought, "I am still a member, in good standing, of *The Church of Jesus Christ of Latter-day Saints*, and that is my leverage." I sent one last email where I referenced my good standing in the church. I pointed out that I had every right to stand in Mormon Fast and Testimony meetings and speak of the true Jesus. I assured him I would do precisely that unless he scheduled an immediate hearing. In a few short days, I received my reply.

26.1 Are You Here to Kill Me?

Two members of the stake High Council stopped by my home to deliver a formal summons to an excommunication hearing. These two gentlemen looked very imposing in full Mormon regalia; white shirt, tie, the works![1]

I met them on the front lawn with a broad smile and a firm handshake. "*Are you here to kill me?*", I asked. They responded with a puzzled look, and so I explained.

> If men turn traitors to God and His servants, their blood will surely be shed, or else they will be damned, and that too **according to their covenants**
> – *Journal of Discourses* (N.p.: n.p., n.d.), 4:375, Heber C. Kimball, emphasis added

> The wickedness and ignorance of the nations forbid this principle's being in full force, but the time will come when the law of God will be in full force. **This is loving our neighbour as ourselves**; if he needs help, help him; and if he wants salvation and it is necessary to

---
[1] See chapter: Of Blue, Beards, and Blasphemy

> **spill his blood on the earth in order that he may be saved**, spill it.
> – *Journal of Discourses* (N.p.: n.p., n.d.), 4:220, Brigham Young, emphasis added

> There is not a man or woman, who violates the covenants made with their God, that will not be required to pay the debt. The blood of Christ will never wipe that out, your own blood must atone for it.
> – *Journal of Discourses* (N.p.: n.p., n.d.), 3:247, Brigham Young & John A. Widtsoe, *Discourses of Brigham Young*(Salt Lake City: Deseret Book, n.d.) 589

One of these high priests claimed to have some knowledge of blood atonement. He tried to make light of the whole thing. The second man was taken unaware. This undeniable truth cut deep, slicing to the center of his heart. He stared at the ground, refusing all eye contact. His discomfort was unmistakable.

I explained that these Mormon prophets clearly described my current state as a bold and vocal breaker of every temple covenant. I explained, "You must kill me now or you do not love me as yourself". I waited ... there was no response. I waited some more ... *"Do you need to borrow a knife?"* I thought this was hilarious. They had a somewhat different view.

26.2 Fields of Grace

The following Sunday morning, I stood in worship service at our local community church. My excommunication hearing was to begin a few hours later, so I was a bit on edge.

The worship band began playing a song I had never before heard. I liked it! I enthusiastically joined in and tried to learn the words and adjust to the unfamiliar tempo. Then came the line that knocked me off my pins.

> There's a place where religion finally dies. There's a place that I lose my selfish pride.
> – Big Daddy Weave. "Fields of Grace" Worship song

The Spirit filled me, overflowed, and spilled out on the floor. I am generally sedate, but not that day. I threw my hands in the air while shouts of joy reverberated through that little church. Somehow, I just knew God had my back, and there was no need to worry.

My reaction surprised everyone in the sanctuary, including myself! Our worship leader started laughing. After the service, he told me why. My arm had been around my wife as we sang. When I forcefully lifted my arms to God, I smacked her soundly on the back of her head. He thought the whole scene was rather comical!

A calm settled over me. I knew I would not stand alone at any time during that day. I knew I would go and do, guided by the Holy Spirit and protected by my defense attorney who is Jesus Christ. From the instant I shouted in unrestrained joy and nearly put Gracie's noggin in orbit, God lifted me. I knew this would be the time and day for me, *when religion would surely die*. I knew I would forever leave behind every religious notion contrived by men, governed by men, and polluted by men. That was the day I was finally and wholly made free!

26.3   No Recording

Before the formal hearing began, the Stake President asked Grace and me to join him in his office. At a previous time, I had informed this man that "I will, for my own protection, record every future meeting." He asked if I intended to record the hearing. I assured him that I did. He indicated that I could not record. I reminded him of Idaho State law that guaranteed me the right to record any conversation of which I am a party. He countered that he would cancel the hearing if I insisted on recording.

I reached into my shoulder bag, extracted an audio recorder, and turned it off. Because he was attempting to block the recording, I asked that Grace be allowed to attend and take notes. He refused, and my sweet wife was ushered into a separate waiting room.

As we stood to enter the hearing chambers, he asked if I had any other recording devices. I responded by telling him that I had many taped to my body under my clothes! He smiled and ushered me into the hearing.

I had three more taped to my body!

26.4   The Hearing

As I entered the High Council room, I immediately noticed twelve men seated on the left and right sides of a long conference table. At the head of the table was the Stake President, his two counselors and the Stake Executive Secretary. The Stake President directed me to take a seat at the far end of the table.

Instead of taking my seat, I paused for a moment and looked at the faces around the table. Most of these men did not know me. Yet, they thought to judge me regarding matters they could not comprehend. I began moving around the table, greeting each man with a smile and a firm handshake. I figured that they should at least look me in the eye before shipping me off to the Mormon gallows, otherwise known as Outer Darkness. As I greeted each man, it became apparent that they were, for the most part, more nervous than I.

This nervousness was confirmed when one of the men opened the meeting in prayer. Mormons have a funny way of praying. They get stiff-lipped, assume an ultra reverent expression, and proceed in a Mormonized, bastardized version of Elizabethan English. At one point, he said, "We thank thou". That's when the stammering began. He stopped, regrouped, and took another run at finding an appropriate word from the 1600s. It's kind of sad. The requirement of speaking to God in a relatively foreign language means they can't just relax and talk with their god.

> For ye have not received the spirit of bondage again to fear; but ye have received the Spirit of adoption, whereby we cry, Abba [Daddy], Father.
> – Romans 8:15 (KJV), emphasis added

At any rate, when he stumbled and stuttered, I smiled. These men are not High Priests.[2] They were merely fathers, husbands, businessmen, and laborers. As is true for all Mormon callings, they were square pegs forcefully driven into round holes. None had a right or any authority to judge another human being. I knew it, and I think they knew it as well. I got the sense that they were anxious to put this ugly business in their rearview mirrors.

I quickly realized that the Stake President meant to harm and used his authority to control and manipulate the men who attended him! He ran the controls while his counselors and High Councilmen sat passively and capitulated. It was a rather sad thing to behold, but it is the Mormon way. There is always the appearance of unity by common consent. In reality, Mormon decisions, actions, and opinions are the fruit of a one-man monarchy. All others who are junior to the ranking member must blindly sustain their leader or be sent away in disgrace.

The Stake President questioned me about my loyalties and to whom I trusted. The questioning was absurd. *Do you sustain Thomas S. Monson as the Lord's chosen prophet?* I answered, *there were prophets until John the Baptist, and after him, we have Jesus alone.*[3] *Do you sustain the other Mormon general authorities as prophets, seers, and revelators?* My answer was essentially the same. He asked if I sustained the local leaders of the church. "*I do not!*" was my response.

I was as bold as I dared be in this statement without being rude. This man wrongly assumed some power or authority over me. I corrected that delusion.

> *Reflections*
>
> As the hearing began, I was asked again if I was recording. I boldly declared, "I am not!" I admit to feeling a bit uncomfortable with this deception. But then, I was supremely confident that this Stake President intended to cause harm and would do any evil to achieve his objective. The recording was a right of self-defense that I was unwilling to surrender. In the end, my fears proved to be justified.
>
> *Lance*

---

[2] See chapter: High Priest
[3] Luke 16:16

I recognized none of that authority and saw only a wolf in sheep's clothing[4] masquerading as a minister of righteousness.[5]

At the time of my excommunication, the *Handbook for Bishops and Stake Presidents* was a carefully guarded secret. I was not supposed to have access to one. This policy was odd because it detailed my rights. Of what value are rights when the accused cannot know what they are?

A little searching on the internet produced a copy which I used to prepare my presentation before these men. I had no desire to defend my choice to become Christian. My decision needed no defense. I had no desire to protect my status as a Mormon because I was no such thing. However, I desired to know what rights I had to speak before the council.

The then-current handbook stated that I had a right to make two statements. Twice, I began to speak, and twice, the Stake President interrupted at around the one-minute mark, taking back the floor.

The handbook further indicated that I, the accused, could call any witnesses to speak for me provided they were in good standing in the church. As I began opening my Bible to a preselected text, I called Jesus Christ, my first witness. The Stake President directed me, use only those witnesses brought.

I was supremely confident that Jesus was with me, especially after the morning's worship service. I did not walk alone, and I knew it. The Holy Spirit attended, and He was mighty.

The Stake President's assumption that I had not brought Jesus with me was most certainly a sad and telling development. If Jesus wasn't welcome, by what power was this body of Mormon leaders operating? If not the power of our holy God, what force presided in that hour? If the power and illumination of God did not lead this council, what evil ruled in those Mormon chambers?[6] At any rate, Jesus Christ was an unacceptable, untrusted and unworthy witness. Consequently, my Holy Bible remained tightly closed throughout.

I called my second group of witnesses, including every man in the room except the Stake President. I had questions specifically prepared for each man. The Stake President directed them not to answer my questions. I remember this moment like it happened yesterday, "Brethren," he said, "you don't have to answer". I reminded them of Peter, who charged us always to have a ready defense for our faith.[7] Then pausing, I looked at these men and asked, "*Do you men have a defense for your faith or are you afraid to speak for Jesus Christ?*" The room went silent. Every man lowered his eyes and focused on the table directly in front of him. I waited ... not a single man lifted his gaze to meet mine. I waited some more ... no man responded. Each one was struck dumb by fear. At the prospect of dealing directly and boldly with the Word of God, Mormon arrogance wilted. To a man, each withdrew from battle.

As Mormon leaders, each man would or should be aware of a unique promise

---

[4] Matthew 7:15
[5] 2 Corinthians 11:15
[6] 2 Corinthians 11:14
[7] I Peter 3:15

from their god. If their belief had been as they claimed, each would have been well prepared and anxious to meet me on the field of spiritual battle. It was not to be. That reality revealed the uncertainty that led to retreat.

> [7] Wherefore, confound your enemies; call upon them to meet you both in public and in private; and inasmuch as ye are faithful their shame shall be made manifest. [8] Wherefore, let them bring forth their strong reasons against the Lord. [9] Verily, thus saith the Lord unto you—there is no weapon that is formed against you shall prosper; [10] And if any man lift his voice against you he shall be confounded in mine own due time.
> – *Doctrine & Covenants*, 71:7-10

Even with the promise of their god's protection, a quorum of top Mormon leaders fell back, fell silent, and failed. They had no answer and dared not respond. They hid behind lowered eyelids and waited for a rescue that did not come.

I had not been allowed to speak. Jesus, the King of Kings, had been rejected and ejected. I watched prominent local leaders wilt. Therefore, I determined to complete the purpose for which I came.

Without requesting permission, I began speaking about what Jesus had done in my life. I concluded by promising each man that Jesus was anxious to do the same for him.

26.5 Temple Guards and Legionnaires

I no sooner began to speak than the Stake President rose from his seat, opened a door, and admitted a Mormon strong-arm intimidation expert. Over my calm and respectfully delivered testimony, the recorded audio reveals this "brute squad" candidate yelling demands of silence and threats of legal prosecution. I had come to tell sixteen men about the miracles Jesus had worked in my life. I took a deep breath and continued speaking.

Over my ongoing and respectful testimony and the strong arm's angry threats, the audio reveals the Stake President placing a 911 call. He reported a disturbance and requested police assistance.

> **disturbance** noun
> **The act of disturbing wherein the peacefully delivered Word of God is employed to frighten and confuse the elect men of Mormonism.**
> – Mormon definition according to Lance

Disturbance? There was no such thing unless the above definition is employed. With respect and calmness that I can only attribute to the Holy Spirit, I spoke of the wonder and power of mighty Jesus.

I completed my testimony in less than three minutes, exited the building, and removed myself from church property. Shortly after that, three police officers arrived to break up and investigate the "disturbance" that never happened.

I have been amazed by how frequently the religious and political elite have turned to false witnesses and manufactured allegations against Jesus and His followers. To lie about the Christians must surely be the top priority. So it was for Jesus, Peter, John, Paul, Stephen, thousands of persecuted Christian men and women; and yes ... even for me!

> [10]Blessed are they which are persecuted for righteousness' sake: for theirs is the kingdom of heaven. [11]Blessed are ye, when men shall revile you, and persecute you, and shall say all manner of evil against you falsely, for my sake. [12]Rejoice, and be exceeding glad: for great is your reward in heaven: for so persecuted they the prophets which were before you.
> – Matthew 5:10-12 (KJV)

26.6 Jesus Stayed

This Stake President underestimated the redemptive power of Jesus and the complete infilling of the Holy Spirit. This silly man had known me only as a Mormon man who struggled in a Mormon world with nothing more than the false Mormon god to sustain me. He may well have been more than a match for the old me. He had no chance against the true and living God who indwelled me that day. He couldn't cause me to act out as I sat in that council of liars. After all, I had peace with God.[8] He couldn't wield his authority against me because Jesus is my King, and I accept no other.[9] He couldn't make me angry[10] because I had the joy of the Lord. He couldn't prevail because evil never does.[11] He couldn't shove his religion down my throat because this was truly the day when *religion finely died!*

I often think of those fifteen men who joined the Stake President to judge and condemn. Each man knows that he shrunk from the defense of his faith. They each witnessed corruption and listened to lies. Each is fully aware of his part in a miscarriage of justice and his willingness to remain quiet when honor demanded a truthful utterance. I'm not angry, nor am I offended. I completely understand the forces that caused them to comply silently.

I pray they will be troubled by the things they saw and did. They watched one man stand against a Stake President whom they would never dare question. They saw me but failed to recognize what was really before their eyes.

> I have been crucified with Christ, and **it is no longer I that live, but Christ living in me**. That life which I now live in the flesh, I

---

[8]Romans 5:1
[9]2 Corinthians 12:9
[10]Proverbs 16:32
[11]Ephesians 6:11

live by faith in the Son of God, who loved me, and gave himself up
for me.
– Galatians 2:20 (WEB), emphasis added

My prayer is ever for these men. God, let them be troubled. Let their memories be harrowed up. Soften their hearts and draw them near. I have planted and watered the best I am able. Dear God, I pray, bring the increase.

So then neither he who plants is anything, nor he who waters, but
God who gives the increase.
– 1 Corinthians 3:7 (WEB)

My only desire for these men is that someday, according to God's timing, they will come to know the better covenant of the Lord. I pray they will live in it forever with joy, truth, and peace with God.

CHAPTER
TWENTYSEVEN

PERSONA NON GRATA

> God has not forgotten us here. He knows of our faith and our persecutions. He knows of our joy and rejoicing. And when we feel too tired and worn down to continue, He is our strength.
>
> *Lance*

Satan loves to divide people. He has a significant advantage when he divides people over points of legalistic theology or degrees of perceived righteousness. When one people finds a reason to pick at and ridicule another, Satan delights. The color of a man's shirt, the number of piercings in a woman's ear, whiskers, skirt length, and even wearing a cross have justified official Mormon disdain and division.

Until it happened to me, I could not imagine the tactics *The Church of Jesus Christ of Latter-day Saints* employ to divide a disciple of Christ from the Mormon-controlled masses. I never comprehended their destructive will until they cast me out of the synagogue![1]

27.1 Sanhedrin Playbook

Predictably, the religious and political elite turn to false testimony and unfounded allegations against all perceived enemies. From the earliest days of Jesus' ministry, this has been the weapon of choice against Jesus and His followers.

---

[1] John 16:2

> But the Pharisees said, "By the prince of the demons, he casts out demons."
> – Matthew 9:34 (WEB)

> But they were filled with rage, and talked with one another about what they might do to Jesus.
> – Luke 6:11 (WEB)

Lying about the Christians to make a case, drive an agenda or establish an advantage has been the tactic of such men for over two thousand years. So little has changed.

> ¹⁰Blessed are they which are persecuted for righteousness' sake: for theirs is the kingdom of heaven. ¹¹Blessed are ye, when men shall revile you, and persecute you, and shall say all manner of evil against you falsely, for my sake. ¹²Rejoice, and be exceeding glad: for great is your reward in heaven: for so persecuted they the prophets which were before you.
> – Matthew 5:10-12 (KJV)

A few days after my excommunication, registered mail arrived from Kirton McConkie, legal representatives for *The Church of Jesus Christ of Latter-day Saints*. Upon opening the envelope, I discovered a PNG (Persona Non Grata) letter. Essentially, it is a trespass ban. The contents were shocking in their open disregard for the truth. It stated that due to my recent behavior, I had caused church *"members to fear for their safety"*. It continued, *"As a result, you are no longer welcome to attend any meeting or activity of the Church, wherever located"*. The letter concluded by indicating that I *pose a risk to the current Stake President and his successor*

When Mormon leaders wrote this letter, they did not know I had an audio record of the entire hearing. The letter exposes the sinister motives of this Stake President. Consider these undisputed facts:

1. He thought he had successfully denied me the right to record the hearing.

2. He drove Grace from the room, thereby eliminating the only witness who might stand against him.

3. He denied me the right to make a statement and have witnesses speak on my behalf.

4. He surrounded himself with fifteen men who would uphold his abuse of power, his violation of the church handbook, and his false police report.

I am fully satisfied that this Stake President intended to deny the rights and privileges guaranteed by Mormonism's handbook. He hoped I would react angrily or violently, thereby justifying a 911 call, police report, criminal charges and possible arrest. When I didn't respond as planned, the disturbance was manufactured in the mind of a corrupt man. He called the police and became a criminal by filing a false police report. The men who watched these things happen and never dared to speak the truth became accessories to that crime.

The audio file exists, and the letter exists. Together, they expose this Mormon leader's false testimony and lawless tactics.

27.2 Out of the Synagogue

The Bible has become such a resource to me. It offers a solution to every dilemma and shines light into every dark corner. I have often wondered why the Mormon leaders would put me out of the church. Many others have stopped believing in Mormonism and are still welcomed on church properties. Why am I banned? According to God's perfect will and timing, He revealed the answer soon enough.

Four years after the PNG letter was delivered to me, the local Stake President called and asked for a meeting. He indicated the purpose of the meeting was to discuss the possible removal of the PNG letter. I arrived at his home at the appointed time and discovered I would be meeting with the Stake President and his Counselor.

I soon discovered that the Stake President had a hidden purpose for the meeting. He made several comments I didn't think much of until weeks later. During the trial of Christ, Pilate asked a question that captured my full attention. He questioned the Sanhedrin about accusations they brought against Jesus. They answered, *"If this man weren't an evildoer, we wouldn't have delivered him up to you."*[2] These words took my breath away. Verified charges of wrongdoing were not necessary or even desired by the Sanhedrin. They had a man to kill, and truth was not a consideration.

I cannot begin to count the many times I have heard similar accusations. A few favorites of this Stake President have been, *"The former Stake President called the police, so you were obviously violent"* and *"the PNG letter states you are a threat to the Mormon people, so clearly you are"*. His favorite, however, has been, *"Men who hold Mormon priesthood keys have taken actions against you. So unmistakably, those actions are appropriate"*.

The meeting wore on for more than an hour. The Stake President continually spoke of changes I needed to make before he could remove the PNG letter. Each demand for change included no discussion of what that change might be, so there was no understanding. I felt something coming and was confident it was coming right at me.

---

[2] John 18:30 (WEB)

Finally, finally, the Stake President revealed his hand, "*Before we leave, let's come to a unity. There's no reason to go down the road of bashing Joseph, let's talk Jesus. Do not come to us anymore and talk about our doctrine that has holes in it. Let's talk Jesus if we're going to get together again. Clearly, we can't do this.*"

There it was! If I want access to important events in my family and friends lives, I must turn my back on the mission to which God had called me. I must turn my back on the Mormon people I love. This modern Sanhedrin member will give my life back on the condition that I never more share the hope of the everlasting gospel. If I deny my God, this Mormon Stake President is prepared to reward me, as it were.

NO!

I do find his demand rather comical, however. If we were to limit the discussion to Jesus alone, we would, by necessity, speak of Joseph Smith. Our conversation would indeed address Mormon claims that Jesus is not eternal. We would be obligated to consider Mormon teachings that the Jews crucified Jesus on charges of polygamy. And what of His blood? Is it really too weak and watered to atone for all the sins of the world? Did He create all things, or did He not? What of Joseph Smith's claim that Jesus was once a mortal and sinful man and that men can become gods equal to the Mormon Jesus? We cannot address these Mormon teachings without confronting Joseph Smith, who is the father of Mormon lies, and a son of Satan who is the father of all lies.

> You are of your father, the devil, and you want to do the desires of your father. He was a murderer from the beginning, and doesn't stand in the truth, because there is no truth in him. When he speaks a lie, he speaks on his own; for he is a liar, and its father.
> – John 8:44 (WEB)

Any conversation about Jesus must include a discussion of the things Jesus said. He spoke boldly of false prophets who are indeed wolves in sheep's clothing.[3] Jesus spoke of the necessity of exposing dark and hidden things.[4] These truths and many more bring us back to the Mormon prophet, Joseph Smith.

27.3 No Fear

So, let this Stake President, this modern-day Pharisee, rage. Let him bring his accusations. Let him lock me out of the church and divide me from family and friends.

---

[3] Matthew 7:15
[4] Luke 12:2

Jesus was the first to be put out of the synagogue. He spoke the truth, and they *rose up and thrust Him out*.[5] He warned His followers that the same would be done to them.[6]

The parents of the blind man feared the Jews because they had power to thrust them out of the synagogue.[7] Consequently, they crawled before and groveled at the feet of evil men. As with the Sanhedrin of old, this Mormon leader wields power to put people out of his church.

True followers of Jesus have no fear. To the churches of Smyrna[8] and Philadelphia,[9] Jesus spoke of evil men who say they are Jews but are not.

This Stake President received a patriarchal blessing from a man who claimed to have the priesthood of God but did not. By that blessing, he is declared a literal descendant of Israel and a member of a specific tribe, probably Ephraim.[10] This Stake President claims to be a Jew, but he is no such thing!

Like this Stake President, evil religious leaders in Smyrna and Philadelphia put people out of the church. They sought to preserve their power by separating those who loved Jesus from others who were still under demonic control.

To the faithful of the church in Smyrna, Jesus promised a *crown of life* and *deliverance from the second death*.

Because the faithful in Philadelphia kept the word of God and did not deny Him, Jesus set before them *an open door that no one can shut*. To these, God promised to make them *a pillar in His heavenly temple and write His name upon them*.

So to this Stake President, I say, "Bring your worst." You are no less blind than every wolf in sheep's clothing who came before. Your power and righteousness are like lipstick on a pig. It does not hide who and what you are. You are outwardly beautiful but filled with dead men's bones.[11] You are the perfectly formed dish and cup, outwardly beautiful and yet, filled with corruption.[12]

> [33]Ye serpents, ye generation of vipers, **how can ye escape the damnation of hell?** [34]Wherefore, behold, I send unto you prophets, and wise men, and scribes: and some of them ye shall kill and crucify; and some of them shall ye scourge in your synagogues, and persecute them from city to city:
> – Matthew 23:33-34 (KJV), emphasis added

In tiny Rockland, Idaho, Grace and I make up the bulk of the church. What might God say to the angel of the church in Rockland? It's not our place to say, but this we do know. God has not forgotten us here. He knows of our faith

---

[5] Luke 4:29
[6] Matthew 10:17
[7] John 9:22
[8] Revelation 2:8-11
[9] Revelation 3:7-13
[10] See chapter: Not Quite White
[11] Matthew 23:27-28
[12] Matthew 23:25-26

and our persecutions. And when we feel too tired and worn down to continue, He is our strength.

> I can do all things through Christ, who strengthens me.
> – Philippians 4:13 (WEB)

CHAPTER
TWENTYEIGHT

GIVEN OVER TO THE COURTS

> I am free from Mormon chains and the grip of false prophets. More importantly, I have the Bible, the very Word of God, to keep me free.
>
> *Lance*

Until the sheriff stopped by to serve me with criminal charges, I never truly comprehended the hideous, depraved nature of the evil one. All my life, the Devil stood before me as a wolf in sheep's clothing.[1] His dark angels were before me as demons masquerading as ministers of righteousness.[2] I accepted all Mormon leadership as men of God, never seeing through the disguise or behind the mask.

28.1 Loss

Six months after my excommunication, Grace's best friend passed unexpectedly. Her body had been ravaged with a sickness that took her so brutally. A few days before her death, Grace and I dropped in at her home. We had a wonderful visit with this beautiful, dying woman and her husband. They were gracious, and our time together was sweet.

Ours had been a friendship that spanned some twenty years. Our children were loved and welcomed in their home, as theirs had been in ours. When we became empty-nesters, we gathered every Monday evening for games, food, and fellowship. Those times are sweet and cherished memories.

---
[1] Matthew 7:15
[2] 2 Corinthians 11:14-15

Predictably, this dear friend's funeral was at the local Mormon church house. It was vital for us to attend and wrap her husband and children in an embrace of love and support. As important as this was for me, it was much more so for Grace. Her bond of love with this sweet, sweet friend was beautiful, profound, and rare.

Together, Grace and I reviewed the *Kirton McConkie letter*[3] and confirmed a key line, *"As a result, you are no longer welcome to attend any meeting or activity of the Church, wherever located"*. The key question became, is a funeral a Mormon church meeting? We concluded that the funeral would not be considered a meeting of the church. Instead, it was a time for all who loved this good woman to come together in unity.

Dressed in our best Sunday attire, Grace and I walked up the sidewalk toward the church house doors. Grace looked up and said, "uh-oh". Standing at the door was a man doing his best impersonation of a *Secret Service Agent*. As we stepped toward the door, the man moved to intercept. He stopped us and indicated that we were not welcome to attend. It seemed strange that this was a decision of *The Church of Jesus Christ of Latter-day Saints* instead of the deceased's husband, who had warmly welcomed us in his home just days earlier.

In a whispered voice, we expressed how much this dear deceased lady

Grace Notes

Awe, My Dear Friend,

From the moment we moved into this community, you were always there. You were the truest of sisters.

How I wish I could have been at your funeral. My heart cried when Lance and I were turned away from the church doors. I so wanted to remember you and share my love with your family and friends.

How can a church profess love for all people and be so insensitive and hateful at a time like that? I was so disappointed but at the same time, not surprised at all.

I miss you every day. May God bring peace and truth to your family.

Grace

meant to us and that we had only come to pay our respects peacefully. Our pleadings made no difference. I drew the Kirton McConkie letter from my jacket pocket and showed the imposing man that the restriction only applied to Mormon meetings and activities. Even as this man apologized, he insisted that we were not welcome. Quietly and respectfully, we turned, retraced our steps, entered our car, and returned to our home.

Out of an abundance of caution, I had an audio recorder running in my jacket pocket. It captured and established every detail of this event.

---

[3] See chapter: Persona Non Grata

28.2 Adding Insult to Injury

In the days that followed, I contacted the Office of *Kirton McConkie* and asked to speak with someone about the letter and its enumerated restrictions. One of the church's leading attorneys returned my call a few days later.

> **If the world hate you**, ye know that it hated me before it hated you.
> – John 15:18 (KJV), emphasis added

I assured the Mormon attorney that I have never caused a disturbance at any Mormon event and never will. He countered with the false accusation that my behavior at the excommunication hearing had been so inappropriate that the Stake President called the police. A simple appeal to the facts could have so easily resolved his accusation. I offered to send him the recording of my hearing, so he could personally confirm that my actions and words were never abusive, inappropriate, or threatening. He had no interest in hearing the audio. Apparently, truth is of no importance to this man and the church he represents.

I appealed to this man's sense of wrong and right by explaining that I am a member of a large Mormon family. I indicated that there would be baby blessings, missionary farewells, homecomings, ordinations, baptisms, weddings and that there would be funerals. I asked him to help me remove the restrictions. I asked him to allow my participation in meaningful and essential family events. He would not be moved.

I appealed to him on behalf of my aging Mother whose funeral will be in a Mormon church. I emphasized my desire to attend. He assured me that the church will contact the authorities and take legal action if I do so.

Once again, this all may be confirmed by captured audio.

28.3 Criminal Charges

Then came the unexpected knock at our front door. I was shocked to see two Deputies from the *Sheriff's Office* on my front porch. They were there to serve me with Criminal Trespass charges.

At my first court appearance, the discussion devolved to a possible sentence of six months in jail and a substantial monetary fine. This all seemed insanely extreme for the offense of attending the funeral of a dearly loved friend. Consequently, I demanded a jury trial.

Immediately, I came to understand that a fair and impartial trial was highly unlikely in the courts of Power County, Idaho. Three undeniable facts supported this conclusion.

1. A vast majority of Power County residents are members of the *The Church of Jesus Christ of Latter-day Saints*. Therefore, the jury that would ultimately decide my innocence or guilt would come from this body of

potential jurors. Some of my jurors were sure to be Mormon and would operate under an irreconcilable conflict of interest. Twice annually at General Conference, twice annually at Stake Conference, and at various times in Mormon worthiness interviews, these church members are required to raise their right hand and swear their devotion and commitment of loyalty to the church leadership. This practice is known as "*Sustaining Church Leaders*". This "*sacred*" covenant with the god of Mormonism is more binding upon them than any earthly oaths or covenants, including those made in the courts of the land. The highest ranking local Mormon leader brought the complaint against me. Church members who would serve as jurors are under a sacred oath to sustain their Mormon leader's wishes. This "sacred" duty would absolutely exceed all others.

2. The County Prosecutor was a Mormon priesthood holder who served under the same Mormon leader who brought criminal charges. He was bound by the same oaths and covenants that held potential jurors captive. Additionally, Mormons make up the largest voting block in the county. Therefore, if the Prosecutor were to decide based on the law of the land instead of his Mormon covenant of loyalty, he may well come into disfavor with the voters.

3. The Judge, in this case, was not Mormon. Like the Prosecutor, he may lose his position if voters felt he ruled against the church.

From the Mormon scriptures, we easily document the stranglehold church leaders have on every true believer of Mormonism. Moreover, we demonstrate that any word spoken by a Mormon leader will have the same binding authority as if god himself spoke it! Consequently, criminal charges against me can only be viewed as an *act of god.*

> What I the Lord have spoken, I have spoken, and I excuse not myself; and though the heavens and the earth pass away, my word shall not pass away, but shall all be fulfilled, **whether by mine own voice or by the voice of my servants, it is the same**.
> – *Doctrine and Covenants*, 1:38, emphasis added

> For his word ye shall receive, **as if from mine own mouth**, in all patience and faith.
> – *Doctrine and Covenants*, 21:5, emphasis added

> For he that receiveth my servants receiveth me;
> – *Doctrine and Covenants*, 84:36

> But if they will not hearken to my voice, **nor unto the voice of these men whom I have appointed**, they shall not be blest, because they pollute mine holy grounds, and mine holy ordinances, and charters, and my holy words which I give unto them.
> – *Doctrine and Covenants*, 124:46, emphasis added

The true Word of God is clear. Every prophet, apostle, preacher, teacher, and evangelist must be tested according to the word God has already revealed. This truth is made clear in the Bible from cover to cover.[4]

> Beloved, don't believe every spirit, but **test the spirits**, whether they are of God, because **many false prophets have gone out into the world**.
> – 1 John 4:1 (WEB), emphasis added

In sixty years of zealous Mormonism, no one ever suggested that I must test the church's leaders. At no time do I remember any teaching or discussion on the necessity of testing. Instead, Mormon study manuals routinely pass over these Bible passages without mention. Mormonism positively rejects the biblical method in favor of a practice the Bible condemns.[5]

> **The Lord does not ask us to prove that the teachings we have read are true, or that they are not true.** That is the kind of objective approach one might take in the academic, scientific world. However, that is not the best way we learn truth from the Lord.
> The Lord offers us the opportunity to let him confirm truth already in our hearts. **But in order to confirm religious truth, one must at least have the idea, or the thought, or the belief (however small) that he has found something true, and then pray to receive the Lord's confirmation.**
> – Gene R. Cook, "Moroni's Promise", Ensign, April, 1994, emphasis added

Every Mormon, therefore, who would play any role in my criminal trial would enter the courtroom with *an idea, or the thought, or the belief (however small) that the Mormon leader who brought criminal charges was acting and speaking convincingly for God.* Consequently, any finding that stood against the Stake President's criminal charges would be a finding against the mind and will of the Mormon god.

I motioned for a venue change, listing the above as grounds to support the motion. After my testimony, the Prosecutor stood and assured the court that

---

[4] Deuteronomy 13:1-6, Deuteronomy 18:20-22, Acts 17:10-11, Galatians 1:6-9
[5] Jeremiah 17:9

his oath to the United States Constitution would be fully honored. Despite his many oaths to a power he deemed supreme to the United States Constitution and the Laws of Idaho, my motion was denied.

28.4 Proceedings

And so it began. The wheels of justice turn painfully slow and are intensely complex. The emotional cost was a burden I did not desire to bear, but bear it I did.

I carried the Word of God to every court appearance. In the waiting room, I opened my Bible and read from its pages while awaiting my time before the Judge. On one such occasion, my phone vibrated. Turning from the Bible, I saw a text from a son-in-law. It read, "Matthew 10:19-20". I soon found the passage and began to read and reread its words. To better understand, I examined the surrounding passages and found context.

> [16] Behold, I send you forth as **sheep in the midst of wolves**: be ye therefore wise as serpents, and harmless as doves. [17] But beware of men: **for they will deliver you up to the councils** [courts], and **they will scourge you in their synagogues**[6]; [18] And ye shall be brought before governors and kings **for my sake**, for a testimony against them and the Gentiles. [19] But when they deliver you up, take no thought how or what ye shall speak: for it shall be given you in that same hour what ye shall speak. [20] **For it is not ye that speak, but the Spirit of your Father which speaketh in you**.
> – Matthew 10:16-20 (KJV), emphasis added

These words took on such power for me. In a strange sort of way, Matthew 10 became my legal strategy. My only plan was to give this thing to God and trust Him to accomplish all things according to His will and pleasure. I must admit that there were days, many, many days when my plan seemed to falter. I was being tried in a Mormon community by a largely Mormon-controlled court. Oh sure, that control was thinly veiled so all could claim impartiality in the face of explicit bias.

One afternoon, following a particularly difficult court hearing, Grace and I discussed the events of the day. I confessed, I seemed to be losing the battle and had every expectation of a guilty verdict and the possible imposition of jail. Together, we committed to praise God, regardless of the outcome. We turned our attention to our right and proper response if jail became a reality. The Bible tells of men, better men than I, who spent time in prison. We determined, should the worst happen, "we will praise God and pray to reach the prisoner or guard who will receive the good news of the gospel."

---

[6] See chapters: Excommunication & Persona Non Grata

28.5 God Is Moving

I stuck to my legal strategy and waited. One day, papers arrived, indicating that the Prosecutor had reduced the charges against me. For me, this was a sure sign that the church had bitten off more than they could successfully chew in a court of law. Initially, the Prosecutor pointed his largest prosecutorial gun at me, hoping that I would make a deal. I had an impression to visit him and ask, "What can we do to make this all go away?" He made an offer that convinced me his gun was, in fact, empty. He drew up a document indicating that he would dismiss all charges if I were to stay off all Mormon-owned property for six months. I accepted.

It's strange. I have a bucket list, and trespassing on Mormon properties is not in the top ten. In fact, it does not appear on the list at all! Grace and I did not enter church property with malicious intent. We went only to pay our respects to a family we loved. Our only desire was to offer support to dear friends. The Prosecutor and *The Church of Jesus Christ of Latter-day Saints* knew it!

I believed then and believe today that godless and misguided covenants to Mormon leaders demanded that the prosecutor attack. His Mormonism allowed no room to do the right thing. He was trapped! I am fully satisfied that his actions were nothing short of malicious prosecution. He needed something to place in his files to validate his faithfulness as a Mormon priesthood holder. His proffered deal gave him the illusion of a win. Meanwhile, he could back away from a no-win situation.

When all documents were signed and the legal mess put to rest, the Judge stood to leave. I was surprised by what he did next. He stopped, turned to face us, and said, "*Houses of worship are supposed to be houses of compassion, we didn't see that in this case.*" Then he turned and exited the courtroom. I did the same with a massive *ear to ear* grin!

Through this experience, there was a strange and wondrous calm. This sense of well-being has become a cherished and familiar friend. In the company of this constant companion, I am free from the chains of Mormonism and the grip of local Mormon leaders. There is nothing to fear.

> And be not afraid of those who kill the body, but cannot kill the soul; but fear rather him who is able to destroy both soul and body in hell.
> – Matthew 10:28 (Darby)

CHAPTER
TWENTYNINE

PEACE IN PERSECUTION

> As long as I draw breath, I will cry out to those who trudge endlessly on the broad way that leads to the wide gate of destruction.
>
> *Lance*

It is difficult to imagine a more universally true proposition than the age-old saying, "The more things change, **the more they stay the same.**" Evil and divisive tactics that may have seemed new and progressive centuries ago remain equally revered and useful today. Past, present, and the foreseeable future combine to prove the adage; *there is not much new under the sun.*

29.1 History Reveals Consistency

The ever predictable Sanhedrin brought false accusations, lying witnesses, and overt lawlessness to accuse and condemn Jesus, even unto death. They did this to justify what they knew they would do all along. Such men do not examine the facts to determine a proper and lawful response. Instead, they establish the desired response and create false evidence to justify it.

> Now the chief priests, and elders, and all the council, sought false witness against Jesus, **to put him to death**;
> – Matthew 26:59 (KJV), emphasis added

> For many bare false witness against him, **but their witness agreed not together**.
> – Mark 14:56 (KJV), emphasis added

History reveals the unchanging nature of evil in the story of two faithful disciples, Peter and John, who stood accused before the council. That they never again speak of Jesus was the demand. The threat of prison was the leverage that enforced the edict.

> ¹⁷But that it spread no further among the people, let us straitly threaten them, that they speak henceforth to no man in this name. ¹⁸And they called them, and commanded them **not to speak at all nor teach in the name of Jesus**.
> – Acts 4:17-18 (KJV), emphasis added

> Saying, Did not we straitly command you that ye should not teach in this name? and, **behold, ye have filled Jerusalem with your doctrine, and intend to bring this man's blood upon us**.
> – Acts 5:28 (KJV), emphasis added

The stoning of Stephen found justification in a mock hearing where false witnesses stood to testify maliciously. By this mechanism, they justified the unconscionable act of murder.

> ¹¹Then they suborned men, which said, We have heard him speak blasphemous words against Moses, and against God. ¹²And they stirred up the people, and the elders, and the scribes, and came upon him, and caught him, and brought him to the council, ¹³And set up false witnesses, which said This man ceaseth not to speak blasphemous words against this holy place, and the law:
> – Acts 6:11-13 (KJV)

The twelve, except John, suffered death by sword, spear, stoning, beating, crucifixion, burning, and more. In the continuing tradition of the Sanhedrin, Christians worldwide have suffered and are suffering every form of persecution, imprisonment, murder, and genocide. Regardless of the perpetrator, be it Jew, Gentile, nation, mob, or ideology, one thing remains universally constant. Evil will always persecute the followers of Jesus simply because they believe!

True disciples share the gospel of Jesus boldly. They can do nothing less. The name of Jesus offends and enrages the ancient and modern Sanhedrin and its derivatives. Jesus was, is, and will always be a threat to evil and designing men. Whenever a man or woman is persecuted or put to death for the gospel truth, traditions of the Sanhedrin will inevitably be in play.

29.2 Modern Sanhedrin

Does the Sanhedrin continue today? There has been a rebranding to present a more modern facade, but the evil that killed Jesus and persecuted the saints remains vibrant and active today.

These tactics were first used against me when a Mormon Bishop, under the direction of a Stake President, issued a gag order. This action's desired outcome was to silence my public voice relative to my faith.[1]

They were used against me a second time at my excommunication hearing when they denied my right to speak, even in my own defense or in defense of God. The desired outcome was to drive me from the church while hearing nothing from me except a defeated whimper. This they did because they fear the word of God![2]

Sanhedrin tactics were used a third time when the PNG letter was issued, complete with provably false accusations of violent threats and criminal behavior.[3]

29.3 The More Things Stay the Same

As of this writing, it's been five years since the gag order, four years since Jesus found and saved us, and four years since the excommunication and issuance of the PNG letter. In the years since the letter, I have missed many events that were important to family and friends. These have included weddings, funerals, baby blessings, Christmas parties, and more.

When a person learns that the church is not true and takes steps to distance himself or herself, there is a turning from the church, not from the people. Loved family members and life-long friends remain dearly cherished. It has been my experience that *The Church of Jesus Christ of Latter-day Saints* will seek to destroy any ongoing relationship between former members and those still tightly entangled in LDS chains. Those loved ones must choose between lifelong kinship and the church. The doctrine of Mormonism will not allow them to love both. And, they dare not love the man who is branded *apostate* and *enemy of god.*

In all the years before and after the PNG letter, Grace nor I disturbed any Mormon event. We have never commented or raised a shadow of suspicion that we may do so. Even though the church worships another Jesus, follows another gospel, and embraces another spirit,[4] the Mormon people have a right to worship in peace according to their desires. Despite their undeniable departure from God's truth, I stand with those people in defense of their right to worship unmolested. I must protect their rights because when the Mormons lose them, so do we!

---

[1] See chapter: The Gag Order
[2] See chapter: Excommunication
[3] See chapter: Persona Non Grata
[4] 2 Corinthians 11:4

29.4 Nehemiah

In the years since my court battle, the church's legal office has contacted me routinely. Their demands came in the form of registered mail. Past experience informed me, these attempts at communication were intended for my harm. If I were to sign for these letters, I would play into their hands by providing evidence that I had been made aware of their ongoing demands.

I read the story of Nehemiah and his rebuilding of the Jerusalem wall. I noted striking similarities between Sanballat, who persecuted Nehemiah, and the Kirton McConkie attorney who harasses me. I noted the legal strategy of Nehemiah and augmented my strategy to incorporate his.

> ²Sanballat and Geshem sent to me, saying, "Come, let us meet together in the villages in the plain of Ono." **But they intended to harm me.** ³I sent messengers to them, saying, "I am doing a great work, so that I can't come down. Why should the work cease, while I leave it, and come down to you?" ⁴**They sent to me four times after this sort; and I answered them the same way.**
> – Nehemiah 6:2-4 (WEB), emphasis added

I have refused to sign for the Kirton McConkie letters. Instead, I respond with a review of Nehemiah's story. I inform them that I have the vital work of sharing the gospel with the Mormon people and have no time to retrieve, review, and respond to their letter. I remind them that Jesus heads up my legal team and request that they send future correspondence to Him.

HE'S IN THE BOOK!

29.5 Jeremiah

Since my court battle, the local Mormon leadership has placed Sunday guards at every entrance to the Rockland, Idaho Mormon church. A local High Priest, who attended my excommunication hearing, indicated that I threatened to enter churches and schools to harm small Mormon children. Captured audio of my hearing proves that no such threat was made or intimated. Captured audio of the High priest establishes his every word.

These guards and this false accusation have a single purpose. The church leadership understands that the people will not receive me if they fear me. Consequently, *The Church of Jesus Christ of Latter-day Saints* has planted seeds of fear and distrust.

My God is so much bigger than their best-laid schemes. By the Word of God, He leads me and sets my feet on the path of His choosing.

> I know thy works: behold, I have set before thee an open door, and no man can shut it: for thou hast a little strength, and hast kept my

word, and hast not denied my name.
– Revelation 3:8 (KJV), emphasis added

My ministry is to find and speak to the Mormon people wherever and whenever possible. This effort includes knocking on the doors of Mormons who once considered me a brother.

At one such home, the door opened, and a beautiful little girl looked up at me. I bent down, gave her a friendly greeting, and asked if her Dad was at home. That's when I saw him rise from his chair, march across the living room while yelling, "*You stay out of my house!*". The door slammed shut, and the sharp click of the deadbolt rang in my ears.

Another man, a Mormon Bishop, indicated that he was too busy to speak with me. He stated that he had to go to his fields and move irrigation pipe, a common chore in our farming community. I responded, "*Great, I will be happy to help you. Maybe we can talk while we work*"? Another door shut in my face.

One woman indicated that she was afraid to let me in her home because of what I might do to her children.

If the world hate you, ye know that it hated me before it hated you.
– John 15:18 (KJV)

I think it is safe to say; God did not open these doors before me. For reasons known only to God, it was not these people's time to hear the good news. Such occurrences are disappointing, but it is all about God's timing and never mine. With a heavy heart, I turned and walked away ... for the time being.

Miraculously, God has opened many doors before me. In these homes, I have opportunities to share the wonder of what God has done for Grace and me. These discussions may not always produce immediate fruit. No matter! Through open doors, I scatter seeds. Some will land on the path and be carried away. Others will land on rocky soil only to spring up and die in the summer heat. Some will grow up among the weeds where they will, in time, be choked out. God willing, other seeds will fall on rich, good ground and bring forth fruit.[5]

With great rejoicing, I often think of the prophet Jeremiah. Jewish leaders were to him as the Mormons have been to me. Dark forces worked tirelessly to shut his mouth as they have worked to shut mine.

> And I said, I will not make mention of him, nor speak any more in his name: but **it was in my heart as a burning fire shut up in my bones**; and I became wearied with holding in, and I could not.
> – Jeremiah 20:9 (Darby), emphasis added

I stand at Mormon temples and church houses, in Mormon homes, and on the public square with Jeremiah as my guide. I will seek my Mormon brothers and sisters wherever they may be.

---

[5] Matthew 13:8

> ²Thus saith the Lord; Stand in the court of the Lord's house, and speak unto all the cities of Judah, which come to worship in the Lord's house, all the words that I command thee to speak unto them; diminish not a word: ³**If so be they will hearken, and turn every man from his evil way** ...
> – Jeremiah 26:2-3a (KJV), emphasis added

29.6 Paul

Jesus called Paul to bring the gospel[6] to the Gentiles. Paul was loyal to the sacred calling, but he could not forget his people, the Jews. Jesus Himself called me to take the gospel to every people and nation[7] This I will do, but my heart and my first love will be the people from which I hail. Paul's message and mine have not been well-received. His heart and mine cry together, *Am I therefore become your enemy, because I tell you the truth?*[8]

> ¹Brethren, my heart's desire and prayer to God for ~~Israel~~ (**the Mormons**) is, that they might be saved. ²For I bear them record that they have **a zeal of God, but not according to knowledge**. ³For they being ignorant of God's righteousness, and going about to **establish their own righteousness**, have not submitted themselves unto the righteousness of God. ⁴For Christ is the end of the law for righteousness to every one that believeth.
> – Romans 10:1-4 (KJV), replacement text inserted, emphasis added

29.7 Peace in Persecution

The Mormon church has its billions of dollars, its team of elite attorneys, and Sanhedrin-like motivations. They may succeed in jailing me or letting my blood as the prophecy of Brigham Young demands.[9] As long as I draw breath, I will cry out to those who trudge endlessly on the broad way that leads to the wide gate of destruction.[10]

> Rescue those who are being led away to death! Indeed, hold back those who are staggering to the slaughter!
> – Proverbs 24:11 (WEB)

And should evil rise again to accomplish a dark work, I will join Peter and John in rejoicing and praising the holy name of God!

---

[6] See chapter: Is the Gospel Everlasting?
[7] Matthew 28:18
[8] Galatians 4:16
[9] See "Are You Here to Kill Me" at chapter: Excommunication
[10] Matthew 7:13

They therefore departed from the presence of the council, **rejoicing that they were counted worthy to suffer dishonor for Jesus' name.**
– Acts 5:41 (WEB), emphasis added

Part V

A HOUSE ON THE ROCK

Surrender to the King

CHAPTER THIRTY

GRACE

> God gave me Grace ... twice. He gave me His grace, and He gave me my sweet Grace! I cherish both.
>
> *Lance*

We can never know who a person is meant to be until God takes hold. That is when we see the impossible happen.

30.1 A Terrible Mormon

Grace was never a very good Mormon. Oh, she played the game, walked the walk, jumped through the hoops, but as a Mormon, she *really, really sucked!*

It was never a question of her goodness. It was a question of her fire or lack thereof. That ol' Book of Mormon, Joseph Smith, Helaman, goddess in embryo fire never quite ignited. At best, it was smoldering soot. I was concerned!

The missionaries told her, we are teaching the Mormon lessons to an elderly gentleman. We don't want him to go through it alone; we don't want him to be uncomfortable. Will you sit in on the lessons ... for him?

To the elderly gentleman, they said, we are teaching the Mormon lessons to a young girl. We don't want her to go through it alone; we don't want her to be uncomfortable. Will you sit in on the lessons ... for her?

It is interesting and telling that her first Mormon experience was based on a lie. By deception, by hook or crook, the Mormon representatives of Jesus Christ coerced her into hearing their message by any means necessary. That same system of half-truths, constant pressure, and persistent coercion eventually led her to be baptized. What a strange thing to realize she came to "Mormon truth" because of a "Mormon lie."

When I was a believing Mormon, I saw those missionary's actions as right, even noble. There was a time when I boasted on them for hooking and landing Grace by whatever means necessary. As a Christian, as a disciple of the Lord Jesus Christ, I see these things in an entirely different light. Truth matters!

> [16] These six [things] doth Jehovah hate, yea, seven are an abomination unto him: [17] haughty eyes, **a lying tongue**, and hands that shed innocent blood; [18] a heart that deviseth wicked imaginations; feet that are swift in running to mischief; [19] **a false witness that uttereth lies**, and he that soweth discords among brethren.
> – Proverbs 6:16-19 (Darby), emphasis added

The absence of truth put my sweet wife in chains.

The missionaries? They were not intentionally evil or deceptive. They were born into a religious system of white lies and half-truths. They had lived it and been submerged in it until they could no longer separate truth and untruth. They were deceived to the degree that they did not recognize the eternal impact of their deceptions. Consequently, they peddled death and called it god. We do not see them as enemies but as fellow victims of a false and pernicious religion.

> ... Yes, the time comes that **whoever kills you** will think that he offers service to God.
> – John 16:2b (WEB), emphasis added

These missionaries never knew that they were killing Grace, leading her to eternal damnation and on to everlasting death!

The elderly gentleman? He didn't bite; he didn't take the bait. He is that one that got away. Praise God!

Grace never openly resisted Mormonism. She went along. When asked to serve, she accepted every calling, and she did serve. But, something was wrong; something was missing. She didn't complain; as she went and did. But, there was no joy, drive, or passion in her service to the Mormon machine.

After endlessly long sessions in the temple, I often talked to her about the endowment's symbolism.[1] I desperately tried to make her see the "imagined and symbolic beauty" of the Mormon gospel[2] as depicted so vividly in the temple ceremony. She nodded and affirmed all my words, but I could tell my pressing was being heard but never profoundly internalized.

Fast and Testimony meetings occur on the first Sunday of every month. This is a meeting when anyone can stand at the pulpit and profess their belief in the truthfulness of the church. Mormon leaders taught that we would lose our testimonies if we did not regularly bear them. Consequently, I stood almost every month to proclaim my belief publicly. Even though my testimony lacked

---
[1] Fig Leaf Apron
[2] See chapter: Is the Gospel Everlasting?

components deemed necessary for salvation, I propped up what testimony I had at every opportunity.[3]

Seldom did a Fast and Testimony meeting come that I did not nudge Grace and ask, "Are you going to bear your testimony?" The answer was always the same; she quietly but firmly refused.

I was deeply concerned about her lackluster approach to our shared religion. My earliest recollections included the understanding that I could be a god someday. That was my passion, that was my drive, and that was my plan for eternity. As a god, I knew there would be many celestial wives and that my sex-life would be ... incredible! Even before I received the whole of my harem, I knew that Grace was, is, and will always be my favorite wife. I desperately wanted her to share in my divine destiny. Yet, I could not deny signs that she was bound for the terrestrial world.

> [78] Wherefore, they are bodies terrestrial, and not bodies celestial, and differ in glory as the moon differs from the sun. [79] These are they who are not valiant in the testimony of Jesus; wherefore, **they obtain not the crown over the kingdom of our God**.
> – *Doctrine & Covenants*, 76:78-79, emphasis added

A crown over the kingdom of our God? What arrogance! What blasphemy to think we could elevate ourselves to a station equal to or above the Mormon god! God's words to Job serve as a reminder of how big God is and how insignificantly insignificant we are in contrast.

> [4] Where were you when I laid the foundations of the earth? Declare, if you have understanding. [5] Who determined its measures, if you know? Or who stretched the line on it? [6] Whereupon were its foundations fastened? Or who laid its cornerstone, [7] when the morning stars sang together, and all the sons of God shouted for joy?
> – Job 38:4-7 (WEB)

As a new creation in Christ,[4] it is difficult to admit these past heresies against our Holy God. It is inconceivable that I ever believed such lies. There was a time when I genuinely sought my wife's salvation by chasing after the blasphemous principles of Mormonism. I now see that I was like the missionaries who deceived for no reason other than to feed the insatiable beast of Mormonism.

I am so grateful for my sweet wife. She suffered so much while she prayed and waited for her stupid man to see the light. Forty years she waited. Forty years she suffered my insufferable pushing and nudging. Forty years she loved me anyway!

---

[3] See chapters: A Testimony of Joseph Smith & Is My Testimony Real?
[4] 2 Corinthians 5:17

30.2 An Awesome Christian Woman

When I finally came around and decided to leave Mormonism,[5] I saw the woman God always intended Grace to be. She bloomed as a tender blossom rising from the desert floor. I watched it happen. It was magnificent in its simple beauty! God moved in her and allowed me to witness the miracle!

The first thing I noticed was an immediate and unquenchable thirst for the Word of God. Morning, noon, and night she was drawn to her Bible. She is so cute and funny with every new discovery of truth and light. Her excitement bubbles up, boils over, and gets on everything. Biblical numerology fascinates her. Old Testament prophecy and New Testament fulfillment make her alive. To my great joy, she shares it all with me.

Grace is the girl who had no interest in joining me for Mormon scripture study. She is the girl who seldom, if ever, cracked open her Book of Mormon. She is the girl who now has four or five bibles to her name and drinks deeply from them until all are tattered and worn.

Grace is the girl who stoically refused to bear her Mormon testimony. Now, she won't stop speaking of her love and devotion to Jesus. The girl just will not shut up, and I do nothing to quench her! In fact, I bask in the glow of her joy. I think back on many years of pushing her to share what our little god had done in her life. I know now that she was silent because the Mormon god was silent to her. All she needed was the truth of the one true God. She is an unstoppable chatterbox, and that is a very good thing.

> *Grace Notes*
>
> As I tried to be a good Mormon wife, a good Mormon mother, and a good Mormon woman, something nagged at my heart. God was drawing me out of Mormonism and to Him. I was at peace and came to know God, but how to tell Lance? Then, He said, "I don't think I can be Mormon anymore." I rejoiced, God is so merciful!
>
> One year after being born again, I felt I had changed but wasn't sure if it was noticeable to others. When Lance confirmed that he could see it, I made a decision. If God can change Abram's name to Abraham, Jacob to Israel, and Sarai to Sarah, then I can be called Grace.
>
> He led me and then Lance to him. I thank God every day for his patient mercy and infinite grace.
>
> *Grace*

I next noticed her new love for me. Our life together had always been good, but there is something more, something deeper, something so beautiful. It is pure joy! There is a new purpose in everything she does. The light in her is unmistakable for any who chooses to see.

---

[5] See chapter: The Words

Sadly, many who once called her daughter, sister, aunt, and friend refuse to see who Grace has become. It is a source of heartbreak for us both.

> And every one that hath forsaken houses, or brethren, or sisters, or father, or mother, or wife, or children, or lands, for my name's sake, shall receive an hundredfold, and shall inherit everlasting life.
> – Matthew 19:29 (KJV)

There are Christian ladies across the country who share a special bond with my sweet wife. Her love has touched many women who languish behind prison walls. She brings life to all who will receive her because she reflects the glory of God. Despite many losses, Grace received at least a hundredfold for every heartbreak, and she receives each with exuberant joy.

On the ride home from church, just a few months after being born again, I asked Grace, "How do you feel?" Her answer was very slow in coming. I glanced at her and waited. When she answered, it was the most profound thing I have ever heard. She said, "*Free*". It was a simple response, yet Grace spoke volumes with a single word.

> Is not this the fast that I have chosen? to loose the bands of wickedness, to undo the heavy burdens, and to let the oppressed go **free**, and that ye break every yoke??
> – Isaiah 58:6 (KJV), emphasis added

Legalism oppressed my sweet wife for so long. Heavy burdens, bands of wickedness, and the yoke of oppression pushed her so low. God has freed her from all these evils. With a single word, she reveled in newfound freedom that only comes from walking with Jesus every day.

We were approaching the first anniversary of freedom from Mormon chains. We were riding to church when she let loose a volley of joy that nearly caused me to run off the road and straight up the nearest light pole.

Grace was not always Grace. Her given name is Melinda. She had always been Mindy for short. She had always been Mindy to me, and she had been Mindy until that very hour. She said, "from now on, I want you to call me by my real name." *Huh?* I wasn't tracking at all. She continued, "To mark God's promise and to celebrate what He was doing in Sarai's life, God gave her a new name. If she can do it, so can I ... *call me Grace.*"

> God said to Abraham, As for Sarai your wife, you shall not call her name Sarai, but her name will be Sarah.
> – Genesis 17:15 (WEB)

Her request instantly made perfect sense. It was a beautiful celebration of God's promise and the cascade of miracles that flooded her life. "Grace", I thought as I played it over in my mind. "Grace", I murmured, trying it on for size. It was a perfect fit like a tailor-made glove. In the twinkling of an eye, she became Grace. It was as if it was meant to be.

She was born Melinda Grace Wehland. Will you look at that? God always knew who he created her to be. For so many years, He patiently waited for us to catch up. She is Grace. It is her name, it is her title, and it is a perfect description of her heart.

In awe, I have wondered at the gifts of God. He gave me Grace ... twice. He gave me His grace, and He gave me my sweet Grace! I cherish both.

CHAPTER
THIRTYONE

ETERNAL MARRIAGE

> There is a marriage that endures through all eternity. Jesus is the bridegroom, and we, the Body of Christ, are his bride.
>
> *Lance*

The hardest thing about leaving Mormonism was the idea that my eternal marriage to Grace would end. Don't get me wrong; I knew the church was a lie and had no confidence in any of its claims. It's just that I love Grace, and I loved the idea of sharing eternity with her.

But there is more to the story, much more.

31.1 Polygamy in Heaven

Plural marriage is foundational to Mormonism. It has never been about sharing eternity with my wife. It was always about wives!

> The man Joseph, the husband of Mary, did not, that we know of, have more than one wife, but Mary the wife of Joseph had another husband. On this account infidels have called the Savior a bastard. This is merely a human opinion upon one of the inscrutable doings of the Almighty. That very babe that was cradled in the manger, was begotten, not by Joseph, the husband of Mary, but by another Being. Do you inquire by whom? He was begotten by God our heavenly Father. This answer may suffice you—you need never inquire more upon that point.
>
> – Brigham Young. Talk, Journal of Discourses 11:268

> The grand reason of the burst of public sentiment in anathemas upon Christ and his disciples, causing his crucifixion, was evidently based upon polygamy, according to the testimony of the philosophers who rose in that age. A belief in the doctrine of a plurality of wives caused the persecution of Jesus and his followers. We might almost think they were "Mormons."
> – Jedediah M. Grant, Second Counselor to Brigham Young. Talk, Journal of Discourses 1:346

In the Mormon heaven, the wife of my youth, the strength in my trials, and the love of my life would become property. In heaven, Grace would become one member of my numberless harem. She would cease to be my cherished wife and exist eternally as a possession, ever submissive to my lustful desires. I would not be hers alone. Instead, she would share me with hundreds or thousands of other wives and concubines.

I am unable to reflect on these beliefs without being sickened. How can a caring husband consider such things for the woman he loves? How can he submit her to such degradation? I don't have a reasonable answer, and I cannot deny my guilt in this thing. I always believed I would die in defense of her, yet I did evil to her and planned evil for her.

31.2 God's Heaven

We don't know a lot about Heaven, but we can know some things. Scripture tells us Jesus prepared Heaven for us.

> ^{2}In my Father's house are many mansions: if it were not so, I would have told you. I go to prepare a place for you. ^{3}And if I go and prepare a place for you, I will come again, and receive you unto myself; that where I am, there ye may be also.
> – John 14:2-3 (KJV)

Left to stand alone, this passage may not mean much. However, when we learn of Jesus and begin to comprehend the measure of His love, we can know something of Heaven.

> But God commendeth his love toward us, in that, while we were yet sinners, Christ died for us.
> – Romans 5:8 (KJV)

You, I, we were rebels to God. We were hateful, belligerent, blasphemes, immoral, idolatrous rebels. Let that sink in. We were all these things and so much more. When Jesus had every reason to hate and destroy us, He willingly went to the cross where He paid the price for every sin. He carried our sins to Golgotha and there nailed them to the cross.[1]

Even we who have given our lives to Jesus still fall short. We habitually sin and deserve total destruction. Despite all the hell we deserve, Jesus instead chooses to justify us. Who can comprehend such love?

> But to him that worketh not, but believeth on him that justifieth the ungodly, his faith is counted for righteousness.
> – Romans 4:5 (KJV)

In Joseph Smith's rewrite of the Bible, Romans 4:5 took a beating. The most significant change was made with the insertion of a single word, "not." The modified phrase reads, "justifieth **not** the ungodly". This textural change recreates Jesus and makes Him an ugly, vindictive, and false god. Mormon men cannot comprehend the love of Jesus. When they become Mormon gods, it is little wonder that they will be so lacking in love toward their wives.

When I think of Heaven, I think of the *love of Jesus*. I consider all I know of His love and then wonder, "What kind of Heaven will love like that prepare?" I can't wait to see it all.

31.3 Me and Grace in Heaven

The Mormon promise of eternal marriage is gone. But, a promise built on a lie is empty. So, what is to become of us, Lance and Grace?

> [37]Nay, in all these things we are more than conquerors through him that loved us. [38]For I am persuaded, that neither death, nor life, nor angels, nor principalities, nor powers, nor things present, nor things to come, [39]Nor height, nor depth, nor any other creature, shall be able to separate us from the love of God, which is in Christ Jesus our Lord.
> – Romans 8:37-39 (KJV)

Grace is secure in the Lord, and she cannot be separated from His love. It is a marvelous and miraculous thing to see the change God has worked in her.

There was once a man named Lance Earl. He looked like me, walked like me, sounded like me, but his heart was so wrong. Like Grace, I have been made new[2], and nothing will ever separate us from the love of God. We are sealed His!

The eternal marriage between Grace and myself was always a lie, but our love is real, and it will endure.

> But now faith, hope, and love remain—these three. **The greatest of these is love**.
> – 1 Corinthians 13:13 (WEB)

---

[1] Colossians 2:14
[2] 2 Corinthians 5:17

More than any other, I love Grace most. Among all those she loves, she says, "I love you more ... well except for Jesus." The love, bond, and connection that is the fruit of a lifetime together will endure because the greatest is love. We are sealed together, not in the way of Joseph Smith, but in the way of Jesus' love. We often speak of our continued journey and can't wait to explore Heaven together. God's way or the Mormon way? What do you think?

31.4 Eternal Marriage

We still believe in eternal marriage. After sixty years of rejecting the Bible, we opened its pages and learned the truth. There is a marriage that endures through all eternity. Jesus is the bridegroom, and we, the Body of Christ, are his bride.

> [5] A voice came from the throne, saying, "Give praise to our God, all you his servants, you who fear him, the small and the great!" [6] I heard something like the voice of a great multitude, and like the voice of many waters, and like the voice of mighty thunders, saying, "Hallelujah! For the Lord our God, the Almighty, reigns! [7] Let us rejoice and be exceedingly glad, and let us give the glory to him. For the marriage of the Lamb has come, and his wife has made herself ready." [8] It was given to her that she would array herself in bright, pure, fine linen: for the fine linen is the righteous acts of the saints. [9] He said to me, "Write, 'Blessed are those who are invited to the marriage supper of the Lamb.'" He said to me, "These are true words of God."
>
> – Revelation 19:5-9 (WEB)

See you at the marriage supper, don't be late!

CHAPTER
THIRTYTWO

PEACE WITH GOD

> He alone gets all the glory, and I alone get the grace!
>
> *Lance*

Jesus sent his disciples, armed with the good news of the gospel, into the highways, byways, cities, and towns. As He sent them, He admonished, " *The harvest is indeed plentiful, but the laborers are few.*".[1] As they went, Jesus reminded them, pray continually that God will send more and more workers to gather the harvest. These first missionaries were sent out with a sober warning to beware of wolves who will hunt and harm them as if they were but small lambs.[2]

These original missionaries, and thousands who followed, prayed, and indeed God has called many to the work. I am but one of these, even one of the least among them all. As one of the very least, I rejoice in what God has, and is, and will do through me. With a new understanding of God, I wonder why He chose me? It is a mystery, and yet, He allows one so wretched as I to join in the work of the kingdom. I am amazed to find myself included as a functioning yet insignificant part of the body of Christ.

> [15]If the foot shall say, Because I am not the hand, I am not of the body; is it therefore not of the body? [16]And if the ear shall say, Because I am not the eye, I am not of the body; is it therefore not of the body? [17]If the whole body were an eye, where were the hearing? If the whole were hearing, where were the smelling? [18]But now hath God set the members every one of them in the body, as it hath

---
[1] Luke 10:2
[2] Luke 10:3

pleased him.
- 1 Corinthians 12:15-18 (KJV)

There are hands, feet, eyes, and ears in the great body of Christ. If these and more are present in the body, there must also be nasal hair. Yes, I am nasal hair, insignificant, sometimes offensive, and even disgusting. Nevertheless, I am nasal hair that believes. I am nasal hair that praises God and sings in full-throated shouts of joy and humble gratitude. I am nasal hair that loves and leans on Jesus alone!

I go into the harvest to share the most excellent news and the greatest story with anyone who will hear. As I go, I try to remember *it is not about me.*

> [19]For I through the law am dead to the law, that I might live unto God. [20]I am crucified with Christ: nevertheless I live; yet not I, but Christ liveth in me: and the life which I now live in the flesh I live by the faith of the Son of God, who loved me, and gave himself for me.
> - Galatians 2:19-20 (KJV)

I sometimes recall that God formed man from the dust of the ground.[3] If He can do so much with a simple handful of dry, parched earth, what can He do with me? What miraculous things will He do with a single, believing nasal hair? The possibilities astound and fill my imagination. With anticipation and endless joy, I ache to see what He will do next!

> [9]He has said to me, "My grace is sufficient for you, for my power is made perfect in weakness." Most gladly therefore I will rather glory in my weaknesses, that the power of Christ may rest on me. [10]Therefore I take pleasure in **weaknesses**, in **injuries**, in **necessities**, in **persecutions**, in **distresses**, **for Christ's sake**. For when I am weak, then am I strong.
> - 2 Corinthians 12:9-10 (WEB), emphasis added

32.1 The Cost of Discipleship

Jesus gave His first missionaries power to do many things, including power over the enemy and a promise that nothing will harm them.[4] As I recall gag orders, false accusations, 911 calls, falsified police reports,[5] ejections from the synagogues (all Mormon properties),[6] criminal charges, court appearances[7] and the forced separation from friends and family[8] who I love, I remember the protection of God.[9] I now know that I was never alone in my most desperate

---
[3] Genesis 2:7
[4] Luke 10:19
[5] Acts 25:7
[6] John 16:2
[7] Matthew 10:17
[8] Matthew 10:21
[9] Deuteronomy 20:4 & Romans 8:31

and despondent hour. Even when I couldn't see God, He has always held me in the hollow of His hand.

32.2 Written In Heaven

Finally, to His missionaries, Jesus said the most amazing and unbelievable thing. When I read His words, I was thunderstruck. Never before had I heard such a thing,

> [20] ... rejoice not, that the spirits are subject unto you; but rather rejoice, because **your names are written in heaven**.
> – Luke 10:20 (KJV), emphasis added

Jesus found me in the darkest pit of legalistic idolatry. He lifted me up and out, and he saved me.[10] I rest and shelter peacefully in the sure testimony of my almighty God.

> [9] If we receive the witness of men, the witness of God is greater: for this is the witness of God which he hath testified of his Son. [10] He that believeth on the Son of God hath the witness in himself: he that believeth not God hath made him a liar; because he believeth not the record that God gave of his Son. [11] And this is the record, that God hath given to us eternal life, and this life is in his Son. [12] He that hath the Son hath life; and he that hath not the Son of God hath not life.
> – 1 John 5:9-12 (KJV)

What a beautiful thing it is that John recorded and affirmed the testimony which he heard so often from the mouth of Jesus.[11] God bless the apostle Jesus loved.[12]

32.3 Give Me a Better Assurance

One summer evening, the local Mormon Bishop and Stake President stopped by for a visit. We sat on the deck in the cool of the evening and enjoyed a long gospel discussion.

At one point, I asked the Stake president if he knew where he would go when he died. I honestly thought he would respond and claim a sure knowledge and certain testimony of his future godhood. His answer was surprising and refreshing. He said none could know for sure, and we all must wait for the judgment. In response, I opened my Bible and began to read:

---

[10] Romans 5:8
[11] John 3:16, John 3:18, John 3:36, John 5:24
[12] John 19:26

> These things have I written unto you that believe on the name of the Son of God; **that ye may know that ye have eternal life**, and that ye may believe on the name of the Son of God.
> – 1 John 5:13 (KJV), emphasis added

In response, the Stake President indicated that John's God-breathed[13] and biblically preserved passage was not entirely accurate. He rapidly named several sections from the Doctrine & Covenants without reading or expounding on any. He said, with the addition of these revealed truths, we know that John's understanding is not complete.

Stunned but not defeated, I urged them to show me something better. I agreed to return to Mormonism if they could give me a better assurance. I assured them that I would race full speed and dive headfirst into the baptismal font for something better.[14] They seemed pleased. However, I insisted on a few conditions. Namely, their "better assurance" must be delivered without conflict or contradiction relative to existing Mormon doctrine. I began a short guided tour of previous teachings from Mormon prophets that I knew would apply to me.

I began by turning to the Book of Mormon.

> And he that endureth not unto the end, the same is he that is also hewn down and cast into the fire, from whence they can no more return, because of the justice of the Father.
> – *Book of Mormon*, 3 Nephi 27:17

It seems clear enough that I have not endured to the end as a valiant Mormon. I am in open rebellion against the destructive teachings of *The Church of Jesus Christ of Latter-day Saints*. Consequently, the option of eternal fire did not appeal much to me. So I continued.

> There is not a man or woman, who violates the covenants made with their God, that will not be required to pay the debt. The blood of Christ will never wipe that out, your own blood must atone for it.
> – *Journal of Discourses* (N.p.: n.p., n.d.), 1:108-109, Brigham Young

I carefully explained Brigham Young's doctrine of *blood atonement* which requires them to slit my throat if they loved me as the Mormon Jesus demands. After my explanation, I looked into the hardened eyes of the Stake President. He was displeased that I brought up this bloody bit of Mormon history. Of more interest were the eyes of the Bishop. They were locked on the evenly spaced boards of my deck. When he finally raised his eyes to meet mine, I asked, "*Do you need to borrow a knife?*" I used that same line a few years earlier when two High Priests delivered a summons to an Excommunication hearing.[15] On both

---

[13] 2 Timothy 3:16-17
[14] Ephesians 2:8-9
[15] See chapter: Excommunication

occasions, my comment was not well received. Apparently, it is the proverbial lead balloon. Is it my delivery, or am I so twisted that I alone think this is uproariously hilarious? Gracie thinks my humor is a bit warped; she is likely correct! At any rate, I was the only one grinning ... again!

Having failed miserably as a stand-up comic, I quickly moved on.

Canonized Mormon scripture describes a group of people who will receive an inheritance in the Telestial Kingdom.

> These are they who are liars, and sorcerers, and adulterers, and whoremongers, and whosoever loves and makes a lie.
> – *Doctrine & Covenants*, 76:103

The Telestial Kingdom is reported to be a part of heaven. Granted, it's not the best and brightest part of Heaven, but Heaven nonetheless. According to Mormon doctrine, it is a degree of God's brilliant, eternal glory. That doesn't sound half bad. However, the Bible presents an almost identical list of people and clearly states *they will have their part in the lake that burns with fire and sulfur.*[16] Mormon doctrine includes two equally binding promises that confirm, certain people will inherit both Heaven and hell. One doctrine or the other may be true, but both cannot be true together. One comes from the Bible and the other from the Doctrine & Covenants. Both are canonized Mormon scripture, so the condition of non-contradiction is violated.

Lastly, I directed the attention of this Bishop and Stake President to my *get out of hell free card.*

> Verily, verily, I say unto you, if a man marry a wife according to my word, and they are sealed by the Holy Spirit of promise ... and he or she shall commit any sin or transgression of the new and everlasting covenant whatever, and all manner of blasphemies, and if they commit no murder wherein they shed innocent blood, yet they shall come forth in the first resurrection, and enter into their exaltation...
> – *Doctrine & Covenants*, 132:26

Having been married and sealed in the Mormon temple, Grace and I have this grand assurance. We can live a life of total and unrepentant debauchery, including murder. That's right; we can commit murder if our victim is not innocent of every offense. Upon meeting these conditions, we will rise up and be exalted as a Mormon god and goddess. While this option sounds intriguing, it sounds just too good to be true.

In the many months that followed, I patiently and kindly reminded this Bishop and Stake President that I was still waiting. I reminded them out of love. Even so, the greater assurance they promised never materialized. I want them to face the reality that their religion offers no promise that equals, exceeds, or even approaches the assurance from God.

---

[16] Revelation 21:8

I am fascinated with this simple pledge from God. With this assurance, long years of uncertainty faded into a distant memory. Jubilant shouts of joy ring out and replace Mormon doubt and fear. At this moment, in this instant, and in this hour, I know with perfect knowledge that I have eternal life with God. This gift is mine, through the loving grace of my King Jesus. No assurance is better than this!

With certainty beyond all certainty, I know I am where Jesus called me to be. He alone gets all the glory, and I alone get the grace! Because of this, I rest in perfect peace with God.[17] Amen and Amen!

---

[17] Romans 5:1

CHAPTER THIRTYTHREE

A PARTING PRAYER

> Flood the hearts of the Mormon people with illumination that reveals You as You actually are.
>
> *Lance*

Jesus is the way, the truth, and the life who came to bring light into the darkness.

> [78] Through the tender mercy of our God; whereby the dayspring from on high hath visited us, [79] To give light to them that sit in darkness and in the shadow of death, to guide our feet into the way of peace.
> – Luke 1:78-79 (KJV)

33.1 A Light Goes Out

With Bible in hand, I stood at a friend's door and knocked. After a short pause, I knocked a second time. That's when the porch light went out. Standing alone in the darkness, my heart hurt for this man. What a tragic thing to be so fearful of the word of God. Quietly I offered a short prayer for the soul of a friend.

I drove to the home of another long-time friend and knocked. Thankfully, he opened the door and invited me in. After catching up with each other, I asked, "Can I read a short passage of scripture and ask a question of you?" He agreed, and I silently praised God.

Opening my Bible to 1 John 5, I began to read,

> If we receive the witness of men, the witness of God is greater; for this is God's testimony which he has testified concerning his Son.
> – 1 John 5:9 (WEB)

Together, we agreed that the testimony of God is significantly more binding and powerful than his, mine or ours. So, I continued reading.

> [10] He who believes in the Son of God has the testimony in himself. He who doesn't believe God has made him a liar, because he has not believed in the testimony that God has given concerning his Son. [11] The testimony is this, that God gave to us eternal life, and this life is in his Son. [12] He who has the Son has the life. He who doesn't have God's Son doesn't have the life.
> – 1 John 5:10-12 (WEB)

I concluded with a reading of John's summation of God's testimony and promise to us. I am fascinated by the simplicity and beauty of this passage. In it, I find endless hope and assurance that no selection of Mormon scripture can equal.

> These things I have written to you who believe in the name of the Son of God, **that you may know that you have eternal life** ...
> – 1 John 5:13a (WEB), emphasis added

I promised my friend that I will immediately return to Mormonism and that he can baptize me if he can give me a better assurance. But, I had a condition. I explained, "The assurance you provide may not contradict the teachings of Mormon prophets, apostles, or official church publications." I continued, "And, it may not contradict the Word God has preserved in the Bible." He studied me for a moment and exclaimed, "It's time for you to go."

I stood, crossed the room, and took his hand. While looking into his eyes, I expressed my love for him and God. In his eyes, I saw what has become a hauntingly familiar sight. They went hard, cold, and dark.

> [22] The light of the body is the eye: if therefore thine eye be single, thy whole body shall be full of light. [23] But if thine eye be evil, thy whole body shall be full of darkness. If therefore the light that is in thee be darkness, how great is that darkness! [24] No man can serve two masters: for either he will hate the one, and love the other; or else he will hold to the one, and despise the other. Ye cannot serve God and mammon.
> – Matthew 6:22-24 (KJV)

My friend was troubled because he wanted to serve God, the real God. However, he was more driven to defend Mormonism. These two masters pulled at his heart.

The pattern of personal attacks is predictable and nearly always repeated. As I said goodbye, the accusations began, "You only came here to prove me wrong, and you right." This accusation is the one I hear more often than all others. It is not about who is wrong and who is right. For me, it is only about

A PARTING PRAYER

who is God. No matter how often I repeat this assurance, most Mormons will not hear. When the light is out and dark blackness grips a heart, the truth will always be rejected. Each time this pattern repeats, I experience a profound sense of loss. It is akin to watching a soul dry up, curl up and die.

I have observed that some men and women who claim to follow Jesus are quickly offended by His Word. How can the word of God offend one who loves God? The truth is, it cannot. The word offends those who are enemies of God. The Mormon people hate God without knowing it. They hate the one true God because they worship another. Consequently, when I speak the Word of God, they are offended.

> Am I therefore become your enemy, because I tell you the truth?
> – Galatians 4:16 (KJV)

> Why do ye not understand my speech? even because ye cannot hear my word.
> – John 8:43 (KJV)

My spirit was heavy as I drove home on that cold winter night. I began to think of the innumerable people who God confounded by that passage from John the Beloved.[1] I marveled at their inability to provide a better assurance. Finally, my heart ached because they cannot or will not see the problem. I thought of a Stake President and Bishop who promised to bring me that better assurance. It's been a year, and they remain silent. I thought of another Bishop who had no response beyond closing his door in my face. A third Bishop said he does not study the scriptures enough to discuss them with me. I thought of those who angrily drove me away or mentally shut me out.

Above all other things, I remembered the eyes of family,

---

[1] 1 John 5:13

Reflections

My Dear Mormon Friends,

I will return to Mormonism if you can give me an assurance as good as 1 John 5:13.

It doesn't matter what you bring. Whatever it may be, it cannot contradict the teachings and doctrines previously espoused by your church. If your god rejects your god, how is he holy? If scripture refutes scripture, how is it trustworthy? With competing doctrines, how will your assurances earn my trust?

My greatest fear is that you will spend the rest of mortality hating me and the balance of eternity hating yourself for choosing death.

Lance

friends, and so many more. Just as the first man physically turned out the porch light, these turned out an inner light. All of them shunned the light and embraced the darkness.

33.2 Pray With Me

Dear God, mighty, sovereign, and eternal, hear my prayer. I have scattered seeds, some, but not as many as I ought. Most seem to fall on hearts, hard as granite. I am pained to see these seeds lay on the surface, waiting for Satan to carry them away.[2] You and I would have all men to be saved.[3] Bless my efforts to that end.

Please, God, let the light come on, stay on, and burn brightly. Flood the hearts of the Mormon people with illumination that reveals You as You actually are. Shine bright white light on every false doctrine, lying prophet, and gospel perversion. Light the dark corners of every hard heart and darkened mind.

> This then is the message which we have heard of him, and declare unto you, that God is light, and in him is no darkness at all.
> – I John 1:5 (KJV)

Almighty God, Father of us all, send more workers, bold and prepared, into the harvest and please Lord, let there be fruit, much fruit.[4]

We thank you for every Mormon soul who hears and responds to the message of hope. We plant and we water, but you bring the increase. To you be the praise and glory forever.

> So then neither is he that planteth any thing, neither he that watereth; but God that giveth the increase.
> – 1 Corinthians 3:7 (KJV)

I pray that You will use this book as a tool to rescue the Mormon people. I lay it in your hands to use as you will.

Finally, God, you saved my sweet Grace and me. There are no words to express the depths of our gratitude. The spirit you put in us leads not to bondage or fear. It is the spirit of adoption, whereby we cry, Abba, Father![5]

AMEN!

---

[2] Matthew 13:4
[3] 1 Timothy 2:4
[4] Matthew 9:38
[5] Romans 8:15

Made in the USA
Monee, IL
27 October 2023